IDM Supervision

Cal D. Stoltenberg

Brian McNeill

Ursula Delworth

IDM Supervision

An Integrated Developmental Model for Supervising Counselors and Therapists

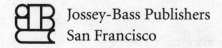

Jossey-Bass Publishers
San Francisco

Substantial discounts on bulk quantities of Jossey-Bass books are available to corporations, professional associations, and other organizations. For details and discount information, contact the special sales department at Jossey-Bass Inc., Publishers (415) 433–1740; Fax (800) 605–2665.

For sales outside the United States, please contact your local Simon & Schuster International Office.

Jossey-Bass Web address: http://www.josseybass.com

Manufactured in the United States of America.

Library of Congress Cataloging-in-Publication Data

Stoltenberg, Cal D.
　　IDM supervision: an integrated development model for supervising counselors and therapists/Cal D. Stoltenberg, Brian McNeill, Ursula Delworth.—1st ed.
　　　　p.　cm.
　　Includes bibliographical references and index.
　　ISBN 0-7879-0846-0 (alk. paper)
　　1. Psychotherapists—Supervision of.　2. Counseling.　I. McNeill, Brian, date.　II. Delworth, Ursula.　III. Title.
　　RC459.S76　1997
　　616.89'14—dc21　　　　　　　　　　　　　　　　　　97-24511
　　　　　　　　　　　　　　　　　　　　　　　　　　　CIP

FIRST EDITION
HB Printing　　　　10 9 8 7 6 5 4 3 2 1

Contents

ᜀ᜵ Introduction

The literature on clinical supervision has undergone a dramatic change since the publication of our first book, *Supervising Counselors and Therapists: A Developmental Approach,* in 1987.[1] What was once an area of practice that was largely conducted in accordance with existing models of psychotherapy and assumed to be important only for training students has become an important part of career-long professional activity with its own theories and research. Although considerable overlap exists between the practice of psychotherapy and the supervision of counseling and psychotherapy, today we understand that being a psychotherapist does not ensure that one is sufficiently able to supervise others' work. Not all good players make good coaches, just as not all good artists make good art instructors. Similarly, our experience tells us that therapists in supervision are confronted with considerably different issues from those typically faced by clients in therapy. Thus, a different framework, one specifically designed to address issues in supervision, is required to allow supervisors to facilitate growth in their supervisees, as well as provide quality assurance for their work.

Our first book grew out of our experience as supervisors and our own theoretical and empirical work. Stoltenberg offered a developmental model of supervision that described a four-stage sequence of psychotherapist development and highlighted supervision environments necessary to encourage this development.[2] His model stimulated considerable research and has been described as the "most heuristic" model of clinical supervision.[3] Delworth and colleagues also advanced the conceptual status of developmental models of supervision in their major article that outlined three stages of development and delineated important tasks required of supervisees to advance from stage to stage.[4] Our collaborative efforts resulted in the evolution of the Integrated Developmental Model (IDM) of supervision, outlined in the first book, that has had a major impact on the field of clinical supervision and remains one of the most important resources for practitioners and researchers in this area. Indeed, developmental models of supervision, of which the IDM is the most complete, have been described as the "zeitgeist" of supervision models,[5] as well as the most researched and visible theme in supervision in recent years.[6] McNeill has provided additional guidance for supervisors in addressing issues of diversity in the supervision process and its effects on the supervisory relationship.[7] These issues are more fully developed across chapters in the book and receive specific attention in Chapters Three through Six.

As we will discuss later in this book, the IDM has proved to be very useful for practitioners engaged in clinical supervision. In addition, the considerable amount of research conducted since the publication of the first book has shown that the model holds up rather well to empirical scrutiny.[8] We have had the opportunity to examine the model in great detail over the past ten years and have explored various aspects of its theoretical underpinnings and practical impact with numerous students, colleagues, and fellow mental health professionals in our direct work in supervision, teaching classes, doing and presenting research, and conducting workshops. Indeed, the three of us have supervised nearly one hundred additional supervisees across levels over the past ten years. These experiences have brought to light deficiencies in the model and the way it was originally presented. More details on certain aspects of the model and ways to apply it are addressed in this book than were included in the first. For example, in Chapter Three we explore issues of therapists in training who appear unable, for a variety of reasons, to develop beyond limited competencies.[9] The importance of considering issues of diversity in the supervision context is covered throughout the book, as is specific guidance in the most appropriate techniques and mechanisms of supervision for various levels of therapists across different clinical activities.

Various formats can be used to provide examples of supervision processes. We have chosen to use supervisory scenarios throughout the book to illustrate important characteristics and processes. In our opinion, scenarios are superior to lengthy transcripts in providing readers with concise and complete supervision examples. All of the scenarios in the book are drawn from our supervision experiences; names and some information have been altered to ensure confidentiality.

Our work with the model over a number of years has brought about additional clarity regarding how other factors, such as persuasion and interpersonal influence, affect the process of clinical supervision.[10] In subsequent chapters, we explore supervisor and supervisee characteristics and supervisory mechanisms that can affect the power of the supervisor to bring about growth and change in the therapist in supervision.

Changes in the health care environment, including the current dominance of managed care organizations as vendors of mental health care, have had a pronounced effect on the training environment. Accountability and efficiency are becoming increasingly important considerations in clinical practice. Who can provide what services to whom under whose supervision for reimbursement is an important consideration for many in the mental health field. Changes in training demands from entry level through postdoctoral and beyond are having an impact on the way clinical supervision is conducted. The call for the systematic implementation of "empirically validated" and "empirically supported" therapeutic interventions has implications for how supervision is conducted, the ethical and legal responsibilities of the supervisor, and the breadth of competence needed to conduct effective supervision.

Finally, ten years of research has accumulated since the first book was published. Although much of this research suggests that the IDM adequately describes psychotherapist development, training environments, and their interplay, this research also points us toward further enhancements of the model that can be subjected to empirical scrutiny, as well as provide useful guidance to practitioners.

OVERVIEW OF THE BOOK

In this book we explore the influences of clinical practice, ethics, the law, health care reform, and research on clinical supervision. In the Introduction, we examine the need for a new book to guide the field of clinical supervision. Chapter One briefly discusses why development is a useful metaphor for the supervision process and presents a case for developmental models of supervision as the most encompassing and useful approach.

Chapters Two through Five of this book carefully delineate the IDM in its current form, articulating psychotherapist development at each stage and the important considerations for supervisors in providing environments that encourage growth. Specific approaches, interventions, and techniques most appropriate for each level of supervisee are presented, along with clarifying case material.

Chapters Six through Ten examine more general issues related to the supervision process and how to address them. The importance of the supervisory relationship is explored with guidance regarding how to enhance its development. The fundamentals of the supervision process also are addressed, dealing with such issues as setting up sessions, initial assessments of supervisee competence, and the impact of various settings. We discuss supervision across disciplines and present the Supervision-in-Context model. Assessment and evaluation of the supervisee, as well as the supervision process, are discussed. Finally, legal and ethical issues that have an impact on the supervision process are addressed.

Other useful resources are provided in the four appendixes. A case conceptualization format, supervisee information form, and the Supervisee Levels Questionnaire–Revised are included as aids to supervisee assessment and training. As well, all relevant research articles on supervision published between 1987 and 1994 are summarized for interested readers.

PURPOSE OF THE BOOK

We believe that this book will have distinct advantages for students, teachers, practitioners, and researchers that are missing in other books on clinical supervision. We are not offering a survey of approaches to supervision, as is commonly found in books intended for beginning students in academic course work. Our intent is not to present a brief summary of numerous approaches to clinical supervision. We believe this book will prove useful in courses on clinical supervision for students and professors because of the way we cover practice, training, and research issues in depth from one comprehensive model. We articulate how to assess supervisee competence and development and supervise across domains of practice for different levels of trainees, and we examine what aspects of the field have empirical support and what remains to be investigated. Thus, rather than presenting thumbnail sketches of many approaches to supervision, some of them rarely used, we provide a detailed model that can guide research, teaching, and practice across professional roles.

Similarly, we are not offering a "techniques" or "how-to" book solely for practitioners who want to be told what to do in supervision. Cookbook approaches certainly are easy to comprehend, but they tend to lose their utility when complex problems are encountered or a breadth of supervisee issues is considered. We are confident that practitioners, whether they are clinicians who do some supervision or professionals who supervise a number of practitioners, will find this book useful. We provide a detailed model regarding which techniques are presented and integrated into a system for supervising therapists across domains of activities and levels of experience. It is a model on which to base practice rather than a presentation of a collection of techniques with minimal coherent organization. Also, we discuss results of research that we use to validate the model rather than asking readers to take our word for its efficacy. Thus, this book should prove useful for students in learning about therapy and supervision processes, as well as seasoned professionals who are confronted daily with complex supervisory and practice issues. All levels of therapists will benefit from a deeper understanding of their own professional development.

Finally, we are not offering a research textbook. We are confident, however, that researchers will find the review of relevant studies, the articulation of the model, and the suggestions for practice useful in directing their investigations into the clinical supervision process. We firmly believe in a scientist-practitioner approach to practice, training, and research. Good practice informs research, good research informs practice, and effective mental health professionals are aware of this interplay and use it to guide their work.

Let us now direct our attention to the utility of using the metaphor of development to understand the path from neophyte counselor to skilled psychotherapist. Chapter One examines the importance of conflict, disequilibrium, assimilation, and accommodation in professional growth.

ACKNOWLEDGMENTS

I am in debt to a number of people who assisted in various ways with the creation of this book. My deepest gratitude is extended to my coauthors, Brian McNeill and Ursula Delworth, without whom this book would never have gotten past the "good idea" stage. We represent three professional generations, linked together by idiosyncratic as well as shared experiences. Now that the book is finished, I can allow myself to begin appreciating the process of working with close friends and colleagues in the writing of this book.

Nearly twenty years of supervisees have given me the opportunity to observe their development and have educated me in the practice of clinical supervision through shared sessions as well as research projects. To name them all would tax my memory and require considerable space. My most recent supervision class, however, deserves mention. Dana Beake, George Blair, Tom Brooks, Sid Dixon, Ric Jerez, Kathy Lasster, and Michelle Thompson provided hours of discussion and insightful critique of earlier versions of these chapters. Rockey Robbins, Elise Berryhill, and Sandra Choney have helped me more fully understand culturally sensitive clinical supervision. I am grateful to Terry Pace, Loreto Prieto, Mark Leach, and Gregg Eichenfield for the hours we spent discussing supervision and training issues.

Finally, I thank my wife, Peggy, and my children, Braden, Ilea, and Kara, for their tolerance with my absence and absent-mindedness while this book took over my life. Dad is ready to do some camping, playing ball, and generally enjoying his family.

Norman, Oklahoma   CAL D. STOLTENBERG
August 1997

I thank my mentors and colleagues, Cal Stoltenberg and Ursula Delworth, for their tremendous influence on my career, as well as others who have helped me along the way. Thanks also to my supervisees and students who provide me with the greatest satisfaction in my work. Finally, and most important, muchas gracias a mi familia, including my parents who have always supported me, and especially Yukiko, Mari, and Kimi, whom I always look forward to coming home to.

Pullman, Washington   BRIAN MCNEILL
August 1997

Thanks to my splendid colleagues, Cal and Brian, especially Cal, who captained this book to completion. I remember and appreciate all the colleagues who, years ago, spent so much time trying to understand and practice this science/art we call clinical supervision. Cal, earlier, and Brian, later, were among them. And I remain grateful to supervisees and students who have shared what is now a twenty-year journey in supervision practice, theory, and research.

Iowa City, Iowa   URSULA DELWORTH
August 1997

CHAPTER ONE

Theoretical Foundations

U nderstanding change over time in one's ability to function as a professional is fundamental in the practice of clinical supervision. Early models of clinical supervision relied heavily on psychotherapeutic processes to describe how to become a psychotherapist. This approach can be useful in providing some guidance to the process of clinical supervision and training, but its applicability tends to be limited to helping the supervisee work through personal issues that stand in the way of effective functioning. Even then, not all models of therapy allow for effective brief interventions for personal blocks and issues that do not subsequently have a negative impact on the supervisory relationship. As we know, dealing in detail with these blocks or disorders is best left to the supervisee's therapist, not the supervisor. The roles differ, as do the goals and, as we shall see, the techniques and interventions.

Another common approach to training and supervision conceptualizes the learning process as skills acquisition and assumes that the process is largely one of acquiring new information and skills, which are added to existing knowledge and proficiencies. Thus, one collects pieces of information, techniques, and concepts and is able to become a better therapist by having a larger armamentarium of tools from which to draw on in working with clients. Although this model may be adequate for entry-level counselors or experienced therapists acquiring training in new areas, it is insufficient to describe higher-order knowledge acquisition and therapist development. This additive model would suggest that therapists will continue to improve in a linear manner directly related to increasing knowledge and experience. Our professional experience, as well as the empirical literature, suggests that this simply does not occur.[1]

Professional, and for that matter, personal, growth tends to follow a less linear path. Although there will be periods of rather smooth growth in knowledge, skills, and proficiencies, change over time tends to occur in spurts and periods of delay (and sometimes regression). Thus, the metaphor of development has been useful in understanding how we change as individuals and therapists. Of additional importance is an understanding of how cognitive processing and motivation affect learning. We will briefly explore the role of cognition, motivation, and attitudes in learning and behavior. We then consider how developmental processes provide an overarching framework that sets the stage for a developmental model of clinical supervision.

COGNITIVE MODELS

The past fifteen years or so have yielded considerable new understanding of the processes of learning and cognition. It is not our purpose here to review this information exhaustively, but we would be remiss in not considering what this research has to say about supervising and training psychotherapists. Anderson has effectively summarized what we know about the development of expertise, which is directly related to what we hope to accomplish in our supervision and training activities. Similar to models of development that are discussed later, three steps or stages explain how people learn skills. The first is a cognitive stage during which a declarative verbal or image representation of the procedure is learned, allowing for a rudimentary understanding of what is to be accomplished. In the second, associative, stage, the person gets feedback, corrects errors, and streamlines the procedures. During the final, autonomous, stage, the student practices and becomes more proficient in performing the skill, until it becomes automatic under the correct conditions. Additional practice, past a critical point, yields limited additional proficiency. However, spacing practice over time, separating out independent parts of a skill and learning them independently, providing immediate feedback, and grouping similar skills to enhance positive transfer are important considerations to incorporate into supervision and training.

Research in related fields can provide some insight into how a psychotherapist learns the trade and becomes a master in his or her practice. Anderson[2] provides some useful descriptions of learning in other content areas. For example, we know that master chess players are not more intelligent than novice ones. Rather, their considerable practice in encountering and dealing with numerous situations allows them to develop a better memory for chess positions and strategies to deal with them. Research on learning geometry also yields some interesting conclusions. Geometry experts are able to learn inference rules and convert them into mental procedures. These "productions" are fine-tuned to specific situations, allowing the individual to develop forward-inference procedures that they can use even when specific goals are not present. Similarly, expert physicists learn to reason forward from known information in a given physics problem rather than reason backward from the problem statement. Physics problems are represented by the experts in abstract concepts that predict a method of solution.

These same processes can be applied in learning psychotherapy and related professional activities. For example, therapists use clinical interview data and other background information about their clients to develop initial hypotheses concerning personality factors and historical and environmental influences, and how these interact to have an impact on the problems the client brought into therapy. These pieces of information will suggest possible diagnoses, which subsequently lead to treatment parameters to deal with the client's situation. Sets, or patterns, of characteristics, including personality style, therapist reactions to the client, and environmental circumstances, will be recognized by expert therapists and lead to "forward thinking" about paths to solutions to problems not even mentioned by the client at intake (for example, the need for personality change as opposed to specific solutions to circumscribed interpersonal difficulties).

Expert versus Novice

Differences between expert and novice computer programmers suggest some patterns that may apply to the practice of psychotherapy.

For example, as programmers become more expert in their field, they learn to represent programming problems in terms of abstract constructs and approach programming tasks from a breadth-first orientation (which allows for more efficient programming than depth first) and acquire better memories for programs and patterns. In short, there appears to be a change over time in moving from novice to expert that exhibits a problem-solving approach that moves from serial processing and deduction to one based in memory retrieval and pattern matching. This movement allows programmers to approach and resolve problems more quickly and efficiently.

We suspect that a similar process occurs for psychotherapists and results in different patterns of activity between novice and experts. For example, the novice therapist observing an expert may be unclear as to why the expert pursues certain avenues during diagnosis and treatment and quickly abandons others. An experienced therapist can match patterns in characteristics previously encountered in work with other clients and therefore approach assessment across a breadth of client experience and abilities rather than honing in on a particular aspect of a presenting problem. Thus, while the novice may collect considerable information related to an initial concern presented by the client, the expert therapist will efficiently assess a number of factors that may, at first blush, seem unrelated to the presenting problem. This information allows the expert to move more quickly to deriving a treatment plan to address core issues, while the novice may end up working on various treatment plans to deal with a collection of circumscribed problems as they arise in therapy. This process is similar to what others have described in developing proficiency in medical diagnosis.

Thus, cognitive research and theory suggests that simply acquiring more facts and skills is not sufficient in explaining how to move from being a novice to becoming an expert psychotherapist. Anderson views memory as a network of nodes and links organized into propositions, which are defined as the smallest unit of meaning that enables us to determine whether a statement is true or false (or, in the case of psychotherapy, relevant or irrelevant).[3] The process of attempting to retrieve information from this network is described as *spreading activation*. Thus, a topic or issue being considered elicits the activation of related concepts in memory, which in turn activate other closely related (neighboring) concepts linked to the first. Recognition occurs when the appropriate proposition is activated and this level of activation reaches a threshold. The strongest links from the concepts that are activated will receive more activation. The strength and number of activated concepts will determine how any given concept is arrived at as important to the problem solution.

Again, this process highlights differences in how expert and novice therapists use information provided by clients. Personality and counseling theory (whether formal or personalized) allows the therapist to attend to certain aspects of client information while ignoring vast amounts of less relevant data. Expert therapists make these decisions relatively quickly and often with limited cognitive processing (in fact, they may not be very aware of how they are making these decisions). Novices are more likely to take a trial-and-error approach and either attend to factors that subsequently prove to be of limited value in diagnosis and treatment or miss other important factors necessary for understanding the client. As expert therapists attend to client factors, other related concepts will be activated (for example, broad patterns of symptoms) and brought into short-term memory for processing. When certain propositions (meaningful concepts) are activated beyond a threshold, understanding of the problem or issues occurs. Strong links from extensive knowledge and experience encoded in the memories of expert therapists increase the likelihood that useful propositions will be activated, which leads to effective problem solving.

Diagnosis and treatment planning is certainly an area where this process is evident. Novice therapists collect information concerning their clients (usually following a procedure taught to them or outlined in agency guidelines) and refer to the *DSM-IV,* searching for lists of characteristics that match what they know about their clients. This process is often one of trial and error, where initial diagnoses are entertained and missing important information concerning criteria is collected until the novice settles on a particular diagnosis.

Next, the therapist moves on to the treatment plan, addressed by consulting the supervisor and other sources to come up with a way to deal effectively with someone displaying a particular disorder. The experts engage in a process of purposeful data collection (objective and subjective) with the client and search their memory for pattern matching, which will tend to help them reach a diagnosis more swiftly and accurately and lead to the development of a treatment plan, which is also the result of pattern matching of concepts learned from prior experience and training.

Cognitive Processing

Anderson's ACT* and ACT-R models are useful in helping us understand how we determine what knowledge is relevant in a given situation and how we retrieve from memory the exact information for which we are searching.[4] As psychotherapists gain in knowledge and experience, the types of information and the strength of associations between them will change. Information (concepts) closely related to initially activated concepts will be more quickly available and moved into short-term memory for use in problem solving. Increasing experience and training can enhance the availability of concepts and strengthen their links. Of course, the possibility exists that inaccurate concepts can be developed and linked together if adequate evaluation of facts and information is not part of the ongoing process of learning psychotherapy. Indeed, in early learning occurring in any domain of the psychotherapy process, initially activated concepts and associated links may be a function of limited knowledge and experience and be inappropriate in solving problems in psychotherapy. The role of the supervisor is to assist the psychotherapist in training to learn additional concepts and reinforce linkages to related ones for particular psychotherapeutic situations. Appropriate supervision environments and experience can lead to the development of expertise, improving the ability to organize information and concepts into patterns that can be quickly recognized, and solutions to these problems activated.

An important extension of this discussion on the importance of cognitive processing on learning psychotherapy is the notion of schemata. We will rely heavily on the discussion by Gagné, Yekovich, and Yekovich in examining schemata and their formulation and refinement.[5] According to this research, information (propositions) regarding the function, categories, parts, and so on of something, as well as images of the entity, are organized together in memory into what are referred to as schemata. Activation of any one element of a schema leads to easy access of other connected elements. Schemata allow us to recognize new examples of something quickly and draw inferences in new situations. We can use knowledge stored in schemata to solve problems encountered in psychotherapy.

Schemata are initially formulated when one notes similarities across more than one example and forms a mental representation that encodes these similarities. Interestingly, during the early stages of schema formation, differences are not focused on or processed. These common elements across examples are abstracted by the learner into a representation that describes the entity across a set of instances. This classification of similarities across examples leads to schema formation, which will be used subsequently to accept or reject new examples into a classification. Interestingly, we might expect that new examples are compared with the recollection of a previously encountered example. Then the new is matched to the old and included or discarded. What appears to happen, however, is that an average set of characteristics is developed into a schema against which any new examples are compared. This schema may not completely match any specific example previously encountered but will serve as the prototype for comparison purposes.

The process appears to be the following. Common elements across at least two examples of an entity are identified. The attributes of example 1 are described, and an image of it is created. The attributes of example 2 are described, and an image of it is created. Then the attributes and images of examples 1 and 2 are compared. This comparison of shared attributes and images results in the creation of a schema. It is important to note that if one does not consciously look for similarities, a schema may not be formed, and the information we collect from experience may not be encoded in a way that benefits understanding and problem solving down the road.

So how does this process work in learning psychotherapy? We might expect that in early course work and clinical experience, psychotherapists in training strive to understand similarities across clients, therapy interventions and processes, and so on. Following the process we have identified, early schemata related to psychotherapy are developed, against which new information and experiences are compared. For example, supervisors will notice supervisees classifying their clients (often erroneously) into diagnostic or conceptual categories based on a limited number of client characteristics. This initial diagnosis may focus primarily on similarities among clients and ignore important differences. As noted, unless one consciously searches for similarities, a schema may not develop, and one's understanding of clients and the psychotherapeutic process will be limited accordingly.

Schema Development and Refinement

Creation of schemata is important, but it is also important to be able to refine an existing schema in the light of new information and experiences. Initial schemata tend to be overly general and are not as useful as later ones in distinguishing among numerous characteristics and suggesting solutions to problems. This tendency to overgeneralize in schema development is a characteristic of novices within a given domain. As we learn more about a particular domain, we can make increasingly refined discriminations.

For this to occur, we need to engage in a conscious decision to understand the limitations of our existing schema. The supervisor's role in highlighting crucial differences between the characteristics of the current client and the schema the supervisee is using for classification (based on prior clients or other information) can help the supervisee refine the schema to be more accurate and helpful. As experienced therapists, we will continue the process of schema refinement. For example, when a psychotherapist decides on a course of action with a client that results in no improvement or, worse, decompensation, a conscious decision to find out why treatment did not work as expected is required. Of note here is also the importance of being able to recognize when something did not work as planned. The current situation is compared to information retrieved from memory concerning a prior situation where the schema was useful. A conscious searching for differences in attributes between the two (or more) situations results in a modification of the schema to include these differences. Discovering that the schema did not work and deciding to set about discovering why appears *not* to be an automatic process. Thus, extensive experience is not sufficient for the refinement of psychotherapy-relevant schemata. Psychotherapists who intentionally monitor and evaluate the utility of their schemata and refine them over time develop expertise.

In general, this process describes the importance and development of, among other things relevant to psychotherapy, differential diagnosis. The process therapists go through in learning to distinguish among a collection of information provided by and about a client in developing a useful diagnosis and case conceptualization occurs over an extended period of time. They continually refine schemata based on similarities across clients and situations into useful diagnostic classifications suggesting treatment alternatives. The more carefully evaluated experience the therapist acquires, the greater is the likelihood of developing schemata that will allow for effective problem solving.

Forming schemata from abstract definitions appears to be difficult. In other words, simply telling someone what an important schema is or describing it will not result in the formation of a useful schema. What appears to be necessary is providing examples, or direct experience with the entity. Learning occurs better with better examples. Without them, the process of constructing or changing schemata will not occur.

Interpersonal Influence and Motivation

In other contexts, we have discussed the utility of examining the role of social influence on clinical supervision.[6] The Interpersonal Influence Model (IIM) has been an important subject of research in professional psychology for decades.[7] Dixon and Claiborn initially applied this model to the supervision process when they proposed how supervisor power and supervisee needs interact in the supervision context.[8] The supervisor's persuasive influence over supervisees is described as a function of the constructs of expert, referent, legitimate, and informational power bases. As their needs change over time, supervisees become more or less susceptible to the influence of the supervisor as a function of his or her perceived expertise. In addition, the similarities the supervisee perceives he or she has with the supervisor form the basis of referent power. As the designated authority figure, the supervisor also enjoys a legitimate power base. Thus, by definition, the supervisor has authority over the supervisee, which usually includes the requirement of evaluation. Finally, the supervisor is perceived as knowing considerably more about therapy and the supervision process than does the supervisee. Therefore, the information and skills that the supervisor can provide to the supervisee forms another basis for the power of persuasion in the supervision context.

We discuss in more detail in subsequent chapters how the needs and characteristics of supervisees at each of three levels of professional development described in the Integrated Developmental Model (IDM) interact with the supervisor power bases in the supervision relationship. We also make recommendations regarding the most effective use of these power bases for each level of supervisee. The IDM relies heavily on accurate assessment of supervisees across a number of domains of professional practice. Once the developmental level is identified for a given domain, specific supervisory interventions can enhance supervisee learning and growth.

Another important consideration in examining how we learn and what behaviors we choose to engage in is motivation. This can have important implications for the likelihood that one will elaborate on information provided in supervision and therapy contexts, which in turn will affect utilization of relevant schemata and their continued refinement. A model of persuasion and information processing, the Elaboration Likelihood Model (ELM), has been used to clarify how situations in supervision and therapy can affect the supervisee's motivation and determine how he or she will use available information and encoded schemata in problem solving.[9] Consistent with our brief overview format in this chapter, we will discuss only the importance of two types of information processing (central route and peripheral route) here and leave the details for exploration in later chapters.

According to the ELM, a continuum of approaches to information processing best describes how we use our cognitive resources in making decisions and developing attitudes. At one end of this continuum is an approach referred to as *peripheral route processing*. This type of processing is characteristic of what we will tend to do when a topic has limited importance or personal relevance or we have limited knowledge or experience related to the topic. Rather than invest a lot of cognitive energy in deciding what our opinion is or determining what to do in a situation, we will rely on contextual cues to assist us. In the supervision context, the credibility of the supervisor can serve as a cue for the supervisee, indicating that little effort needs to be expended to consider the merits of the supervisor's recommendations if he or she is seen as an expert with considerable experience in this particular area. Although this may simplify things for the supervisor (and boost his or her ego), an uncritical acceptance of supervisor recommendations or interpretations may result in the supervisee's becoming more of an extension of the supervisor than an autonomously functioning therapist. There are a number of problems with this position that we highlight later in this book.

The other pole on the continuum is *central route processing*. Here the supervisee is sufficiently motivated and knowledgeable to elaborate on information provided in supervision, as well as in therapy, rather than uncritically accept it. This allows the trainee to utilize fully relevant schemata developed over time to evaluate the pros and cons of various options, including those supplied by the supervisor. This effortful process should also assist the supervisee in schema creation and refinement, which should then have a greater impact on that person's future behavior in supervision and therapy.

Thus, motivation needs to be considered as well as ability in examining the learning environment related to supervision and training in psychotherapy. Cognitive activity related to schema creation, refinement, and subsequent therapist behavior tends not to be automatic. The learning environment must be modified to encourage optimal understanding, integration, and retention. A number of models of human development offer guidelines for understanding how people grow and the types of environments that encourage this growth. However, we will now focus on more general developmental constructs to guide the discussion and consider their utility in understanding how we grow as professional therapists.

MODELS OF HUMAN DEVELOPMENT

Lerner notes that a general interpretation of the concept of development requires systematic and successive changes to occur over some period of time in an organization, usually how an individual organism is organized.[10] The concept of development, originally applied in a biological context, has been applied in a more general way to include the organization of an organism that changes over time as an adaptation to the environment.[11] A refinement of this idea suggests that only movement from a general global organization to one that is highly differentiated and integrated into a hierarchy, the orthogenetic principle, adequately describes development.[12] This latter conceptualization fits more closely what we see happen in the professional development of therapists.

In our earlier book, we addressed two general models of development: the mechanistic and the organismic models. The mechanistic model uses the machine as its basic metaphor. This view of human development is one of antecedent-consequent relationships and posits a reactive conceptualization of human behavior characteristic of stimulus-response behaviorism.[13] This approach reflects a natural-science view of the world, which is reductionistic and sees change as continuous, additive, and quantifiable.[14] In the therapy context, we would view development as a rather smooth, continuous adding of skills and knowledge over time that eventually leads to expertise.

The organismic model takes the organism, with its qualitative changes over time, as its basic metaphor for development. These theories rely on an active organism model, epistemological constructivism, where the organism plays an important role in constructing knowledge and reality.[15] This epigenetic viewpoint maintains that qualitative change cannot be reduced to a quantitative organization of elemental components. Rather, something new, with a higher level of complexity, characterizes different stages of development. This view of the world reflects an antireductionistic, discontinuous, and qualitative perspective where interaction between the organism and the environment results in goal-directed behavior and growth.[16] In short, the whole is considerably greater than the sum of the parts.

In considering human learning and development, the mechanistic approach relies heavily on additive elements, many of them a function of the environment or accumulating information in a stimulus-response framework. The organismic model, on the other hand, posits a biological goal-oriented framework on the process of learning, where changes in the organization of the organism are largely dictated by qualitatively different stages of development. In practice, most organismic theorists, for example, Jean Piaget and Freud, assume that general laws govern development across all stages of psychological functioning, and specific laws affect development within stages.[17] In the context of therapist development, as we have suggested in our earlier work, one would expect a general continuous development whereby therapists accumulate additional knowledge and skills and achieve qualitatively distinct development that defines changes for various stages.[18] Thus, we find a general increase in therapist knowledge and skills over time but qualitative differences in the level of complexity of these and how they are used, which differs from level to level. In short, according to the IDM, the Level 1 therapist not only knows less than Levels 2 and 3 but is characterized by a different way of viewing therapy (and related activities) than each of the two higher levels of therapists. Consistent with Lerner's developmental-contextual perspective, the learning environment provided in supervision and therapy will interact with the level of development of the therapist, resulting in change.[19] As we shall see in Chapters Two through Five, the context or environment provided by supervisors for supervisees plays a crucial role in the rate and ultimate level of therapist development.

———

As we have seen in this chapter, an understanding of cognitive and human development theories is important in considering how we become psychotherapists. Learning and doing psychotherapy is not an isolated specialty. We can gain insight and avoid reinventing the wheel if we use knowledge already available to us. In addition, we may avoid making mistakes concerning the learning process if we attend carefully to what experts in the field of learning have to tell us. Exhaustive reviews of the supervision literature by Worthington and Stoltenberg, McNeill, and Crethar have come to similar conclusions regarding the validity of developmental models of supervision.[20] Stoltenberg and colleagues summarized the research on supervision as indicating "there is support for general developmental models, perceptions of supervisors and supervisees are consistent with developmental theories, the behavior of supervisors changes as counselors gain experience, and the supervision relationship changes as counselors gain experience."[21]

The remaining chapters examine the issues raised here in more detail and apply them specifically to the education and training of psychotherapists. We are hopeful that the discussion and examples will serve to assist all therapists in the creation and modification of schemata that will positively improve their work in clinical supervision and other professional activities.

CHAPTER TWO

An Overview of the IDM

Although developmental models of supervision have probably been the most influential in recent years and have generated considerable research, critics have argued that the theory has not readily translated into concrete applications.[1] As we have noted, providing more details regarding the application of the IDM is one of the reasons for this book. Nevertheless, sometimes simple cookbook solutions and directions are not possible, or at least may be misleading. Also, simple models are easier to understand, while more complex ones require more time and effort to grasp and integrate— but the more elegant the model, the more supervisory issues are addressed.

We have noticed that some researchers and practitioners tend to use earlier, and simpler, presentations of our developmental model for their research and practice.[2] Although these earlier models may be more easily comprehended, they lack the breadth to guide the supervision process fully. Related areas of inquiry have faced similar problems. Clinical intuition has suggested that flexibly applying therapeutic interventions is superior to rigidly adhering to treatment approaches set out in manuals. Evidence now indicates that this notion has merit.[3]

Therefore, to meet the needs of the specific supervisee adequately, the supervisor must be well versed in the model of supervision and able to adapt to changing needs within and across sessions.

Our task here is to introduce the IDM briefly, with only limited attention paid to elaborations and specific applications; those will come later. Just as a good novel requires time for character and plot development, a good model requires an adequate framework on which one can hang the specifics of therapist trainees, their development, and the supervision process across contexts.

OVERARCHING STRUCTURES AND SPECIFIC DOMAINS

Other earlier models of psychotherapist development have suggested that growth occurs in broad stages, with supervisees labeled as Level 1, Level 2, and so on. Clinical practice, and now research, however, suggests that this view is too simplistic and does not reflect reality. Professional practice consists of a diverse collection of responsibilities and activities requiring a wide range of skills, knowledge, and experience. It is simply not useful to categorize a trainee this broadly, although a general "level" designation may prove efficient in considering the degree of expertise and capacity for assuming responsibilities within a particular context.

In practice, we all tend to function at different levels of professional development across areas of mental health service delivery. For example, a supervisee may function with a relatively high degree of confidence and autonomy when conducting individual psychotherapy with a depressed client but, due to little experience and training, may lack this confidence and autonomy when working with childhood sexual abuse. This effect was demonstrated in a recent study two of us conducted with other colleagues.[4] Similarly, Tracey and colleagues found that supervisees desired different types of supervision, varying in degree of structure provided by the supervisor, depending on their experience with particular client presenting problems.[5]

This perspective on trainee development complicates life for supervisors. We not only need to know how to provide optimal supervision for different levels of supervisees, we also need to be able to assess their level of development across the professional activities in which they are engaged while they are under our supervision. Furthermore, we need to move from supervision appropriate for a particular level of development in one domain, to supervision appropriate for a different level of development in another domain, and often within the same supervision session.

Before we discuss how to provide this differential supervision, we explore how to identify the level of trainee development in general. We then move on to discussing how this plays itself out in specific domains.

Overriding Structures

We have found it useful to monitor trainee development by attending closely to three overriding structures that provide markers in assessing professional growth. Within any given area of clinical practice, these structures reflect the level of development at which the trainee is currently functioning. We consider three distinct levels of development and how these structures differ for each level.

SELF AND OTHER AWARENESS   This structure has both cognitive and affective components and indicates where the individual is in terms of self-preoccupation, awareness of the client's world, and enlightened self-awareness. The cognitive component describes the content of the thought processes characteristic across levels, and the affective component accounts for changes in emotions such as anxiety.

MOTIVATION   This structure reflects the supervisee's interest, investment, and effort expended in clinical training and practice. Changes over time tend to go from early high levels through a vacillation from day to day, and client to client, and culminating in a stable degree of motivation over time.

AUTONOMY   Changes in the degree of independence demonstrated by trainees over time accompany the other structural changes. Beginners tend to be rather dependent on supervisors or other authority figures and eventually grow into a dependency-autonomy conflict, or professional adolescence. Clinical experience and supervision allows therapists to become conditionally autonomously functioning professionals. This awareness of strengths and weaknesses allows the individual to assess accurately the need for additional supervision or consultation regarding professional issues.

Specific Domains

Before we go into detail in examining the role of the overriding structures, it may be helpful to look at some of the specific domains of clinical practice for which these structures provide guidance in assessing
developmental level. The degree of specificity with which we can
approach the discussion of domains varies a great deal. As a starting
point, we consider eight specific domains of clinical activity.

INTERVENTION SKILLS COMPETENCE   This domain addresses the therapist's confidence in and ability to carry out therapeutic interventions. The developmental level in this domain will differ depending
on the therapist's familiarity with a given modality (for example, individual, group, marital, or family therapy) and the theoretical orientation used.

ASSESSMENT TECHNIQUES   This domain addresses the therapist's confidence in and ability to conduct psychological assessments. Of course,
numerous assessment devices and protocols exist, and the developmental level of the therapist will vary depending on experience and
training across approaches (for example, personality, vocational, neuropsychological). Our discussion of this domain shares some com-
monalities with other recent work in the area of assessment.[6]

INTERPERSONAL ASSESSMENT   Some professionals may consider this
domain a subset of assessment techniques in, for example, considering the test-taking behavior of a client across the assessment period
and integration of clinical interview data with formal assessment data.
We tend to consider it separately because the nature of interpersonal
assessment may extend well beyond a formal assessment period and
incorporate the use of self in conceptualizing a client's interpersonal
dynamics. Again, the nature of this domain differs depending on the
theoretical orientation of the therapist.

CLIENT CONCEPTUALIZATION   This domain includes, but is not limited
to, diagnosis. The inadequacy of current diagnostic criteria for guiding treatment is well documented.[7] This domain goes beyond an axis
or V-code diagnosis and includes the therapist's understanding of how
the client's characteristics, history, and life circumstances blend to

affect adjustment. The nature of this conceptualization varies depending on the therapist's worldview or theoretical orientation.

INDIVIDUAL DIFFERENCES   This domain includes an understanding of ethnic, racial, and cultural influences on individuals, as well as the idiosyncrasies that form the person's personality. Various elements of this domain will surface or submerge across time depending on the themes addressed in therapy, assessment, or other enterprises.

THEORETICAL ORIENTATION   This domain includes formal theories of psychology and psychotherapy, as well as eclectic approaches and personal integrations. A therapist may vary in rather significant degrees of complexity of understanding across orientations used in clinical practice.

TREATMENT PLANS AND GOALS   This domain addresses how the therapist plans to organize his or her efforts in working with clients in the psychotherapeutic context. The sequencing of issues and interventions leading to achievement of therapeutic goals and objectives will vary depending on the therapeutic orientation, the therapist's skill level, and situational resources and constraints.

PROFESSIONAL ETHICS   Different mental health professions are guided by their own professional ethics, which in turn are affected by their professional practice. This domain addresses how professional ethics and standards of practice intertwine with personal ethics in the development of the therapist.

STRUCTURES ACROSS LEVELS OF THERAPIST DEVELOPMENT

Now that we have summarized our overriding structures and presented some domains for consideration, we examine how these structures vary across levels of therapist development. Later, we expand this discussion by considering how these structures define the levels across domains.

Level 1

Supervisees who are functioning at the early Level 1 stage for a particular domain display some common characteristics. If they are new to the field in the initial phases of education and training in psychotherapy, they often have limited directly relevant experience, although they may have considerable indirectly related experience such as general interpersonal skills. Their background knowledge will usually be limited to an introduction to theories and techniques. The supervisor can choose various approaches to take, but typically a focus on relationship skills and simple intervention strategies is predominant.

Supervisees who may have had considerable experience in other domains of clinical activity (for example, other therapy orientations, other modalities, or related mental health experience) nevertheless will be functioning at Level 1 if these experiences are significantly different from the primary training focus in supervision. For example, it is common to encounter supervisees with significant training and experience in individual counseling or psychotherapy, within one or two orientations, but little or no knowledge or experience in another orientation or another therapeutic modality (for example, marital, family, or group therapy). Similarly, supervisees may have engaged in significant training in assessment but little in psychotherapy, or vice versa.

Level 1 trainees will have limited background in the particular domain of focus in at least part of what occurs in supervision. New trainees will be Level 1 across most or all domains; advanced supervisees, sometimes even relatively seasoned professionals, will have limited background in certain domains of the clinical experience under supervision. In Chapter Three we discuss in more detail how to deal with this variety of Level 1 therapist, but for now we generally examine the characteristics of the overriding structures for this level.

SELF AND OTHER AWARENESS   Learning new skills, theories, strategies, and so on tends to result in considerable confusion and anxiety in Level 1 supervisees. At this level, their evaluation of self-performance is often guided by a perception of accuracy in faithfully performing a given technique or following a particular strategy with a client. This self-focus leaves little attentional capacity for considering the client's perspective or even processing the therapist's own affective or cognitive reactions to the client. Research has confirmed that this self-focus tends to elicit significant anxiety in the supervisee, which can complicate effective performance.[8]

In considering the awareness structure, supervisors need to monitor both *cognitive* and *affective* components. The confusion, lack of certainty, or loss of a sense of what to do is characteristic of the interference on therapist cognitions at this level. Due to the need to reflect constantly on the rules, skills, theories, and other didactic material being learned, it is difficult for trainees to carefully listen to and process information provided by the client in session. It is also difficult for them to recall relevant information from memory immediately in the session when they are struggling to understand the client's perspective. The trainee's schema related to this aspect of practice within this clinical situation is not sufficiently developed and integrated to allow for quick and easy access. Add to this the trainee's concern with evaluation by the client and the supervisor, and it is easy to see how confusion can reign. We recently heard a university football coach refer to this effect as "analysis paralysis" in bemoaning the hesitation and mistakes his young charges made.

The *affective* component in self-awareness accompanies the cognitive confusion. Developmentally, we know that the state of disequilibrium caused by a perception of insufficient understanding often elicits conflict or discomfort in a given situation. Add to this the fear and anxiety often associated with the anticipation of a negative evaluation by others (client and supervisor), and it is easy to understand the range of negative emotions that Level 1 therapists potentially experience.

Level 1 supervisees are characterized by a focus on the self, and it is often a negative focus rather than an insightful self-understanding. Whereas it is typical for trainees at this level to be excited about learning how to engage in professional practice, even the more mature and personally developed trainees tend to experience the confusion and anxiety associated with this stage.

As Level 1 supervisees gain experience and are exposed to a facilitative supervision environment, their confidence and skills increase, and they begin to feel less of a need to focus so intently on their own performance. They then begin the transition to switching their focus more toward their clients and away from monitoring their own skills, anxiety, and recall of clinical directives conveyed during the educational process. They are now more able to notice the impact of the therapeutic process on the client, as well as attend more carefully to the client's communications.

MOTIVATION   Level 1 supervisees are typically highly motivated. Some of this motivation is a function of their desire to become a fully functioning clinician. Often some "end-state" model of a professional based on personal acquaintances or depictions of therapists in books or film serves as a developmental goal for the beginning trainee. The desire to move quickly from neophyte to expert can be a strong motivator. In addition, some of this early motivation is a function of wanting to grow beyond the uncertainty, confusion, and anxiety associated with this stage. This motivation to learn and grow is often reflected in a desire to learn "the best" or "the correct" approach to dealing with clinical problems. There is often also a desire to share this understanding and expertise with clients, and the perception of professional effectiveness can result in a measure of confidence and serve to reinforce the person's selection of career path.

Getting past the early perception of inadequacy and experiencing some measure of success begins the transition to Level 2. Here we may see a reduced desire to learning new approaches or techniques as the supervisee may prefer to enjoy a feeling of self-efficacy as a clinician.

AUTONOMY   Novice clinicians, whether across the board or in a specific domain, tend to show considerable dependency on the supervisor, an appropriate response to their lack of knowledge and experience and their scant understanding of the processes involved. They typically rely on the supervisor to provide structure in supervision and their behavior in the focal domains. They are looking to the supervisor, other authority figures, or other sources to provide information (productions) they can elaborate on and integrate into an overall structure (schema) from which to understand the clinical process and direct therapeutic behavior.

Again, early successes tend to decrease the supervisees' perception of the need to depend on the supervisor and lead to a desire for more autonomy in supervision and clinical practice. A rather simplistic understanding of a complex phenomenon may lead supervisees to desire more autonomy in practice than is warranted. Other supervisees will need to be encouraged to take risks beyond the point where skill deficiencies would be considered a hindrance.

A METAPHOR   In conveying the model to trainees and others, it has sometimes proved useful to use a simple metaphor to encapsulate the developmental process conceptualized by the IDM. One of us has had experience and training as a rock climber in his younger years. Let us imagine the client to be a novice climber who has slipped into a crevasse (a hole) and is calling to our supervisee for help. The Level 1 climber (supervisee) may stand at the edge of the crevasse, mountain climbing manual in hand, and yell down advice to the stranded climber. Or the supervisee may go off and seek guidance from you, the experienced expert team leader, concerning how to assist the stranded person (client). In either case, the supervisee is attempting to assist the client having had little or no experience with or personal understanding of the process. He or she is standing on the edge, sending interventions down to the client (reach for that rock, stretch for that hand-hold, you can do it!), hoping the client will find his or her way out. Sometimes this is sufficient, and the supervisee feels the power of therapy and begins to develop confidence.

Level 2

Resolution of Level 1 issues allows the supervisee to move into Level 2. This transition can be facilitated, or hindered, by the supervision environment. Of course, we must not forget that this developmental sequence occurs within domains, so we may expect to find differential growth across domains. This differentiation may be a function of more of a focus on some domains rather than others during prior supervision, resulting in greater growth in these domains than others. Additional training opportunities may result in more development in certain domains. Also, the trainee's personal characteristics may be better suited to particular domains of practice, and there may be more rapid growth in those domains.

SELF AND OTHER AWARENESS   The transition in switching away from a primary focus on the supervisee's own thoughts and performance toward more of a focus on the client enables movement into Level 2. With the freeing up of awareness from self-preoccupation, the trainee has more attention to be available to direct toward the client and can understand the client's world more fully, marking a structural shift in the area of *cognition*. This additional perspective may, however, confuse the supervisee. A trainee in late Level 1 may have a fairly naive and simplistic view of the client and clinical processes; now these processes may seem complex, confusing, and overwhelming to the Level 2 supervisee.

In the *affective* area, the opportunity to develop empathy more fully with the client now becomes possible. It is difficult to feel someone else's pain when you are preoccupied with your own anxiety. The supervisee's newly developed ability to focus on the client can yield a sensing of the emotional experience of the client. Rather than guessing what emotions the client may be experiencing at any given time, the Level 2 therapist can develop the ability to pick up on verbal and non-verbal cues that communicate the inner emotional experience of the client. This can add considerable depth to the supervisee's understanding of the client. It can also increase the likelihood of enmeshment, countertransference, or an "intervention paralysis" for the supervisee, who may now be nearly as emotionally overwhelmed as is the client.

For the Level 2 supervisee, the lifting of the veil of anxious self-awareness can result in a deeper and more accurate understanding of the client. Taken to the extreme, it can also lead to an inability to get beyond the confusion or intense emotion stimulated by a singular focus on the client. The transition beyond Level 2 to Level 3 consists of altering the focus to include more reactions of the therapist to the client and reflection on what is known by the supervisee regarding the clinical processes at work or tapping into relevant schema while engaged in clinical activity.

MOTIVATION   The confidence that accompanies perceptions of self-efficacy in clinical practice has been shaken by the increased knowledge of the complexity of the enterprise. The effects on motivation can be significant. Some supervisees react to this confusion by seeking additional support and guidance and display high levels of motivation to learn. For others, reacknowledging confusion and frustration can reduce motivation to learn as well as engage in clinical activities. The confusion and, at times, despair contrasting with feelings of confidence and effectiveness can be reflected in vacillating motivation in this supervisee.

The transition issues for this level of trainee revolve around the goal of personalizing an orientation to professional practice. A self-understanding that can develop from learning how one's personal characteristics interact with clinical practice issues forms the basis for the work of Level 3.

AUTONOMY   The dependency of the early Level 1 trainee has given way to a sense of efficacy and a desire for some autonomy by the Level 2 supervisee. This will often take the shape of a dependency-autonomy conflict, not unlike what we all experienced in adolescence. At times, confidence will be high, and the supervisee will want to develop his or her own ideas assertively. A level of independent functioning may be possible with rather specific requests for help. At other times, when things are not going so well, the supervisee may become dependent or, on occasion, evasive. This person will show lowered confidence in clinical work and, sometimes, behavior similar to early Level 1 trainees.

As the Level 2 therapist transitions to Level 3, a more consistent conditional autonomy will appear. This supervisee is better able to understand the parameters of his or her competence, and the dependency-autonomy conflict will fade.

THE METAPHOR   Our mountain climber has moved from standing on the edge of the crevasse and sending down instructions, to climbing down into the hole with the stranded climber (client). The stranded climber now feels more understood, realizing that the supervisee can better see the problem from his or her perspective. The new challenge is for someone to figure a way out. Our supervisee may become as stranded and fearful as the client. They may now both be crying up to the supervisor to help them out, or giving up on the possibility of rescue.

Level 3

The turbulence and uncertainty associated with Level 2 give way to a more stable, autonomous, and reflective Level 3 therapist. The transitional phase to Level 3 brings about more of a focus on a personalized approach to clinical practice and a greater use and understanding of the self.

SELF AND OTHER AWARENESS   Some of the focus on the self that we saw in Level 1 returns in Level 3, although the quality of the self-focus is remarkably different now. Here the supervisee begins to be more accepting of himself or herself with all the professional strengths and weaknesses. The high empathy and understanding, an important developmental milestone in Level 2, remains. However, the therapist now is able to focus on the client and process the information provided, while being able to pull back and reflect on his or her own reactions to the client. This reflection can be fairly objective and include a memory search to identify relevant schemata and bring the information into awareness for use in decision-making. This therapist, through the self-knowledge that has developed, is better able to use himself or herself (personal characteristics, genuine responses) in sessions.

MOTIVATION   The fluctuating motivation we observed in Level 2 has been replaced with a more stable high level of motivation for professional development and practice. Periodic ups and downs will continue, but within a narrower range of motivation. Remaining doubts about one's clinical effectiveness are not disabling, and there is considerably more concern for the total professional identity and how the therapist role fits into it.

AUTONOMY   A commitment to retaining responsibility for one's clinical work is characteristic of this stage. While there is a solid sense of when consultation is necessary, the firm belief in one's autonomy and professional judgment is not easily shaken. The notion of independent practice is now less of a goal and more of a realization. Supervision is useful in solidifying gains and broadening one's perspectives, but tends to become more collegial at this point, with less of a difference in levels of expertise between supervisor and supervisee.

THE METAPHOR   Our mountain climbing guide in Level 3 is able to lower himself or herself down into the crevasse and effectively communicate to our stranded climber his or her understanding of the emotional, cognitive, and environmental aspects of the problem. With calm and confidence, our climber assists the stranded colleague in developing a plan to climb out, examining options and working from experience as well as a detailed understanding of rock climbing technique and the mountain. While success is not guaranteed, the likelihood of both climbers' rising out of the crevasse is considerably increased.

Level 3i (Integrated)

Once the therapist has reached Level 3 in a number of domains, the goal becomes one of integrating across the domains. The therapist now learns to move smoothly from, for example, assessment through conceptualization, developing treatment goals, and implementation of interventions.

SELF AND OTHER AWARENESS   The transition to Level 3i is characterized by a personalized understanding of clinical practice that crosses
domains. The therapist is able to monitor the impact of personal life
changes on professional identity and performance. This self-understanding is apparent from the therapist's awareness of how his or her
personal characteristics affect various clinical roles, as well as an integration and consistency of identity across these roles.

MOTIVATION   Relatively high and stable motivation will be evident
across a number of domains. The therapist is likely to be aware of
domains where this motivation is lacking and understand the reasons
for it. Decisions concerning professional and personal goals will dic-
tate which domains and professional roles will emerge as most important. A refocusing of one's practice to new areas may occur,
necessitating a revisiting of Level 1 or Level 2 issues, depending on the
similarity of the new domains to those in which professional development is high.

AUTONOMY   The therapist is able to move conceptually and behaviorally from one domain to another with a high degree of fluidity. The
possibility of refocusing one's practice to new domains will bring
about changes in autonomy consistent with the level of professional
development of related domains. However, professional identity is
solid across most domains relevant to the person's practice.

THE METAPHOR   Our Level 3 mountain climbing guide was able to help
our stranded climber emerge from the crevasse. Perhaps we can extend
our metaphor for the Level 3i guide to an ability to handle most types
of emergencies and challenges confronted by his or her charges on the
mountain. In addition, this individual may be particularly adept at
training other guides to provide similar assistance to climbers who are
attempting to scale everything from rocks to glacier covered peaks.
Table 2.1 summarizes descriptions of the overriding structures by level
of development, including transitions between levels.

INTERACTION OF STRUCTURES
AND DOMAINS

We will leave a detailed discussion of the structures across domains
for each level of professional development for the next three chapters.
Some general discussion of this process here will help set the stage for

subsequent details. It is important to keep in mind that supervisees commonly are functioning at different levels of development for various domains at any given point in time. The range of levels, of course, will tend to be less for very inexperienced versus experienced professionals. The novice therapist will be functioning largely at Level 1, while the therapist with considerable experience is be expected to be functioning primarily in Level 3. It would be an error, however, to assume that all experienced clinicians function at Level 3 across domains. We know therapists who seem to be unable to progress beyond Level 2 or, at times, Level 1 structures for particular domains.

The Level 1 Therapist

Across domains, the Level 1 therapist has skills to learn and needs opportunities to practice them. In the domain of intervention skills competence, the Level 1 therapist tends to focus on how the skills should be performed and when to use them. The therapist's evaluation of his or her effectiveness will be primarily based on self-perceptions of the adequacy of performing the techniques. Little awareness exists as to the effects of these interventions on the client.

The high motivation of the Level 1 therapist across relevant domains is at least partially a function of the fear and anxiety present. There is a strong desire to emulate experienced therapists, often the supervisor, as a means of developing skill and confidence and moving beyond the anxious neophyte role. The theoretical orientation beginners adopt is often directly tied into the perceived orientation of a role model. Often the more easily understood or unambiguous models are those to which these therapists are initially drawn. At other times, rather complex theories are "abstracted" by the Level 1 therapist into some fairly simple and understandable constructs to make the information more digestible. Another common approach is to be attracted to a theory that fits most closely one's own personal (often informal) theory of human behavior. This has the advantage of allowing the beginners to fill in the blanks in their knowledge of the theory with common sense, as they perceive it.

Typically the Level 1 trainee is quite dependent on the supervisor or others in authority. This is, of course, quite acceptable and usually imperative. The supervisor is the source of answers to the many puzzling questions with which beginners struggle. For example, producing a comprehensive, or even marginally inclusive, conceptualization or diagnosis of a client is often quite difficult for beginning therapists.

Level 1

Motivation	High motivation
	High levels of anxiety
	Skill acquisition focus
Autonomy	Dependent upon supervisor
	Needs structure from supervisor
	Positive feedback
	Minimal direct confrontation
Awareness	Self-awareness is limited
	Self-focus is high
	Evaluation apprehension
	Unaware of strengths/weaknesses

Transition to Level 2

Motivation	May decrease for new approaches/techniques
Autonomy	May desire more than is warranted
Awareness	Begins to move toward client, away from self

Level 2

Motivation	Fluctuating, sometimes highly confident
	Increased complexity shakes confidence
	Confusion, despair, vacillation
Autonomy	Dependency-autonomy conflict
	Can be quite assertive, pursue own agenda
	Functions more independently
	May only want requested, specific input
	Other times dependent or evasive
Awareness	Focuses more on client
	Empathy more possible
	Understanding client worldview more possible
	May become enmeshed, lose effectiveness
	May become confused, lose effectiveness
	Appropriate balance is an issue

Transition to Level 3

Motivation	Increased desire to personalize orientation
Autonomy	More conditionally autonomous
	Better understands limitations
Awareness	Focus begins to include self-reactions to client

Level 3

Motivation	Stable motivation
	Doubts remain, but not disabling
	Total professional identity is the focus
Autonomy	Firm belief in own autonomy
	Knows when to seek consultation

Table 2.1.   The Supervision Environment.

	Retains responsibility
Awareness	Accepts own strengths/weaknesses
	High empathy and understanding
	Focuses on client, process, and self
	Uses therapeutic self in sessions

Transition to 3i

Motivation	Strives for stable motivation across domains
Autonomy	Moves conceptually and behaviorally across domains
	Professional identity solid across relevant domains
Awareness	Personalized understanding across relevant domains
	Monitors impact of personal on professional life

Table 2.1.   (*continued*)

[handwritten marginal note: not apparent in my types]

Paging through a copy of the *DSM-IV* and trying to fit the client into appropriate categories can be at best a hit-or-miss enterprise. The supervisor can provide the necessary insights, mechanisms for data collection, and integration of information for the trainee. As the trainee develops this skill, the supervisor is still needed to validate or improve upon the initial versions.

In summary, across domains, the Level 1 therapist is characterized by a predominant self-preoccupation, a strong motivation for learning how to become as proficient as other professionals, and a desire to be instructed and nurtured by a more experienced clinician.

The Level 2 Therapist

The change in focus from the self to the client that occurs with Level 2 has many implications for practice across domains. In this stage, we can expect to see a considerable increase in the therapist's sensitivity to individual differences across clients. The increased empathic focus on the client allows the therapist to experience greater depth of emotional and cognitive understanding of the client, which increases the therapist's appreciation for the client's life circumstances. This greater depth and breadth of understanding of the client's world can be quite useful to the trainee in developing more adequate case conceptualizations. On the other hand, this wealth of information, with all of its idiosyncratic nuances, can present real problems for the therapist in wading through the data and reducing the information down to a concise conceptualization or diagnosis. At times, we may find a negative reaction to diagnosing or "labeling" a client because of the impersonal evaluation such processes can convey. This flood of information may also cause the therapist to freeze up in terms of making clinical decisions in treatment. By experiencing the client's emotions and thoughts, solutions that may have appeared quite workable at Level 1 may now appear overly simplistic and naive. Indeed, in terms of specific therapist behaviors and client progress, our Level 2 therapist may sometimes be less effective than our naively confident late Level 1 therapist.

This increase in perceived complexity of clinical practice and confusion concerning one's ability to function as a professional can produce day-to-day (and sometimes hour-to-hour) fluctuations in motivation. While our early Level 1 therapists may lack sufficient clinical knowledge to make decisions, our Level 2 therapist may perceive too many, or no adequate, options and become immobilized. The domain of individual differences often remains quite relevant and has implications across the other domains. The desire to know and understand the client's situation and view of the world is typically strong, except when the confusion or emotions get too strong, and the Level 2 therapist retreats to the relative safety of inactivity.

Regular reminders of professional ethics are important for Level 2 therapists. The dependency-autonomy conflict can create tension in the supervisory relationship that may limit the willingness of the therapist to share feelings and thoughts with the supervisor. Becoming too enmeshed with a client, or assuming too much responsibility for one's well-being, can result in unfortunate consequences.

The Level 3 Therapist

The Level 3 therapist is more able to use insightful self-awareness in addition to the awareness of the client's experience developed during Level 2. Both come into play in practice, giving a breadth of perspective to the therapist. His or her treatment goals and plans may reflect this integration of sources of information. Knowledge of a guiding theory, conceptualization of the client's difficulties, and confidence in one's own abilities will result in more adequate treatment plans. The Level 3 therapist is able to integrate information acquired through empathic listening to and skillful assessment of the client, monitor his or her own responses in the clinical situation, and be able to separate from the process in order to make more objective third-person observations. This results in an improved ability to plan and carry out effective treatments. In addition, we find little variation in how this individual functions across different professional roles in domains where development has reached Level 3. In other words, the integration of personal characteristics with professional behavior is high.

Motivation is stable and relatively high as the therapist makes great strides toward developing an idiosyncratic therapeutic style. This personalization of clinical practice allows for considerable autonomy for the Level 3 therapist. The therapist's idiosyncratic understanding of theory and implementation of interventions makes supervision consultative rather than didactic. Recommendations for changes or observations of other effective therapists are sifted through the Level 3 therapist's understanding of self and how this translates into his or her therapeutic behavior. This will not appear as defensiveness in supervision but rather as a thoughtful translation of one person's strengths and understandings into another's repertoire.

The Level 3i Therapist

This therapist is fully functioning across domains relevant to her or his practice. Level 3 structures are in play, and a fluidity of movement among them is apparent. In our experience, Level 3i is not often fully achieved, but clinicians who reach this point are considered masters by their colleagues.

The growth experienced as movement into Level 3i is less vertical (moving up the levels) and more horizontal in spreading understanding across domains and linking relevant schemata. Piaget's notion of *horizontal d'ecalage,* the unfolding from within, characterizes this level. Development within each domain is utilized to generate new awareness through integration and linking of schemata, as well as learning in response to input from others. The Level 3i therapist is creative, able to integrate previously retained knowledge across areas, learn from others, and evolve strong and appropriate accommodations and assimilations throughout the life cycle. Gilligan's notion of relational context of supervision is consistent with this stage.[9] The ongoing work of this therapist is to reestablish networks of knowledge with self-understandings that change as the individual continues to mature.

——◊——

This brief description of the IDM introduced some of the characteristics of the levels of professional development and provided some general examples. The next three chapters examine in detail each of the levels across domains, with considerable attention paid to how the supervisor can augment development of the supervisee. Specific examples of how the therapist characteristics are evident in therapy and in supervision, and guidance in providing supervisory interventions, are provided. Each chapter describes the prototypical therapist at each level, with particular attention to identification of status on the three overriding structures. How the structures are assessed across domains will be presented, with examples of therapists who exemplify these characteristics. Finally, specific guidance for supervisors who are working with supervisees at each level will be addressed. A general framework for providing a facilitative supervision environment will be augmented by specific recommendations for supervisory interventions that are effective for each level of therapist. Again, examples of implementation of some of these interventions with supervisees will be examined to give life to the model.

CHAPTER THREE

The Level 1 Therapist

———⟡———

After we have discussed the characteristics of the Level 1 therapist, we will turn our attention to the supervision environment most suited for this level of trainee. General orienting assumptions as well as specific useful techniques will be explored. We will also spend a little time examining examples of trainees who often have difficulty developing beyond entry level status. These Sublevel 1 trainees[1] pose challenges to trainers that may not be solved by traditional training methods.

Finally, we will address transitional issues that the Level 1 trainee will face just prior to moving on to Level 2. Identification of these issues signals to the supervisor that the Level 1 therapist is poised to begin dealing with Level 2 issues.

THE ENTRY-LEVEL TRAINEE

When we think of Level 1 trainees, the entry-level therapist is often the person who comes to mind. Those of us involved in training programs have the opportunity to work with a new group of beginning therapists-in-training on a yearly basis. The excitement (and anxiety), fresh perspectives, and zest for learning are always a welcome reminder of the optimism and promise that can characterize our profession.

Backgrounds of entry-level trainees vary considerably depending on the type of training program they are entering (psychology, social work, mental health counseling, psychiatry, and so on), but typically they have some content knowledge of the psychotherapy process, personality theory, systems theory, and other relevant areas. Their actual applied experience is usually limited, however, and may simply reflect an interest in human nature, being labeled a good listener by friends, or having experienced (or observed) critical life events that have emphasized for them the importance of psychotherapy and related practice.

Learning and Cognition

Most programs that train mental health professionals typically expose new students to course work and some type of prepracticum experience before they begin working with clients. This work provides the initial basis for understanding the process (therapy, assessment, and so on) and controlled opportunities for practice. In terms of cognitive models of learning, declarative verbal or image representation of the process begins here, allowing for a simple initial understanding of what is to be accomplished. These early concepts and the linkages created between them provide the initial framework from which trainees develop schemata. These schemata are derived from classifications of similarities across examples of processes, client types, assessment devices, and so on, addressed in training.

Trainees evaluate much of the information provided in early course work against their personal experience. Where similarities exist, schemata will more quickly be developed that will provide the early basis of understanding. Information less congruent with their prior experience may take longer to integrate or may be inaccurately integrated into existing schemata. It is useful to keep in mind that an initial schema will tend to be overly general and cannot accommodate numerous characteristics.

Another way of describing this process is to note that beginning trainees typically develop rather simplistic understandings of complex constructs and processes. Exceptionally bright trainees may learn complex material rather quickly and be able to regurgitate it on demand, but the actual ties to clinical processes will be weak at best. Once the schema of "hammer" is developed, nails are seen everywhere.

Motivations for Entering the Field

The motivations or reasons for entering training can have an impact on early development. A number of new trainees have a strong desire to help others in need. They want to gain the skills necessary to reduce the suffering of others and consequently have a tendency to prioritize their learning experiences directly related to psychotherapy interventions. Their interest in studying research methods, assessment techniques, or general information on biological, cognitive, emotional, or social processes may be limited. Those attracted to the field because they found the issues and processes intellectually stimulating may be less concerned initially with allaying the pain or problems of potential clients and more with the challenge of understanding human nature.

Depending on the focus of the training program, some new trainees are primarily interested in the science associated with clinical issues. They may prioritize learning experiences associated with research methodologies, statistics, and examination of empirical literatures on particular clinical issues.

Another rather common initial motivation for entering the field is the desire to learn more about oneself or another important figure in one's life. This can be in response to childhood experience, relationship issues, or any number of other life experiences. These trainees have a strong interest in issues most closely associated with aspects of personal experience and less interest in areas they perceive as unrelated.

Finally are new trainees whose primary motivation appears to be prestige or status. They are sometimes quite motivated to learn a breadth of knowledge and skills to earn the prestige or status to which they aspire. Others quite simply want the degree that leads to the license so they can begin the lifestyle they envision.

In our experience, no single initial motivational framework ensures success. Often these trainees' initial views of the field will change, and sometimes radically, over the course of training. And some trainees may be more resistant than others or unable to benefit from training.

ADVANCED SUPERVISEES

Although we typically think of entry-level trainees when we consider Level 1, much supervisory work will be with therapists who are functioning at Levels 2 or 3 in one or more domains but remain in Level 1 for others. The characteristics, needs, and exemplification of structures for these trainees still fit the Level 1 classification, but the overall

professional development and experience may mask some of the
naiveté apparent in true beginners.

Sam was an experienced therapist who had worked as a master's-level counselor in a
community mental health center for a number of years prior to returning to school for
advanced training. His supervisor was pleased with Sam's ability to work with clients
in individual therapy. He could quickly assess his clients and provide accurate diagnoses, as well as develop and carry out thoughtful treatment plans. It became apparent to the supervisor, however, that Sam lacked experience and understanding
regarding the modality of marital therapy. Couples who were assigned to Sam
inevitably were moved into individual therapy to deal with personal issues rather than
seen in marital therapy to address relationship problems. When this tendency was
explored in supervision, Sam noted that there always seemed to be a number of personal issues that each person could benefit from addressing and, frankly, he felt more
comfortable doing this than trying to engage in couples work.

A danger with advanced trainees who remain at Level 1 in domains
in which they practice is that they may reconceptualize issues, clients,
or processes to fit modalities with which they can comfortably perform at a higher level. This is, of course, not always the case. Fortu-
nately, a majority of therapists seek out training for new domains or
areas of practice and work diligently with the supervisor to develop
in these new areas.

LEVEL 1 STRUCTURES

Let's now move our attention to the overriding structures discussed
in the prior chapter. After we examine how each of these three structures characterize Level 1 therapists, we will see how they are evident
across the domains of professional practice.

Self and Other Awareness

Recall that Level 1 therapists are characterized by a primary focus on
themselves. In contrast to a rather enlightened self-focus or self-understanding that we will see with Level 3 therapists, the early Level 1
supervisee's awareness is primarily focused on his or her own anxiety,
lack of skills and knowledge, and the likelihood that he or she is being
regularly evaluated (and negatively, it is feared). These preoccupations
interfere with the supervisee's ability to perform the tasks associated

with clinical practice adequately and to focus on the task at hand or the client.

Prior research has consistently documented the anxiety and uncertainty of beginning trainees.[2] Hale and Stoltenberg conducted a study of new trainees and were able to parcel out the anxiety they felt into two types.[3] Students interested in counseling were offered the opportunity to work with a client concerning a relationship problem. They all were shown a videotape presentation of rather simple fundamental counseling skills to give them some exposure to the counseling process. Conditions were varied so that some trainees saw the client (a confederate) in a room with a visible video camera (and were alerted to this) while others used a room with no visible camera (and were unaware of one). Half of each of these groups were told that their counseling would be critiqued by a supervisor after the session, and the other half were told that such supervision would be available to them at some future time, should they desire it. Students were told to use as many of the skills they observed on the training tape as possible. Students who were to see the supervisor were told that their session would be critiqued according to the skills demonstrated in the training videotape.

The results of this study indicated that the lowest level of anxiety was reported by students who were in rooms with no visible video camera and were not scheduled to see a supervisor after the session. These students also tended to stay in the counseling session longer (which was left open-ended) than other students. The students who were in rooms with visible video cameras and were scheduled to see a supervisor after the session reported the highest levels of anxiety and tended to stay the shortest time in the counseling session. The other two groups fell in between and were similar in levels of reported anxiety.

The authors concluded that some of the anxiety the students experienced was associated with evaluation apprehension, or the concern of being negatively evaluated by the supervisor. Another component of the anxiety for some was a function of a process referred to as objective self-awareness,[4] or a personal negative appraisal of the self by an individual who does not think he or she is meeting acceptable standards of practice. Both of these components fit well with the cognitive and emotional aspects of self-awareness as it pertains to Level 1 therapists.

In the cognitive area, these supervisees are concerned with learning information, understanding the process, and performing the skills in an appropriate manner. Their attention tends to be directed toward searching their memories for clues as to what to do (scanning relevant schemata), monitoring their own behavior in performing newly learned skills, and trying to fit what the client is telling them (in assessment and psychotherapy) into a meaningful category for conceptualization purposes. This concerted effort leaves little attentional space available for focusing their thoughts directly on the client and understanding his or her perspective.

Affectively, supervisees in the early phase of Level 1 experience considerable anxiety, and sometimes fear, related to their lack of confidence in knowing what to do, being able to do it, and being negatively evaluated by the client or the supervisor, or both, for doing it poorly. It is difficult, if not impossible, for the trainee who is suffering through performance anxiety to experience empathy for the client and truly resonate with his or her emotional experience.

Although the early confusion and uncomfortable levels of anxiety lighten as the trainee gains experience, this progress does not signal an end to Level 1. The self-awareness and lack of other awareness will continue for a while. The trainee's initial negative assessment of his or her own performance will usually give way to more confidence in the ability to exercise certain skills and understand certain processes. The focus nevertheless remains on how the therapist is performing and understanding rather than on insightful perceptions of the client's reactions to the process.

Motivation

Early in the training experience, Level 1 therapists will be characterized by fairly high levels of motivation, though tempered, of course, by the anxiety associated with this stage (for example, relief or feeling off the hook when a client no-shows or cancels). Nonetheless, embarking on a new career and learning a new profession is an exciting time, and most new trainees want to learn, and quickly. For most supervisees, the first practicum experience after preparatory initial course work represents the first experience relevant to the "real work" in terms of becoming a therapist. Thus, a high investment in the learning of therapeutic skills adds to the beginner's high motivation. No doubt some of this motivation is related to wanting the anxiety to end and the confidence to take over, but the impact remains. The early Level 1 therapist is typically enthusiastic, committed, and attentive.

These characteristics are facilitative of quick learning of material and skills and, for most, fairly rapid progress in learning and performing some fundamental tasks.

This early motivation to learn may dissipate somewhat as trainees hit the latter phase of Level 1. Although the motivation to practice usually remains high, an overconfidence may emerge from a perception of competence in performing fundamental tasks and confidence in one's grasp of limited information. Positive evaluations by the supervisor may add to this state of overconfidence, which is not tempered by the more complex understanding of clinical processes characteristic of later stages of professional development.

Autonomy

Level 1 therapists are usually, and appropriately, highly dependent on the supervisor, primarily during the early phase of training. The supervisor and other authority figures are seen as sources of support and knowledge and viewed as crucial to the trainee's desire to get beyond the lack of knowledge and anxiety. The supervisor is, at least to some degree, a role model for the beginner. Thus, supervision is an opportunity to receive support, direct information, specific advice, and training in helping the trainee negotiate clinical practice—all appropriate to the Level 1 trainee who, by definition, lacks the knowledge and skills necessary to perform as an autonomous professional.

Toward the end of Level 1, trainees tend to become less openly dependent on supervisors. If the training experience has been structured in such a way to allow the therapist to achieve success in early attempts at interventions, he or she may develop sufficient, although unjustified, confidence and desire more autonomous functioning. With therapists who are functioning at advanced levels in other domains, we may see relatively high levels of initial confidence in functioning in the new domain based primarily on the assumption that their other clinical knowledge and skills will carry them through.

STRUCTURES ACROSS DOMAINS

General descriptions of Level 1 supervisees are inadequate to conduct a careful assessment. It is necessary to evaluate the therapist across domains that are relevant to his or her practice under supervision. To do this, supervisors must be cognizant of the structural status for each of the domains of interest. As we have noticed, there are also transitions between levels that mark development that occurs prior to a stage change. Although a therapist will usually be functioning at more than one level across a number of domains, he or she should be at similar levels across closely related domains if sufficient experience and training have occurred. Stoltenberg and Delworth[5] described how Level 1 trainees exemplify the overriding structures across eight domains.

Intervention Skills Competence

This rather broad domain reflects many different skills associated with numerous types of interventions flowing from various theoretical frameworks. In addition, different modes of delivery necessitate the use of a range of skills. Supervisors must consider the specific therapeutic activity of focus when assessing a therapist in this domain. Are they evaluating intervention skills from a cognitive-behavioral framework in working with an individual depressed woman? Or evaluating intervention skills from an object relations framework in working with a narcissistic man? Perhaps supervisory attention focuses on marital therapy, where conjoint sessions with the couple are the modality. It is important to consider the supervisee's level of development for this domain in context and realize that he or she may be quite developed within a given theoretical framework, working with a particular type of client, and from a certain modality, yet be considerably less developed when one or more of these conditions is altered.

Beginning therapists usually desire training in some understandable set of skills, preferably within a fairly structured framework, that will provide some guidelines for working with clients. If, for example, some variation on fundamental listening skills is the initial focus of training, the supervisee will strive to understand how to perform these skills in sessions and self-evaluate how effectively they have been implemented. This situation fits rather well with the initial self-focus of Level 1 trainees, who tend to imitate another or apply a cursory understanding of the process to their sessions. They will try to remember how to implement a skill and decide when to use it, focusing primarily on their own internal frame of reference. This reflects the cognitive focus.

The affective dimension of this self-preoccupation is anxiety or feelings of apprehension. There can be a real lack of self-efficacy in a trainee's ability to perform a skill adequately or time it appropriately. Should the supervisor be unaware of or unresponsive to this anxiety and create more ambiguity, the trainee's anxiety will accelerate.

Beginning therapists typically latch on to a particular orientation and become a devotee. Although expert experienced therapists also often work from a primary orientation (although most tend to be eclectic), novices are likely to make a less well-informed decision. They find it easier to select an approach, often the first one to which they are exposed, and stay with it than learn more than one and stay confused that much longer. This approach is not a bad one. Developing a therapeutic base can allow the trainee to move more quickly to advanced Level 1, feeling comfortable and opening up awareness to the client, which in turn may stimulate more exploration into other approaches and techniques. This sense of power or mastery can open the trainee up for more challenging experiences, eliciting more growth.

Still, it is fairly common for novices to take a given set of skills to the limit before investing themselves in learning new or more comprehensive frameworks. For example, in our training clinic at the University of Oklahoma, our master's students may find themselves seeing couples fairly soon after they begin to feel somewhat comfortable with individual clients and often before any formal didactic course work in marital approaches to therapy. Usually the trainees begin by using fundamental listening skills, taking turns if there are two therapists, focusing on one client at a time. They often show some initial resistance to learning a mode of therapy more suited to couples because this necessitates a step back to uncertainty and learning new skills. Thus, an early motivation to learn can be inhibited by moving the trainee too quickly and demanding too much.

Early dependence on the supervisor is to be expected, and even encouraged, within limits. The therapist relies on the supervisor to show how to apply skills learned in laboratories or discussed in class. Expansion of new skills to move the therapy process along is expected to come from the supervisor when needed. Occasionally this dependency can be extreme and nonfacilitative. Nearly every year we seem to have one or more new trainees who have the need to call the supervisor at nearly any hour, day or night, to check out what to do with a client or request other resources for learning techniques. If the supervisor is an advanced student, this dependence can be annoying. If the supervisor is a senior psychologist, this is often viewed as intolerable.

However, therapeutic ego strength is quite limited, and constructive ways to redirect the trainee's energies are needed to keep the situation from becoming aversive. Positive reinforcement and rewarding appropriate behavior go a long way in making trainees feel effective and confident in their potential for growth.

Assessment Techniques

Early course work in assessment approaches and instruments, along with intake training, marks the beginning of work in this domain. It is common for trainees to assume initially that assessment information is unequivocal, rather than indications of a certain likelihood of personality characteristics, cognitive styles, career interests, and so on. Some trainees may pursue an early preference for "interview data" as the primary source of information for assessment, while others may become intrigued with objective, norm-based assessments. The strong cognitive self-focus can be quite useful in this stage as novices learn to administer assessment devices in a standardized way, but it can present problems when they have to listen carefully to responses, decide when to push for elaborations, and code according to criteria. There can be a tendency to want to fit clients into neatly defined categories, which reduces some of the ambiguity of therapy. Indeed, we find an "assessment clinic," in which we focus primarily on conducting contract assessments, to be quite popular with newer students. Some seem to be initially more attracted to what they perceive as the more structured and straightforward process of assessment than the "fuzzy," less structured process of therapy. Nonetheless, their motivation is usually high, as expected. The supervisor is expected to be there to help decide on the assessment strategy, train in administration and scoring, and interpret results.

Interpersonal Assessment

Somewhere in between intervention skills competence and assessment techniques is the process of interpersonal assessment. Here the therapist must learn to use himself or herself in the session either to elicit responses from the client that aid the assessment process or use his or her own reactions to the client as an indication of social skills status or the presence or absence of certain personality characteristics. In the early phases of focus on this domain, the therapist is inclined either to ignore certain processes that are occurring in therapy or attribute too much pathology to reasonable responses by the client to anxiety-provoking situations. Therapists' self-focus limits their ability to take the perspective of the client and their ability to monitor their own reactions accurately (due to the uncertainty they feel). Getting locked into a set of expectations concerning client responses will make it difficult for the trainee to respond to unexpected statements or recognize clues to client characteristics that were unanticipated. The motivation to learn to assess clients is high, but, again, the supervisor plays a crucial role in serving to validate, redirect, interpret information, or offer alternative conceptualizations for the therapist.

Client Conceptualization

Formal case conceptualizations can take many forms, often varying according to the theoretical model the therapist uses. This process should not be confused with diagnosis (for example, using *DSM-IV*). Although trainees need to learn the process and utility of an accurate *DSM-IV* diagnosis, reference to the manual often does not advance an understanding of the client that leads to a subsequent treatment plan (another domain). The literature is fairly clear on the limitations of diagnostic classifications in making treatment decisions,[6] so it is important not to limit the focus on client conceptualizations to simple diagnoses. We use a rather detailed format to guide therapists in developing a more complex understanding of their client's dynamics as well as forcing them to attend to and integrate relevant data (see Appendix A).

Novice therapists tend to focus on specific aspects of the client's history, current situation, or assessment data and exclude consideration of other relevant information. This can be a function of seeing the world through their own experiences, or simply forcing a familiar template on all new situations. They may make rather grand conceptualizations based on somewhat sparse information or discrete observations. Diagnostic criteria can be bent to the will of a therapist in search of a parsimonious diagnosis. Consistency of diagnosis, or of information congruent with a given orientation, may direct thinking rather than a search for information and a conceptualization salient to the client's presenting problem and life circumstances. There can be a tendency to either "psychopathologize" fairly functional responses by the client or "normalize" fairly pathological ones. Early on, there is a strong interest in learning about clients and understanding them, so novices' motivation is high. Their initial attempts at conceptualizations may be inordinately long (but lacking in organization and integration) or incredibly brief. Nonetheless, they rely on the supervisor to provide direction, affirmation, and confirmation of therapist conceptualizations.

Individual Differences

Schneider[7] asserts that the time has come for educational models to include the "unselfconscious integration" of issues of gender, sexual, ethnic, and socioeconomic diversity as a simple reflection of the way the world is. Many training programs have attempted to address this issue by including more course work on the counseling issues of diverse populations, along with the infusion of diversity issues across course work. Although it is increasingly likely that Level 1 trainees are being exposed to these issues early in their training experiences, they still often rely too heavily on their own idiosyncratic experiences and perceptions of the world in attempting to understand their clients. Their own cultural background may serve as the "ground" on which a given client is viewed as the "figure." Although it is probably advantageous for therapists to have had broad experiences across various cultures, this is not the norm. Additionally, the impact of gender is salient for many issues, and an understanding of this issue may initially be lacking or unarticulated. Many trainees, even with the growing emphasis on multicultural issues, may assume that they share a similar worldview with most of their clients, therefore not acknowledging the importance of differences in background, culture, gender, or physical or mental abilities. On the other hand, trainees are often highly motivated to learn about other cultures, genders, people with disabilities, and other important individual differences. In therapy, however, these therapists may see themselves as having little or nothing in common with clients from different backgrounds or life circumstances, which can make therapy appear to be an overwhelming task. On the other hand, they may attempt to use what they have learned in multicultural courses and apply fairly rigid, although often positive, stereotypes to their clients.

Cheryl had not worked with many ethnic minority clients before she was assigned a fairly traditional American Indian boy as a client. After the initial session, she remarked to her supervisor that she did not feel comfortable with the boy. "He's awfully quiet, and I think he's keeping some important things from me. He never looked me directly in the eye during the entire session and offered very little without prompting. I almost wonder if he wasn't high on something." Cheryl's supervisor explored with her other aspects of the client's behavior and noted that it is often considered disrespectful for American Indian children to maintain eye contact with adults. "His quiet demeanor and lack of eye contact might well be a function of his respect for you rather than a sign of resistance, inattentiveness, or substance abuse."

Personality characteristics form another factor in individual differences that can create challenges for the therapist. Classification of clients into various "disorders" can immobilize the trainee (How can I work with a crazy person?), or these differences may be minimized as one approach to therapy is assumed to work in all cases. If the therapist relies primarily on his or her own life experiences, or the authority of a given theoretical orientation to therapy, the important information that can be provided by the client is lost. The supervisor provides a useful resource in learning how to collect important information and integrate individual differences into the therapy process.

Theoretical Orientation

Training programs approach teaching theoretical orientations differently. Some are closely identified with a particular orientation, while others are more diverse. However this training occurs, it is unusual for beginning therapists to have a detailed and integrated knowledge of any orientation when work begins with clients. Even in programs that attempt to expose trainees to diverse models, there is a tendency for novice therapists to discover the "best" or most correct orientation. Once identified, they can expend considerable effort in disciple-like fervor to learn all about the approach.

Some of our students have responded quite well to a focus on "empirically validated/empirically supported" approaches to therapy, thinking initially that this would simplify the process of learning therapy. As they come to realize that no one approach works in all cases and that specific guidance is lacking as to the superior approach across many situations, they can become disheartened. Even when a particular theoretical orientation shows promise for being effective with a breadth of clients and presenting problems, the moderating factors that need to be considered in planning and carrying out treatment often defy simple solutions. Nonetheless, in Level 1, ease of understanding and conservation of effort can be the rule. Motivation is high and energy expended in learning is significant, so supervisors can provide direction that can result in a firm foundation in a particular approach. Although knowledge based in a single approach will subsequently encourage some tunnel vision and can limit flexibility, it also serves to reduce anxiety and provide a cognitive structure for understanding the process. The early dependence may result in strong imitation of the supervisor's orientation, but may also reflect adherence to course work or other sources of information available to the therapist.

Treatment Plans and Goals

Many of us have had the experience of asking a supervisee after four or five sessions to give a detailed explanation of the treatment plan— and find that none exists. In one of our training clinics, we require a treatment plan by the third session, but with beginning therapists the plan can be very brief and very general, or it may be more of a work of fiction than a guide for therapy. It is difficult for Level 1 therapists to conceptualize the treatment process from intake through termination. Frankly, their initial focus is often more on keeping the clients coming than of expecting facilitative change. It is common to find treatment plans where there are limited short-term or long-term goals, outcome criteria, or intervention approaches tied to any of these. Sometimes the trainee has techniques in mind to use, but cannot tie these into the goals, or he or she may have some goals in mind but no idea how to reach them.

Therapist behaviors within a given session may stand independently from behaviors in prior or subsequent sessions and may be a response to situational influences as opposed to an overall plan. While it is not uncommon for experienced therapists to shoot from the hip in a given session, he or she is relying on a wealth of information available in the session, in addition to prior knowledge and experience. The beginner's approach is likely to be more random or based more on a predetermined sequence of interventions as part of a structured program. In either situation, the self-focus inhibits using all available client data, and the reaction to any ambiguous information will either elicit a more highly structured response or retreat to the supervisor for direction.

Professional Ethics

All mental health service providers are exposed to professional guidelines of ethical behavior and relevant state laws as part of their training programs. Initial utilization of these guidelines follows a fairly rigid application of rote memorization, or at least learning to look up specific guidelines for particular situations. If they are not emphasized, however, a laissez-faire approach can emerge in which the guidelines are viewed as being for the guidance of others and not for the therapist. More often, however, the guidelines are taken seriously to the extent that they are understood. Integrating ethics with personal and professional values and identity will come more slowly during later development. When details are lacking in the guidelines, ethical dilemmas can ensue, and the trainee usually consults with colleagues, the supervisor, and others in authority. If the guidelines are not adequately discussed and continuously highlighted, however, they may not be seen as relevant across all situations where they should guide professional behavior. In these situations, a lack of clarity or understanding can result in an ethical bind for therapists.

SUPERVISING THE LEVEL 1 THERAPIST

In this examination of approaches to supervising Level 1 therapists, guiding assumptions will form the framework from which we consider some specific techniques that have proved helpful. We prefer to provide orienting structure and concepts rather than attempting to develop a cookbook approach to supervision. The latter approach may be easier to grasp initially and provide more specific direction, but it tends to wear thin and lose its utility as more complicated issues take center stage. For example, interpersonal process recall and microcounseling were initially developed to guide the training of skills for new counselors.[8] These approaches, and their variations, have proved useful in this regard. In addition, resources exist for beginning supervisors that include activities, tables, and charts to help the novice approach supervising beginning trainees.[9]

Our approach is to provide a "map" for the "territory" of clinical supervision across developmental and experience levels. Thus, certain techniques take precedence at given points in time, while others prove more useful in different situations. Also, because therapists will be simultaneously at different levels of development, one approach may prove inadequate across domains, perhaps even within a given supervision session.

We have described in some detail how we view the Level 1 therapist according to the overriding structures and how these characteristics will make themselves evident across different domains. Considerable support exists for aspects of this view of therapists within the empirical literature. For example, Guest and Beutler examined trainees over time during a training program. They noted that beginning therapists valued support and technical direction from their supervisors.[10] Similarly, Krause and Allen found that supervisors viewed themselves as varying their supervisory approach for trainees at various levels in ways quite similar to Stoltenberg's developmental model.[11] Although trainees appeared not to be aware of this difference in approaches, supervisor and supervisee dyads that agreed on the supervisee's developmental level showed the greatest satisfaction and impact of supervision for the trainees.

Other studies have examined the supervision process and have provided evidence consistent with our developmental view. Studies have reported that supervisors tend to vary their approach to supervising therapists by providing more structure and instruction during the early phases.[12] Beginning therapists tend to want greater structure provided by their supervisors,[13] are less self-aware,[14] and feel more uncertainty regarding expectations and evaluations in supervision.[15]

General Considerations

A consistent finding in the empirical literature on clinical supervision, and a basic tenet of our developmental models since their inception, is that the supervisor of Level 1 therapists needs to provide structure for the supervision experience, as well as assist the supervisees in structuring their clinical work. This structure removes some of the uncertainty from the process and helps limit the anxiety associated with early training.

One of the advantages of being associated with a clinical training program is having the opportunity to teach courses on clinical supervision and supervise doctoral students who are learning to supervise. In our program at Oklahoma, our second-year doctoral students (who usually have a master's degree before beginning the doctoral program) supervise beginning master's students over two semesters. One of the issues commonly addressed is the need to organize the supervision sessions for the supervisees. Taking a nondirective approach in this early phase is usually problematic and raises the already significantly high anxiety level of the new supervisees.

This level of therapist typically views the supervisor as a role model and, perhaps, an expert. Minimally, the supervisor will usually be seen as knowing more about clinical practice than do the supervisees. This is, of course, usually a positive experience for our student supervisors. It can also be rewarding for experienced supervisors, although the degree of dependency of some beginning therapists can become tiresome for the supervisor who is continually working with this level of therapist.

Janet was a first-year master's student in a community counseling program whose direct supervisor was Kim, a second-year doctoral student in counseling psychology. Janet was particularly anxious, even for a novice, about beginning her first practicum in the clinic. The initial supervision sessions were spent getting to know one another. Kim described her orientation to therapy and supervision (which, frankly, was just developing), and Janet discussed what she had learned thus far and how her interest in counseling had developed. They covered how to do intake assessments and the format for the initial counseling session Janet would have with her first client. Kim role-played the client and then the therapist with Janet to give her practice in using the fundamental counseling skills she had been studying. As time for the initial session approached, Janet asked for additional supervision time and called Kim at home nearly every day to discuss issues that had occurred to her. After the initial session, Janet wanted an extended supervision session to study the videotape of the session completely. As was common in this setting, other first-year students observed the counseling session live via video and gave Janet some feedback after the session. This resulted in more phone calls to Kim to process the feelings of inadequacy and anger Janet felt in response to this feedback from her colleagues.

Confidence can build slowly, although sometimes it comes far too quickly, with Level 1 trainees. Becoming a therapist can be viewed as something more threatening and much more an extension of one's personality than other learning experiences. Thus, for some trainees, criticism of their therapy skills is viewed as criticism of them and their level of maturity rather than a comment on what they have learned and what they have left to learn. This perspective can be attenuated somewhat by approaching this early training as a process of learning skills and behaviors. By breaking down the process into fairly discrete and observable actions, it becomes less threatening and more easily learned.

As the clarity of understanding concerning at least some of the processes associated with clinical practice develops, the trainee's confidence will build. It is often facilitative to work from a fairly consistent and rudimentary framework to allow understanding of theory and skills to proceed at an acceptable speed to enable the trainee to function adequately in the domain of interest. For example, an initial focus on fundamental counseling skills can reduce the complexity of the therapeutic process to an understandable level. Behaviors that encourage the client to explore issues and communicate attentiveness and concern by the therapist can move along the therapy process, even if these behaviors are performed without the optimal level of underlying understanding. It is possible, of course, for a novice therapist to learn to reflect content and some client feelings without a deep understanding of the client's experience or true empathy. This can come later.

It is also important to encourage early responsibility for one's role in the therapeutic process. Although considerable information will need to be conveyed to the Level 1 therapist by the supervisor through fairly didactic means, supervisors should remain alert for the opportunities to encourage the supervisee to engage in problem solving about his or her clinical work and engage in a self-examination. This process needs to be carefully monitored so that it facilitates early attempts at autonomy without endangering the client or confusing the therapist or frustrating his or her development. Appropriate risk taking should also be encouraged. The trainee may tend to stay with what he or she knows rather than explore new skills or interventions. On the other hand, fools often go gladly where the experienced would fear to tread. Risk taking is not always good or appropriate, and the experience of the supervisor needs to be brought to bear in clinical decision making. Remember that a facilitative level of discomfort or disequilibrium is necessary for growth. On the other hand, sufficient information and experience need to be assimilated for the trainee to be able to develop useful and relevant schemata related to clinical practice. A careful balance must be maintained.

Client Assignment

It is not always possible to exert total control over the types of clinical experiences available to Level 1 supervisees. In the best of all worlds, which is rarely possible, it is probably most beneficial for clients with fairly mild presenting problems (certain "V" codes, problems in living, mild depression) to be assigned to beginning therapists. Sometimes "maintenance" cases are appropriate, even if the level of pathology is significant. In these latter cases, the primary goal may be monitoring the client with limited expectations for improvement. The goal is to assign clients to the therapists who will present minimal risks and have some potential for positive therapeutic experiences. With mildly troubled clients who have adequate personal resources, fundamental counseling skills implemented by the therapist can result in significant improvement. Other clients whose problems are fairly specific, for example, simple phobias, can benefit from a structured approach to therapy (systematic desensitization) that can be quickly learned and adequately implemented by the beginning therapist. Clients with whom the therapists can develop a degree of comfort in the therapy situation, and with whom he or she can practice some fundamental skills, are ideal for beginners. In the absence of such clients, very careful intensive supervision with considerable instruction (or even cotherapy) may be necessary to ensure client welfare and protect the supervisee from early failure.

Interventions

Loganbill, Hardy, and Delworth described supervision interventions that can form a useful basis for understanding the supervision process.[16] For Level 1 therapists, *facilitative* interventions are perhaps the most important. These interventions are intended to communicate support to the supervisee and encourage development. Praise, reinforcement of appropriate demonstrations of skills, careful and attentive listening, and other indications of appreciation of and consideration for the supervisee are particularly useful at this time.

Prescriptive interventions are also very necessary for Level 1 therapists. These supervisees will have limited knowledge of therapeutic orientations, interventions, and client dynamics. It is important that the supervisor be prepared to advise the therapist concerning what might be done at a given point with a particular client. It is best, when possible, to present the supervisee with alternatives, in order to encourage central route processing by supervisees and support early attempts at autonomy. By presenting options from which the therapist can select an intervention, supervisors encourage the assumption of responsibility for treatment and engaging in a critical evaluation of alternatives.

In some cases, a direct prescriptive intervention for novices, such as, "Do not ask any questions in the next session," is helpful and takes advantage of their need for structure. Phrasing this directive as a challenge may be considered a catalytic intervention (see below), but serves to take advantage of the beginning therapist's high level of motivation.

Another useful class of supervision interventions for Level 1 therapists is *conceptual* interventions. Remember that the self-aware (or self-conscious) Level 1 trainee will tend to focus primarily on what he or she should do with the client, or how anxious he or she is, rather than thinking through a rationale for a given intervention. This therapist's ability to make conceptual ties between theory and practice will be limited, so the supervisor should begin the process of linking the two together for the supervisee when the opportunity exists. The better a therapist is able to begin to think of the theory, diagnosis (or conceptualization), and treatment continuum, the more quickly he or she will develop autonomy.

Confrontive interventions are sometimes appropriate for Level 1 therapists, but they are usually best used when the early anxiety has lifted and some confidence in ability has developed. Recall that as the therapist becomes comfortably established in Level 1, he or she can adequately perform (at least by his or her own standards) certain skills and feels confident about understanding the process. At this point an increase in the desire for autonomy will be noted. Therapists who have had the opportunity to experience success in their clinical work and have found that they can be effective may become quite confident and comfortable with their level of understanding and skills. This is the time when confrontation can be effectively used. Earlier in the training experience, confrontation may freeze the supervisee and halt development. Once the comfort level has grown, however, confrontation may be necessary to move the therapist beyond what is safe and to try new interventions or work with more challenging clients. We find that the use of videotapes is often important at this stage. This technology enables the supervisee to evaluate his or her work critically and begin the process of focusing attention more on the client and seeing the impact of the interventions. These confrontations need not always be dramatic or inflammatory. Simply pointing out mistakes, miscues, or things overlooked by the therapist can provide sufficient confrontation.

Catalytic interventions are typically reserved for late Level 1 rather than beginning therapists. Catalytic interventions are intended to expand the awareness of the therapist in aspects of clinical practice that have escaped his or her attention, due to limitations in available awareness as a function of the person's self-absorption. While we will use these interventions liberally in Level 2, they can also be useful in redirecting the attention of the advanced Level 1 trainee. Catalytic interventions challenge the comfort level of the supervisee. Again, this is often made easier by having access to videotapes of the supervisee's work with clients. Commenting on the therapeutic process, focusing the therapist's attention on the client's reactions, or focusing attention on the therapist's thoughts and feelings at a given point in the session are examples of interventions that can broaden the view of the trainee. We might also highlight the potential for, or the exhibiting of any, countertransference reactions by the therapist. The therapist's emotional reactions to the client, or the supervisor, can be highlighted and pursued as avenues for exploration of the therapeutic, and supervision, process. By pushing the therapist to attend more to the client as well as understand the clinical process at a more complex level, the supervisor is setting the stage for movement into Level 2.

Supervisory Mechanisms

There are a number of techniques or mechanisms that the effective supervisor can draw on in clinical supervision. In our opinion, the power is not usually in the technique but rather in how effectively it is used. No one technique or mechanism is adequate for all situations. Skilled supervisors will use a breadth of mechanisms to further supervisory goals and encourage the growth of the trainee. We will discuss a number of mechanisms, but our list is neither exhaustive nor prescriptive. The mechanism chosen at any given point in time for work with a particular therapist depends on available resources and the current needs of the situation.

In working with Level 1 (and Level 2) therapists, observation of their clinical work is imperative. Although some training settings rely heavily on verbatims (attempts by the trainee to write down everything that was said during a given session) or other variations on self-report, these are inadequate. Level 1 therapists are not able to perceive accurately what they are doing in the session, let alone what is going on with the client. Supervisors who rely on their perceptions, and their memories, will be supervising in the dark. Observation is crucial, whether it is by videotape, direct observation, immediate, or delayed. To know what went on in a session, supervisors need to see it or, minimally, hear it.

Live observation, sometimes with "consultation teams," is an approach that has grown in popularity, particularly in marriage and family training programs. This approach is increasingly viewed as a strong modality in professional psychology programs as well.[17] Live observation—whether phone consultations, "bug-in-the-ear" technology, or pulling the therapist out of the room for a consultation is the technique of choice—has much to offer. The advantages include providing immediate structure for the session for the supervisee, being present to provide support and feedback, giving immediate advice or prescriptions, and seeing the process unfold as it happens. There are also some drawbacks to this approach. The time investment by the supervisor and distraction to the flow of the session can be significant. In addition, these approaches tend to take the responsibility away from the supervisee and give it to the supervisor or consultant. There is some advantage to having the supervisee struggle to deal with a clinical situation without the security blanket of the consultant or supervisor being immediately available. Nonetheless, if used with care, there can be real benefits. If used inappropriately, growth can be stagnated.

Skills training is necessary in the early stages of development for nearly any domain. One of our students is fond of saying, "Fake it until you make it," as his model of therapy. This slogan can be useful for supervision of the therapist as well. As Alfred Korzybski once said, the map is not the territory.[18] In a similar vein, the skill is not the intervention. Therapists can learn the behavior but not understand the intent or the nuances of its application or implementation. Nonetheless, the skills provide mechanisms for moving therapy along. Practice of skills in supervision, role-playing therapy interactions, reversing roles, and playing those interactions out again can be very useful in building the skills necessary for early work in therapy.

Perhaps introducing a sports analogy here will be helpful. Many of us have had the opportunity to teach our children, or other people's children, how to play baseball. If left to their own devices, they will learn how to hit a ball with some degree of effectiveness. However, when a coach steps in and begins to instruct the child on how to hold a bat, pay attention to the strike zone, or watch for the curve ball, the ability of the child to hit the ball can be compromised. Nonetheless, some of these skills may need to be developed (even overlearned) before the child can anticipate the pitch and hit to the opposite field and score a runner from third base. We might also note that children will pick up on certain behaviors when observing more advanced ball players that have little, if anything, to do with effective hitting. One of our nephews was soundly convinced that banging the bat on home plate was the most important part of being a batter. The behavior was learned before the meaning became evident.

Supervisees also tend to rely on their supervisors to interpret dynamics for them in their work with clients. This is useful and appropriate as long as it is done within the confines of their understanding of the process. The supervisor who "takes off" on hypothesizing about interpersonal or family dynamics of the client may leave the therapist in the dust. The supervisee may still be wondering how to get the client to talk, considering other more esoteric material may fall on deaf ears or add to the confusion.

Level 1 therapists have limited information regarding clinical practice at their disposal. They are often eager to learn and respond well to lists of readings or other resources the supervisor provides to them. It is important, however, to keep the breadth of this material somewhat limited. For example, the novice therapist may have difficulty integrating cognitive therapy material with object relations readings. It may be better to stay within a given orientation initially and expand the range of information and resources as the therapist is able to implement material that has already been presented.

Group supervision can be a good mechanism for learning for the Level 1 trainee. We discuss this subject in more detail in Chapter Seven, but suffice it to say at this point that this presents another opportunity to learn by example from colleagues. Appropriately handled group supervision can present the therapist with additional options for interventions, other conceptualization perspectives, and additional skills to practice. It can also serve as a supportive atmosphere for exploring the clinical process and one's understanding of it. If not handled carefully, however, it can become an aversive situation that adds to the level of anxiety of the therapists. The supervisor must take care to encourage positive feedback and constructive comments while normalizing the growth process for the supervisees. Competition is common and, if left unfettered, can create a negative environment that does more harm than good. We have summarized some of the points of this discussion in Table 3.1.

General considerations	Provide structure and keep anxiety at manageable levels
Client assignment	Mild presenting problems or maintenance cases
Interventions	Facilitative (supportive, encouraging)
	Prescriptive (suggest approaches, etc.)
	Conceptual (some, tie theory-DX-TX)
	Catalytic (late Level 1; see Level 2)
Mechanisms	Observation (video or live)
	Skills training
	Role playing
	Interpret dynamics (limited, client or trainee)
	Readings
	Group supervision
	Appropriate balance of ambiguity/conflict
	Address strengths, then weaknesses
	Closely monitor clients

Table 3.1.   Level 1 Supervision Environment.

Final Considerations

We need to be constantly aware of striving for the facilitative balance of ambiguity and conflict versus clarity and comfort. Too much ambiguity, anxiety, or disequilibriums will frustrate trainees and inhibit their growth. Too much perceived clarity or naive understanding of the process, comfort, and confidence will also stagnate growth. The balance must be struck and restruck again throughout the supervision process.

It has been demonstrated in related research that perhaps the optimal approach to providing feedback for beginning therapists is to highlight strengths and positive behaviors first, then move on to areas where growth has yet to occur or corrective feedback is necessary.[19] This process sets up the supervisee to hear what the supervisor has to say. By first acknowledging areas of strength, supervisors reinforce the initial attempts at competence and early development of confidence. They are informing the supervisee that they are aware of the progress he or she has made and the skills already developed. Then focusing on areas for growth can build on these strengths and remind the therapist that development is not complete, and there is more to learn.

Finally, supervisors must always take great care to monitor client welfare. They have the dual responsibilities of encouraging and enhancing supervisee growth while maintaining quality control of the services provided to clients. We make it very clear that the purpose of our clinic is to train therapists. Thus, most therapy will be provided by students under the supervision of licensed professionals. The fact is that most clients would benefit more, and benefit more quickly, from therapy provided by a skilled and seasoned professional than they will by working with a trainee. Our fee schedule reflects an awareness of this. However, we would quickly run out of skilled, experienced, seasoned professionals if supervisees were not allowed to work with clients or were merely used as extensions of the supervisor's clinical expertise. Nonetheless, we should be sure that no harm is done and, hopefully, quality services are provided by our supervisees, regardless of level of therapist development.

SUBLEVEL 1 TRAINEES

Some aspiring therapists, new to the field and lacking in experience, do not seem to be able to progress in their development. Sometimes these problems arise early in prepracticum experiences, but they can surface later when these young (in terms of experience) therapists are working with clients in the clinical setting. Although occasionally our selection procedures are lacking and students with serious disorders enter our programs, this remains rare. More common are situations where there appears to be developmental stagnation or personal blocks that preclude effective growth as a therapist.

Eichenfield and Stoltenberg have described these trainees as Sublevel 1.[20] These individuals are unable to meet entry-level expectations in training as psychotherapists. For some, it appears to be a lack of prerequisite skills in interpersonal relationships, communication, ability to attend or listen to others, language adequacy, or cultural awareness and knowledge. This becomes a greater risk of occurring for programs that rely heavily on Graduate Record Exam (GRE) scores and college grade-point averages, to the exclusion of personal interviews and informative letters of recommendation. Occasionally these difficulties are transient and become problems only because the progress of the student is slower than what is expected by the faculty. Additional time, if permitted, may be sufficient for this person to progress to acceptable levels.

Some supervisees may suffer from an inability or lack of motivation to learn about and develop skills in therapeutic interventions. Although the number of mental health professionals continues to grow and, some believe, may have already reached the point of saturation, applications to many training programs remain strong.[21] Thus, one can assume that the intellectual potential of most students will be sufficient to enable them to meet the demands of graduate school. Development as a therapist, however, goes beyond the ability to memorize facts, work calculus problems, and do well on admissions exams. It also requires an ability to develop interpersonal sensitivity, read nonverbal communications, and develop empathy—skills not adequately measured by the GRE or required to excel in most college course work.

One of the major sources of lack of progress in clinical training, however, is due to unresolved interpersonal or intrapersonal concerns of the trainees. Eichenfield and Stoltenberg have described some categories of these types of students. The following scenarios illustrate some of the characteristics of these trainees.

THE REINCARNATED TRAINEE

Jan's supervisor had noted that she was assuming too much responsibility for her clients. She was a new student in the program in her first practicum in the clinic. Although it was not particularly uncommon for new trainees to become perhaps too involved with their clients, Jan seemed to take more of an active role in "mothering" her clients than was apparent in the work of others in her class. Upon exploring this issue in supervision, Jan explained that she felt an inadequate childhood was the primary reason her clients were experiencing difficulties: "If they can just find the kind of nurturing that they should have gotten from their parents, I'm sure they will be fine. My own parents didn't give me the love and support I needed, and I'm not going to let that happen to my clients."

THE SAVIOR TRAINEE

Jack had experienced a powerful "reawakening" a couple of years before entering the program. As he noted to his supervisor, he had been without direction, and feeling lonely and depressed, when he had a profound religious experience. For him, this allowed his attention to move away from his distressing life and focus on more "positive" emotions. The conversion experience had been very effective for him, he noted, and he was sure it would work as well for others. "How can I work with a distressed client and not show them the way to eternal salvation?" he would ask in supervision. "If they would just let go of their negative emotions and think more positively, they wouldn't need to be in here talking to a stranger."

UNFINISHED CLIENT/DENYING TRAINEE

Kate was a mature woman in her early fifties who had decided to return to school to learn more about helping people work through their problems. She had always been a good listener and was able to develop high levels of trust in people rather quickly. "Folks always seem to open up to me and tell me their problems. I thought I should learn more about how to help them work through these difficulties." Kate's supervisor, an advanced doctoral student, had noticed a troubling change in her behavior while observing a videotape of a couples counseling session. Kate had developed good rapport with the couple during their initial sessions, but halfway through this one, the wife disclosed that her husband had struck her in the face twice over the past two years. After hearing this in the session, Kate became very directive, telling the wife she needed to "get out of the relationship before you really get hurt." She became very protective of the wife and quite aggressive toward the husband. In reviewing the videotape with Kate, the supervisor paused at one point and asked Kate what she was feeling and if she had felt this way in other situations. Kate broke down in tears and stated that her twenty-three-year-old daughter was in an abusive relationship and refused to take action to change it or leave. Indeed, her own first marriage had been plagued with violence. "I guess I just see my sweet daughter sitting there in the room and I need to save her. I just can't help it; it's wrong and something must be done."

SUSPICIOUS, DISTRUSTFUL TRAINEE

Bruce's supervisor had quickly noticed a tendency toward being judgmental and quite selective concerning the kinds of clients with whom he was willing to work. In group supervision one day, he had challenged a colleague who was working with a lesbian client to "force this girl to face up to how she is hurting her family and reconsider pursuing this kind of lifestyle." Problems occurred again shortly after when one of Bruce's clients came to session very distressed because his wife was leaving him "for another man." Bruce responded with anger and suggested that it is difficult to trust women because "you never know when you'll get burned, you just know it will happen sometime." Exploration of this reaction in supervision yielded information about a series of unsuccessful relationships in Bruce's past and anger toward women as being unworthy of trust and vindictive.

THE ADDICTED OR NONPRACTICING ADDICTED TRAINEE

Jack had spent years struggling to overcome a serious addiction to alcohol. His past was a series of starts and stops concerning his dependency on alcohol. He began his training program after having stayed "clean" for three years. It was obvious that he was a bright and motivated student who had made great strides toward reaching his goal of abstinence and success. The major problem with Jack's professional development was his reliance on his perspective that "an addictive personality" was at the root of most of his clients' problems and that "the twelve-step approach" was always the best way to address these problems. Jack's supervisor was constantly exploring this perspective with Jack and discouraging him from referring most of his clients to Alcoholics

Anonymous, Narcotics Anonymous, and other twelve-step programs whether or not substance abuse appeared to be a predominant problem.

Very few therapists are so well adjusted that their own personal limitations or blocks never present problems in their clinical work. However, when these issues inhibit professional growth and affect work with clients, care needs to be taken to mobilize resources to deal with them. We have previously noted in this book that supervision is not psychotherapy, and supervisors are ill advised to engage in therapy with supervisees. Nonetheless, supervisors must be sensitive to the presence of therapists' blocks or disorders that will put either them or their clients at risk. Sometimes these issues can be adequately addressed in a reasonably short period of time in therapy, allowing the therapists to limit the focus of their clinical work for a while or take a short sabbatical from seeing clients. In other situations, more time is necessary to allow the therapists to work through these difficulties before they can be allowed to resume (or begin) clinical work. Sometimes a complete termination of training is required, and a new career is warranted. Thus, the power of the supervisory relationship cannot be assumed to be sufficient to correct all deficiencies or problems brought to training by supervisees. Taking an active role in addressing these problems and pushing for the appropriate plan of action is one of the many responsibilities of clinical supervisors.

OTHER CONSIDERATIONS

Numerous sources of influence exist in the supervision relationship. Some of these have been investigated in research, while others remain untested. Some are based on theory and are consistent with clinical experience and anecdotal reports. Among these latter sources of influence are issues of power and routes to persuasion. Social psychological research has long been suggestive in terms of relevance for clinical practice with some support emerging over the years for its clinical relevance.[22]

We have argued in other contexts that the Interpersonal Influence Model (IIM) and the Elaboration Likelihood Model (ELM) provide some conceptual clarity regarding how the supervisor can have an impact on the trainee within the supervision relationship.[23] This persuasive power can have a positive impact, or it can inhibit the kind of development the supervisor hopes to encourage in the therapist.

To varying degrees, the supervisor will have certain social power bases (expert, referent, reward, legitimate, and informational) that can be used to influence the supervisee. The ELM provides some guidance regarding how to utilize these power bases effectively. The danger presented in implementing the social power inherent in supervision is that the supervisee may not engage in sufficient information processing in evaluating and integrating supervisor recommendations.

Remember that one must have sufficient motivation and ability to critique input from others (engage in central route processing). Level 1 therapists will generally be highly motivated in desiring to learn about clinical processes and improve their performance. However, their ability to evaluate input adequately will be limited. Few relevant schemata will exist from which the therapist can draw information to compare and contrast recommendations offered by the supervisor. Thus, the risk exists that supervisor recommendations, perspectives, and information will be uncritically accepted and not sufficiently processed to allow for conceptual integration. In short, the supervisee may buy into what the supervisor says, but without any understanding as to why and how these recommendations should be implemented.

We can see this effect in supervisees who continually seek advice from the supervisor, often for situations similar to ones previously addressed in supervision. We may also see a tendency to use recommended skills or interventions appropriate for one situation across a number of others for which they are inappropriate. This reflects a lack of understanding, or inadequate elaboration of information, so that the emerging schema lacks sufficient complexity to guide behavior effectively. Of course, this level of understanding will come slowly, but it can be enhanced by encouraging a critical evaluation and processing of material covered in supervision. Prescriptive interventions in supervision are appropriate for this level of supervisee. Using these interventions without adequate elaboration and processing is likely to result in a poor understanding and short-term impact on the supervisee. Without developing an understanding of the processes involved, the therapist is more likely to seek out additional advice in the future and not be able to evaluate that information critically. Perhaps an example is in order.

Lauren was fairly young when she began the program. She was a very bright undergraduate student who had graduated early and was accepted into a counseling program. Her first supervisor worked from a cognitive therapy orientation, which made some sense to Lauren. Their supervision sessions generally followed a skills training format in which Lauren would ask what to do each week with her clients and would receive specific directives from her supervisor. Her performance was evaluated as adequate over the semester, largely because she would work from her notes (taken in supervision) and implement the recommendations in the next counseling sessions. The following semester Lauren was assigned to a supervisor whose therapeutic orientation was object relations. Being the eager student that she was, Lauren was soon requesting specific guidance for interventions consistent with the object relations framework and would diligently attempt to implement them in the next counseling session. Negative feedback from clients came quickly as they became puzzled regarding the rather dramatic shift in the focus of their sessions. Lauren was confused and initially had trouble seeing any inconsistencies.

Theoretical arguments aside, one can see the benefit of being exposed to various orientations and techniques during a training experience. However, when the therapist is serving primarily as a vehicle for carrying out the recommendations of the supervisor, inadequate learning occurs. The benefits of the different perspectives are not processed, evaluated, or integrated, and a learning opportunity is lost. Supervisors who take the time and make the effort to use their social power to encourage the therapist to elaborate on and integrate information and perspectives provided in therapy are enabling the development of a professional and setting the stage for Level 2 issues to emerge.

TRANSITIONAL ISSUES

Success in supervision of Level 1 therapists will result in increased confidence in their ability to understand and implement interventions. Although this understanding is limited in terms of complexity and breadth, the troublesome anxiety has diminished while motivation remains good, the self-focus has lessened, and the movement toward some autonomy has begun. It is at this point that some Level 1 therapists may appear overconfident or even cocky to their supervisors. Here is where the increasing attention to client reactions, assigning more difficult cases, and expanding the therapists' views of clinical processes are crucial. In our training clinic, this is the time when we are most likely to assign a client with a personality disorder to the therapist. It is time to "shake the tree" and move the therapist to the next level. There is often some resistance to the realization that therapy is complex and simple solutions are few, but the change is necessary for the therapist to continue to develop and not stagnate at a rather perfunctory stage of development.

Within the domain of individual differences, it is important at this stage to broaden the experience of supervisees with culturally diverse clientele. Lopez and colleagues, in an examination of multicultural aspects of developmental supervision, stress the importance of exposure to cultural differences through supervision and course work (if possible) at this stage of therapist training.[24] This breadth of experience will facilitate the transition of these therapists to Level 2.

There is sometimes a manifest desire on the part of the trainee to skip the complexity of Level 2 issues and move directly to the self-aware, confident effectiveness we see in Level 3 therapists. Unfortunately, this is no more likely than skipping adolescence and moving directly into adulthood. The turbulence of Level 2 is necessary for the therapist to develop the next level of skills, understanding, and perspective required to reach his or her professional potential.

CHAPTER FOUR

The Level 2 Therapist

At the point of reaching what we conceptualize as Level 2, supervisees are making the transition away from being highly dependent, imitative, and unaware in responding to a highly structured, supportive, and largely instructional supervisory environment. With successful counseling experience comes an increased desire and confidence to make one's own decisions concerning client cases. An increasing mastery of basic facilitative and attending skills results in less of a self-focus, reduced anxiety, and more of an ability to attend to the client experience. At the same time, however, difficult and unsuccessful cases may cause supervisees to question their effectiveness as therapists, affecting their previously high levels of motivation.

The Level 2 therapist is making a transition across the various domains from dependence on the supervisor to a sense of independent functioning, from primarily a self-focus to a focus on the client experience, and from a previously high and fairly stable level of motivation to fluctuating levels. Unless this transition is successfully negotiated, this period can be a difficult time for supervisee and supervisor alike, characterized by conflict consisting of disruption, resistance, ambivalence, and instability. It is during this stage that many supervisors experience failures. However, it is also a time when the supervisor can effectively resolve conflict, resulting in a deeper understanding of therapists' skills and personal characteristics, and using this understanding to mentor a supervisee, leading to significant professional growth.

In our experience, therapists who have gone through at least two or three semesters of practica, or a year or so of postmaster's degree work primarily in agencies working directly with clients, often begin to demonstrate characteristics of Level 2 structures in one or more domains. By this point, the therapist has been assigned clients who afford the opportunity for mastering basic listening and attending skills, along with some rudimentary intervention strategies and methods. Consequently the therapist has experienced some success in work. As you will recall, we recommend the assignment of more difficult clients (for example, personality disorders) during the latter part of Level 1. As a result, the supervision process has identified not only the supervisee's strengths but also weaknesses, as the therapist struggles to understand why he or she is unable to be effective with some clients. Therapists now begin to realize the complexity and the very real limitations of the therapy process, and these struggles may have a negative effect on their level of motivation.

The Level 2 therapist's manifestations of Level 2 structures are highly dependent on previous experience across the eight domains, exposure to a variety and diversity of client types and problems, and quality as well as quantity of previous individual and group supervision. Previous supervision consisting of only brief meetings every other week simply to monitor caseloads may indeed force a therapist to function independently, but not necessarily to function effectively. Thus, it is entirely possible that a given supervisee may demonstrate a high level of autonomy in the assessment domain after working for a number of years administering and interpreting assessment instruments. However, in beginning to focus more on therapy, the supervisee may exhibit fluctuating levels of autonomy and motivation in regard to this less developed domain of intervention skills competence. Consequently, given the various practica and experiential requirements across training programs and state regulating agencies, supervisors cannot simply assume that a given supervisee truly represents Level 2 on the basis of previous global experience, especially when this experience has been unsupervised.

We can expect therapists who have just reached Level 2 in a particular domain of practice to be functioning at Level 1 in others and perhaps Level 3 in one or more domains. As a result, supervisors must make a thorough assessment across the various domains to ascertain an accurate picture of the range in levels of supervisee functioning. In order to facilitate assessment of the Level 2 therapist, we will now turn to our discussion of the attributes and structures characteristic of these therapists, descriptions of Level 2 behaviors within the eight domains, and recommendations for the supervisory environment and interventions.

LEARNING AND COGNITION

The Level 1 therapist has worked to develop some simple understandings and relevant schemata in an initial response to what is the very multilayered complex process we know as psychotherapy and its attendant functions across the eight domains. However, the increase in complexity and diversity in current clientele, along with the realization that a single approach to all problems is ineffective, provides more information that is discrepant with previous simple and somewhat tentative formulations and resultant schemata. If the supervisor is providing effective supervision at this stage, the Level 2 therapist is being exposed more to alternative conceptualizations and diagnoses of client processes along with a wider array of treatment approaches and orientations while at the same time being challenged to function more independently. The supervisor's role is also to encourage the therapist to explore and understand the limitations of the therapist's existing schemata.

The supervisee at this level is seemingly being bombarded by information from a number of fronts, including client perceptions, supervisor interventions, and colleagues' diverse viewpoints. These sources of new information and feedback are often discrepant with existing productions (declarative verbal or image representations of information) in overly general schemata. These challenges to previously established beliefs and methods of operation contribute to a state of confusion (or general associative stage) for the therapist, and a major task now becomes one of integrating and synthesizing these diverse viewpoints. As we will see, supervisees can easily become overwhelmed by these challenges. However, the openness that Level 2 supervisees generally demonstrate toward seeking new information helps in successfully resolving and comprehending these complex processes. This work leads to a more complete integration and synthesis as they strive to develop a personalized approach in their therapeutic work.

LEVEL 2 STRUCTURES

We will now focus on the three overriding structures and examine how changes in these structures mark development in Level 2.

Self and Other Awareness

At this stage, the supervisee exhibits less of a self-focus and is able to focus more on the client, attempting to understand his or her perceptions of the world while also trying to empathize more with the client's affect. The additional cognitive focus on seeing the client's perspective can introduce confusion and result in frustration for the trainee, as the complexity of the therapy process has now been increased and the supervisee struggles to understand the client's world more fully.

Within the affective realm, the therapist exhibits an increased capacity to empathize with the client that did not previously exist because of the predominant self-focus. The supervisee shows an increased sensitivity to the verbal and nonverbal behaviors that communicate clients' inner emotional experiencing, adding considerably to the depth of the supervisee's accurate empathic understanding of the client. The danger for the therapist at this point is overidentification with the client to the extent of being unable to provide effective interventions. Overidentification also increases the potential to engage in countertransference reactions. The supervisee may become enmeshed in the client's viewpoint, losing the objectivity necessary to provide effective treatment. Common general manifestations of this overidentification include strong beliefs in the veracity of the client's subjective reporting of presenting concerns, a desire to advocate strongly for the client in various realms, or taking the client's position regarding attitudes toward significant others. Supervisees at this stage can become so affectively overwhelmed by immersing themselves in the client's perspective that they may freeze up and be unable to make clinical decisions in treatment.

Anecdotal evidence and gender research suggest that gender differences may emerge in the tendency of therapists to rely on either a cognitive or affective focus on the client. Male therapists, through socialization, may tend to want to resolve the client's problems and focus more on cognitive problem-solving aspects of therapy. On the other hand, perhaps due to a greater learned focus on relationships, female therapists may demonstrate more of a focus on the emotional experience of the client.[1] In terms of challenges, male therapists may need to be encouraged to focus more on the client's affect (empathy) rather than attending only to struggling with solving problems and understanding the client's worldview. Female therapists may need to be encouraged to focus more on cognition and problem solving and resist the temptation to overidentify emotionally with the client. In other words, males may tend to retreat to tight constructs and assimilations, and females may tend to overaccommodate to the client's world.

Autonomy

The primary conflict for the therapist at this level is a vacillation between autonomy and dependency. On the one hand, supervisees are developing their own ideas and gaining knowledge through experience, individual and group supervision, and workshops or course work (if students) regarding effective interventions with clients. Thus, they tend to have an appropriate tendency to move away from imitating the supervisor. Supervisees become more confident, and sometimes reactive, in asserting their independence in intervening with clients. In addition, they may resist discussing certain cases if they suspect that the supervisor will disagree or suggest an alternative approach. Essentially, supervisees desire to function independently in counseling situations concerning certain client types and problems with which they have experienced success. In these cases, they will function quite capably and appropriately on their own. At the same time, however, they remain dependent on the supervisor for advice and direction in various cases or domains where they lack experience or confidence, or both. At these times, the supervisee still functions as a Level 1 therapist. The Level 2 therapist may also resemble the Level 1 supervisee when the added complexity associated with an increased focus on the client reduces the level of certainty and creates confusion regarding issues that may have seemed clear during Level 1.

Thus, we expect the supervisee to oscillate between independent functioning and continuing dependence on the supervisor. The extremes in dependency and autonomy will vary according to the previous counseling experience and the effectiveness of supervision the therapist has been exposed to, as well as the personal characteristics of the supervisee (for example, openness to feedback). This effect is illustrated in a study by Tracey, Ellickson, and Sherry.[2] In this investigation, beginning students, in contrast to advanced students, preferred a more highly structured supervision environment overall, and advanced students who were high on reactance preferred a low-structured environment more than advanced students low on reactance. However, under crisis therapeutic conditions (such as suicide), where advanced trainees lacked experience and anxiety remained high, they still preferred the structured supervision regardless of their level of reactance. Lack of experience with an unfamiliar domain (suicidal clients) appears to have resulted in these advanced therapists' functioning in Level 1 with this clientele. In response, they appropriately preferred a highly structured supervision environment.

At this point, therapists are struggling with the complexity of the therapeutic process and resultant confusion while attempting to consolidate the gains they made during the first stage. Some may resist appropriate dependency at times because they believe they *should* be able to function autonomously. Conversely, they may become overwhelmed and react negatively to supervisors who suggest new ways of conceptualization or intervention as an expression of their frustration in resolving the confusion surrounding this dependency-autonomy conflict. Other therapists who have been led to overestimate their skill level through previous laissez-faire supervision may view any dependency on the supervisor as a weakness and resist sharing their thoughts and feelings in supervision as an expression of autonomy. In some cases, supervisees ignore supervisor suggestions and directives and may inappropriately intervene in cases where they lack expertise, negatively affecting client welfare. Finally, some supervisees with fluctuating levels of confidence or assertiveness will operate in a predominantly dependent mode, constantly seeking supervisor approval when in fact they have the knowledge and ability to function more independently.

Motivation

The dependency-autonomy struggle also affects the motivation level of Level 2 therapists. They desire to function independently, but when they are exposed to more difficult client types and problems and more complex theories, methods of intervention, and diagnostic categories, they may not be effective with some clients. They may start questioning their skills, and the experience may shake their level of confidence and sense of therapeutic efficacy. For some therapists, this confusion manifests itself in high levels of motivation as they seek additional guidance and support. Others will wallow in confusion and frustration, and sometimes despair, which can reduce their motivation to learn and engage in clinical activities. Most commonly, their motivation level fluctuates as they vacillate between these feelings of confusion and discouragement versus personal efficacy and confidence when experiencing success. Therapists may become discouraged or distant in their work one week and exhibit a high level of enthusiasm the following week.

These fluctuations typically manifest themselves as "forgetting" tasks discussed and agreed on in previous supervision sessions or as a lack of preparation for current supervision sessions. Fluctuations in the quality of taped sessions will also be apparent from client to client or on a week-to-week basis. At this time, trainees in graduate school settings may begin to question their career decision to become a therapist and distance themselves cognitively or affectively from the therapeutic process. Instead they may immerse themselves in other forms of activity, such as research or teaching, while shortchanging therapeutic responsibilities. Therapists in postgraduate work settings may manifest more overt signs of discouragement by "giving up" on certain clients, facilitating referrals, or expressing the need for a vacation or a break from clients. Nevertheless, in most cases, the therapist who is discouraged or distant one week returns the next week with increased enthusiasm for clinical work.

INTERACTION OF DOMAINS AND STRUCTURES

The complexity of learning psychotherapeutic skills is such that we should not expect a Level 2 therapist to demonstrate consistently effective performance across all of the domains. Experience or past exposure to training in any one domain, as well as the personal characteristics of a given supervisee, interact to influence progression through the levels for each domain.

Intervention Skills Competence

The characteristics of the Level 2 therapist are especially apparent in this domain as the supervisee is increasingly comfortable with a wide array of intervention skills, although these skills are not well integrated within an overriding theoretical orientation or conceptual scheme. Exploration of various approaches and the most current developments in the psychotherapeutic arena may be pursued and attempted, including the latest fads. It is fairly common to see these therapists as intentionally seeking to learn interventions and approaches dissimilar from those used by their supervisors. Supervisees will make repeated requests for more experience with diverse client types and problems, yet fail to acknowledge or even resist supervisor recommendations to expand their repertoire. Given the strong cognitive and affective focus on the client's experience, therapists may become enmeshed and demonstrate a temporary inability to make decisions regarding client welfare or treatment. With the intent of establishing the therapeutic alliance, they also will readily express support to clients in appropriate ways. Unfortunately, they may also cross the line in terms of what is therapeutic by expressing overt agreement with client viewpoints through summaries, reflections of feeling, content, and so on. In addition, the therapist may be affectively overwhelmed and confused by the seemingly insurmountable complexity of the counseling process and be unable to progress.

Assessment Techniques

In this domain Level 2 therapists demonstrate an increased knowledge of diagnostic classifications and assessment instruments. However, with the increased focus on the client's perspective, they often have difficulty integrating information from assessments and interviews that may be inconsistent or discrepant with their view of the client. As a result, they may demonstrate a confirmatory bias in their approach to gathering information in clinical interviews, asking leading questions, or directing the interview toward information that they believe fits the client's worldview. This bias may also be demonstrated in their interpretation of psychological instruments and other assessments. There is often a tendency to weight heavily certain consistent or discrete pieces of information in the formation of pet hypotheses that fit the client's perspective or the supervisees' bias, to the exclusion of disconfirming or inconsistent information. They may also lose interest in, reject, or even view the use of assessment instruments as somehow harmful to clients. In addition, *DSM-IV* diagnostic categories may be viewed as cold, impersonal, or irrelevant in providing useful information or implications for treatment. The formal, unflattering description included in diagnostic categories can seem too harsh or pessimistic when applied to their clients.

Interpersonal Assessment

The ability of the therapist to be self-aware and to monitor his or her cognitive and affective reactions toward clients is also severely limited due to the strong focus on the client's perspective. In essence, the therapist may be overacommodating to the client's worldview. Thus, the therapist may be unable to separate responses to clients based on accurate perceptions of the client's interpersonal interactions versus countertransference reactions outside of immediate awareness.

Level 2 therapists may exhibit a naive lack of insight regarding this process. Supervisors are often initially surprised when their attempts to increase supervisees' awareness in this domain are met with confusion or disbelief by their supervisees. This may appear as a reticence to consider one's reaction but may often be simple surprise that this information may be relevant at this time.

Client Conceptualization

While written and verbal conceptualizations of therapeutic dynamics and processes are based on a more complete understanding of the client's perspective, they may also be largely based on the client's viewpoint, without integration of other sources of information (for example, objective or projective psychological testing). Again, obvious discrepancies or inconsistencies in information gathered are often ignored or overlooked. They may make a case for exceptions to specific diagnostic classifications, or misclassifications, largely based on their perception of the client's worldview. Many times, obvious discrepancies between several parts of the client's story are overlooked and not integrated into the diagnosis or conceptualization. For example, the ruminations and negativistic thinking patterns associated with various forms of depression may be misinterpreted as the recurrent thoughts demonstrated in Obsessive-Compulsive Disorder, because the therapist is convinced by the client that the latter is really the problem and outside his or her control. It is during these times that many therapists fail to acknowledge the manipulative behaviors of Antisocial Personality Disorder clients or may be easily charmed by the attention-seeking qualities of clients exhibiting features associated with Histrionic Personality Disorders.

Susan was considered a very strong, advanced trainee in her graduate program and was consistently viewed by most supervisors as having strengths in relationship-building skills, as evidenced by her low "no-show" and premature termination rates. Early in her contact with an ongoing client who expressed difficulty in "choosing" between two romantic relationships, Susan was convinced that his strongly avowed guilt and anxiety were sincere. Her written conceptualization prepared for a group case conference emphasized nonpathological aspects and the concerns that the client expressed regarding interpersonal relationships, while results of the client's recent Minnesota Multiphasic Personality Inventory (MMPI) indicated high antisocial tendencies with a current low level of state anxiety. Presumably Susan had reviewed the MMPI results prior to the case conference presentation. However, when confronted again with these discrepant findings, Susan replied, "I just know he would not lie to me. After all, he shows up every week, and he just tries so hard in our sessions."

Individual Differences

In terms of awareness of issues surrounding lifestyle, gender, and culture or ethnicity, Level 2 supervisees are more willing to acknowledge the influence of sociocultural and environmental variables on behavior and the limitations of conventional counseling modalities for working with diverse clientele. However, they are still vacillating between general culture-specific characteristics they believe apply to all individual members of various groups (for example, females, Asian Americans) and the idea that every client is so unique that defining cultural values, attitudes, and behaviors may be ignored. As a manifestation of this confusion, they may tend to apply this new information garnered from other training experiences (for example, in-service training, workshops, course work) in a rigid and stereotypical fashion. As supervisors, we have regularly been provided with basic information regarding a client's gender and ethnic background with a look from the supervisee reflective of, "So, now what do I do?"

Alternatively, despite their attempts to understand diverse clientele, Level 2 therapists may be overwhelmed with what they perceive as yet another dimension of behavior that they need to understand and integrate into their work. Thus, they may believe that differences between cultural groups are so vast that they feel incapable of understanding the experience of a client with a background different from their own. Lopez and colleagues[3] suggest that therapists at this level feel "overburdened" by issues of culture or individual differences as an extension of the search for culture-specific or ethnic components and that this burden is a necessary step that is characteristic of the Level 2 supervisee's struggle with confusion and ambivalence. It is within this domain, however, that some of the most crucial and productive work in Level 2 is done. Although the therapist may be confused and vacillating, he or she simultaneously has greater openness and interest in learning about other groups and exhibits a genuine attempt to understand the varieties of human experience and the effects on the counseling process. Thus, in addition to other types of training experiences that Level 2 therapists are being exposed to in the realm of individual differences, it becomes crucial for supervisors to strike while the iron is hot. Supervisors must encourage the attempts of Level 2 supervisees to understand and intervene to resolve conflicts and increase knowledge in this important domain.

Theoretical Orientation

Therapists at this stage often demonstrate movement away from a strict allegiance to a specific theoretical orientation identified with the program, faculty member, or supervisor to more experimentation with a wider variety of techniques and strategies. Similar to the domain of intervention skills competence, supervisees may be seeking the most current therapeutic developments to learn and may be susceptible to faddish approaches lacking empirical or consistent theoretical support. The therapist at this point is attempting to find a perspective or approach that fits with his or her own view of human behavior and personal counseling style, but runs the risk of forcing clients to fit into a particular theoretical model. As a result, Level 2 therapists often have difficulty explaining why they used a certain orientation or technique and justifying this choice. They will also tend to have questions regarding how supervisors derived their own working approaches in searching for a personal orientation. This search is a necessary task for all effective psychotherapists and should be encouraged in Level 2 supervisees, although within the bounds of concern for client welfare.

Treatment Plans and Goals

Setting basic treatment goals and plans seems functional and concrete for the Level 1 supervisee and serves to reduce anxiety. However, the overaccommodation demonstrated by the Level 2 therapist may result in anxiety or despair concerning the difficulty of providing effective treatment or discouragement when initial treatment plans fail. Level 2 therapists may lose sight of the necessity and practicality of jointly formulating treatment plans with clients by attempting to experiment with alternative treatment strategies and theoretical orientations. Thus, treatment goals may reflect experimentation with a new approach or be overly vague or general (for example, "working on the relationship"), ignored when viewing open-ended sessions with clients as sufficient, or deferred until the client articulates concern over the direction of therapy. Finally, in the act of overaccommodating to the client's perspective, treatment goals may simply reflect the client's initial reasons for seeking counseling, ignoring the relevance of therapist assessment and conceptualization in the goal-setting process.

Professional Ethics

The implications and ramifications of formal professional ethical guidelines are generally better understood by Level 2 therapists. At this level, however, supervisees may place more emphasis on client welfare in situations where both client welfare and counselor welfare may be at stake. They may sometimes view ethical standards as imposed limitations on practice that may be violated and justified by exceptions to the rule. For example, one of us was shocked to learn one day that a supervisee had scheduled a lunch date with a current client diagnosed as Borderline Personality Disorder in order to foster a successful termination! This person would have been considered a Level 2 or Level 3 therapist across any number of domains.

In situations concerning the welfare of two or more clients, such as in family or group work, supervisees may be torn by their allegiance to one of the clients versus the necessity to behave ethically (for example, reporting child abuse). For example, one of our supervisees was in a therapeutic relationship with a man desiring help with controlling his anger. The supervisee had gained an appreciation for this man's past experiences of being beaten by his father and ignored by his mother. The therapist had begun to understand how this man saw the world and could feel the depth of his pain and anger. During one session, the client reported that he had struck his child the night before, resulting in some bruises but no permanent physical harm. The client felt awful and was experiencing considerable guilt and fear. He asked the therapist to help him find ways to avoid such behavior in the future. The supervisee felt caught between his legal responsibility to report the client to child protective services and his caring and empathy for him. After processing his reactions in supervision the following day, the therapist alerted the client that he needed to call child protective services, which he then did.

In many instances in discussions of professional ethics with Level 2 trainees, we have heard the justification that potential violation of an ethical principle may be warranted because a supervisor, faculty member, or other professional committed the same act (for example, dual role relationships). Consequently, supervisors should be well aware of the necessity to behave as a role model for *all* levels of supervisees in the domain of professional ethics. This consideration is especially relevant to Level 2 supervisees in the midst of ambivalence and confusion.

SUPERVISING THE LEVEL 2 THERAPIST

One of the basic tenets of the IDM is that the supervision environment should change in response to the differing needs, issues, and perceptions of the developing supervisee. The supervisor must be extremely vigilant in early supervision sessions in order to (1) assess carefully the current level of functioning of the therapist, (2) be prepared to make a shift in supervisory style in order to respond effectively to the changing needs of the Level 2 therapist, and (3) facilitate development to the higher levels. Many of the recent research studies cited in Chapter Three also examined characteristics of advanced trainees. These studies provide support for the notion that supervisors vary their supervisory styles and alter the supervision environment to meet the changing needs of more advanced trainees[4] and that supervisees increase in their level of independence[5] and thus require less structure within the supervision environment.[6] Indeed, more recent studies of developmental supervision processes mirror the conclusions of early research regarding changes that occur in supervisor and supervisee behaviors across developmental levels.[7] However, although the research literature has been able to identify the changing needs and characteristics of therapists as they increase in experience, what has been more difficult is the identification of *specific* characteristics descriptive of the Level 2 supervisee. This difficulty appears to be reflective of the complexity associated with Level 2 as trainees address the issues confronting them across multiple domains. In addition, the ambivalence, confusion, and fluctuation that supervisees exhibit during Level 2 add to the challenge of researching this level. Similar to working with Level 1 trainees, the cookbook approach may seem appealing in dealing with the conflicts, complexities, and transitions demonstrated by the Level 2 supervisee, especially for readers who have experienced supervision with this level of therapist. However, such an approach remains unrealistic; instead, flexibility on the part of the supervisor characterizes the approach to the Level 2 supervision environment. Consequently, let us now turn to discussion of supervision approaches and guidelines with the Level 2 therapist.

Therapeutic Adolescence

The characteristics of the Level 2 therapist have led Stoltenberg and Delworth to characterize this stage as one of "Trial and Tribulation and liken it to a period of therapist adolescence."[8] Thus, the task of the supervisor with Level 2 supervisees is to provide a fine balance between guidance and support, and a degree of autonomy and challenge in fostering the independence and confidence of the therapist. Supervisors must recognize and provide a supervisory environment that is qualitatively different from that of the Level 1 therapist by increasing autonomy and decreasing structure. Highly structured directives and didactic advice appropriate for Level 1 supervisees are likely to be met by resistance and even anger by the Level 2 therapist. Of course, the supervisor must always be aware of the overriding concern regarding issues of client welfare by providing appropriate structure and guidance in domains where the supervisee is in need of further development. Level 2 therapists will not always be receptive to the kind of guidance supervisors provide to Level 1 therapists, even when it is necessary. Thus, the supervisor must be prepared to articulate his or her rationale for providing direction in certain situations and respond to supervisee resistance and anger in a nondefensive, facilitative manner. For neophyte supervisors, Level 2 therapists often provide the first difficult test of their supervisory skills as well as their patience.

Client Assignment

Recall that our recommendation in Chapter Three was to shake up the Level 1 therapist to help the transition to Level 2 by assigning more difficult and complex client cases. Indeed, in most training agencies,

Level 2 supervisees, because of the amount of their prior experience, are typically assigned clients reflective of higher degrees of psychopathology who may be less amenable to change through the facilitative skills and structured approaches applied during Level 1. The Level 2 therapist may also be receiving training and experience in a wider variety of domains—individual, group, marital and family counseling—some of which may be unfamiliar. In postgraduate job settings, however, therapists may not be receiving training and exposure across various domains, and they may exhibit Level 2 structures in only a couple of the broader domains (for example, intervention skills competence) consistent with job requirements. Additionally, in these settings, therapists may be functioning at Level 3 in any number of domains, but in seeking additional expertise in a new modality, they may function at Level 2 in the newer domain.

An increased diversity of clientele and presenting concerns is exciting and challenging, as well as frustrating and anxiety producing. Previously effective counseling behavior may prove less than adequate in ameliorating more complex client problems. As a result, client assignment should reflect a blend of cases with which the therapist exhibits confidence and independence, with more difficult challenging cases requiring the application of underdeveloped skills. This allows the supervisee to consolidate previously learned skills, while challenging the supervisee's ability to respond in a flexible manner to new problem situations. Training agencies that assign clients exclusively on a "space available" or "next-in-line" basis miss crucial opportunities to attend to or enhance the development of the Level 2 supervisee and may actually impede growth.

Supervisor Interventions

Research investigations appear to indicate that support is a necessary ingredient across all developmental levels.[9] Thus, facilitative interventions that express ongoing support and concern for supervisee development continue to remain important for the Level 2 therapist, especially during times of supervisor-supervisee conflict. A little added support and overt expression of this support does wonders for the fluctuating motivation level of the Level 2 therapist. Sharing or disclosing one's own past experiences or difficulties with similar issues serves to accomplish this function.

Prescriptive interventions, although slightly less frequent for Level 2 therapists than Level 1 therapists, are also necessary at times to encourage growth across the domains. That is, the Level 2 therapist will require supervisor knowledge and expertise across relevant domains. However, prescriptive interventions suggested for domains in which Level 2 therapists adequately function again run the risk of eliciting trainee reactance and defensiveness and impeding supervisee growth and progress. It is especially important in utilizing prescriptive interventions with Level 2 supervisees to offer multiple alternatives and encourage some collaborative decision making while allowing for some autonomous choices. Conflicts over supervisor prescriptions are usually defused when the supervisor is able to articulate a clear, cogent rationale, underscoring the importance of client welfare.

In order to enhance growth, Level 2 therapists must also be challenged to provide their rationales for responding to various client concerns. This is especially true for cases where supervisees may resist input, feel uncertain, or become angry and impatient. Thus, for Level 2 supervisees, conceptual interventions are effective in requiring them to articulate their own or alternative intervention plans. In addition, introducing different conceptualizations of the same client by supervisors serves to challenge the supervisees and expand their level of understanding. It is important, however, that conceptual interventions be accompanied by high levels of support and empathy so they are not misinterpreted by supervisees as covert or disguised prescriptive interventions or demonstrations of the supervisor's superior conceptual or diagnostic skills. This would elicit defensive reactions.

Level 2 therapists may be most susceptible to overt or covert client manipulations due to their tendency to overaccommodate to the client's perspective, setting the stage for countertransference reactions. Thus, the increased use of catalytic interventions with Level 2 therapists, in the form of process comments by supervisors, can increase supervisee self-awareness when they are enmeshed in only the client's viewpoint. Supervisor comments are most frequently directed to the therapist's reactions and feelings toward clients in moment-to-moment session interactions of which they may be only marginally aware. Process comments may also be issued in the form of a direct challenge to stir things up in the Level 2 therapist and, in essence, force the supervisee to focus on and monitor his or her feelings and reactions during an interpersonal interaction. This can help provide an impetus to move away from an exclusive focus on the client's perspective. Examination of moment-to-moment reactions is best achieved through the review of taped counseling session excerpts in a search for expanded learning and increased self-insight. Process-type comments may also be employed to assist the supervisee in examining the dynamics of the supervisory relationship (see Chapter Six).

Lorraine was a fourth-semester trainee who was generally well regarded by the training faculty in her program, and she had received positive evaluations of her clinical performance. During the first meeting with her new supervisor, she acted somewhat surprised when he informed her that she needed to tape all counseling sessions and bring the tapes to her weekly supervision sessions. The supervisor inquired about the availability of taped sessions during the next couple of supervision sessions. Lorraine reported that none of her clients had provided her with written permission to tape, and she quickly moved to a discussion of clients. It became clear that Lorraine had definite ideas regarding the way she believed therapy should be conducted, even while she seemed to accept supervisor recommendations. Attempts to process possible evaluation anxiety as resistance to taping were brushed aside as Lorraine demonstrated little insight into the reasons more of her clients were not providing permission to tape. At this point, the supervisor strongly reaffirmed the necessity of obtaining session tapes as relevant to both client welfare and supervisee evaluation and development. An intervention was employed that contained prescriptive as well as catalytic elements. Lorraine was told that she must provide a taped counseling session at the next supervisory meeting. The intervention was prescriptive in the sense that it was made clear that there was no negotiation on this requirement. It was catalytic in that it was strongly presented to Lorraine in order to get things moving and promote a behavioral change.

At the next supervisory meeting, Lorraine did indeed provide a tape, and she was overtly anxious about playing it in the presence of the supervisor. Prior to viewing the tape, the supervisor processed with Lorraine his observations of her present as well as recent reactions and behavior related to this issue of taping. It turned out that Lorraine was indeed anxious regarding issues of evaluation and believed that she was going to be challenged on skills that she thought she performed very well. It soon became very apparent that the rationale presented to clients in obtaining permission to tape was negatively biased such that most clients would not routinely provide permission. Lorraine also reported that she had never provided a tape to her previous supervisor but had simply responded with various excuses during the entire supervisory relationship. Lorraine began bringing tapes on an ongoing basis, and, with continued processing of her evaluation anxiety, she was soon able to relax and review tapes with the supervisor. As Lorraine came to appreciate the role of interpersonal process within counseling, the supervisor reviewed the examples of this process within the supervision sessions as a conceptual intervention designed to illustrate the value of process interventions in counseling.

Consistent with the ELM,[10] we expect Level 2 therapists to be less predisposed to engage in the peripheral route processing characteristic of Level 1 therapists, who often uncritically accept supervisor recommendations. Thus, the Level 2 supervisee will often need to be convinced of, or challenged, regarding the usefulness of an intervention suggested by the supervisor. This challenge should result in a better understanding of the counseling process with an increased likelihood of lasting effects on the therapist's counseling and supervision behavior. This occurs because the information is effortfully evaluated and elaborated, and, thus, more centrally processed and integrated into relevant schemata.[11] However, if the therapist strongly adheres to a particular approach or perspective, biased processing may occur as the supervisee is unwilling to entertain alternatives. Although the purpose of clinical supervision is not to indoctrinate therapists into a particular approach or orientation, in our view it is inappropriate for supervisees to remain close-minded toward alternative methods of intervention simply because they may be unfamiliar with them. Thus, in order to facilitate more central processing and address possible biased processing, supervisors must expose to therapists diverse approaches that have been demonstrated to be effective with certain client populations and problems. Because all supervisors cannot work comfortably within all theoretical orientations, the Level 2 supervisee may benefit from exposure to supervisors who adhere to differing approaches to therapy.[12]

Challenging catalytic or conceptual types of supervisor interventions can be uncomfortable for supervisees who are sensitive to evaluation, because they may perceive that the supervisor is questioning their skills or knowledge. Nevertheless, what is comfortable, reassuring, or viewed positively by supervisees is often not what produces further growth. Challenge within a supportive supervisory environment is needed for the Level 2 supervisee to progress to higher levels of competence. Supervisors who use what the trainee may perceive as confrontational types of interventions do not need to present them in a punitive, aggressive, or superior manner. In our experience, powerful confrontations can be presented to supervisees in a low-key,

straightforward manner. In most cases, the content of the confrontation is sufficient to produce the needed challenge or internal conflict
in the supervisee, which may be facilitated by an honest discussion of
therapist strengths and weaknesses across the domains. Level 2 therapists, however, often will be taken off-guard or initially react defen-
sively to confrontational interventions, perceiving them as a threat to
their autonomy. Thus, it is important for supervisors to process these
reactions in the here and now while at other times backing off and let-
ting understanding occur. Some less sensitive or reactive trainees
require more forceful confrontations in which supervisors challenge
and directly follow up on recommendations in order to produce the
challenge or conflict necessary to stimulate growth. However, it is not
unusual for Level 2 therapists to return to a subsequent supervision
session having carefully considered and processed the supervisor's
confrontational intervention. One of us had the opportunity to follow our own advice—in order to enhance your own credibility,
acknowledge credibility—in working with an experienced, potentially
reactive Level 2 therapist.

Mel was an experienced therapist who held a master's degree and had returned to
school for his doctorate. His supervisor was new to the program, although not inexperienced. They began their year of supervision with Mel's informing the supervisor
that he preferred to consider their weekly meetings as "consultation" rather than supervision. He noted his rather extensive experience and said he felt less a need to be supervised than simply to have someone available for periodic consultations should the
need arise. The supervisor fought the urge to use his legitimate power and inform Mel
that he would be required to be supervised because he was now a student in a training program. Instead, the supervisor invested considerable time in having Mel describe
for him the extent of his experience and give great detail regarding his theoretical orientation (which happened to be different from the supervisor's). The supervisor
showed interest and noted that his approach differed somewhat and that it should be
interesting for both of them to learn more about their views of therapy over the coming year.

　In subsequent supervision sessions, the supervisor continued to show interest in
understanding Mel's approach and asked for clarification when he did not understand
an intervention or interpretation (or, frankly, when he disagreed with one). He also
asked to see videotapes of Mel's work with clients so he could better understand Mel's
approach to therapy. This "inquisitive" approach seemed to put Mel at ease, and fairly
soon he was noting his confusion with certain clients, dissatisfaction with his work

with some, and asking for direct input regarding other options. The supervisory relationship ended after a year with Mel's remarking about his surprising growth as a therapist and his appreciation for all he had learned from his "supervisor."

Despite the difficult issues that supervisees at Level 2 experience, research studies suggest that therapists at this level begin to demonstrate an increased readiness and openness to discussion and processing of personal issues of self-awareness, defensiveness, transference and countertransference, and the supervisory relationship.[13] A recent phenomenological investigation of "good supervision" events by Worthen and McNeill[14] with intermediate to advanced trainees seems to capture from the perspective of supervisees much of what we consider descriptive of Level 2 therapists. This study also indicated support for the ability of Level 2 supervisees to respond positively to process issues in supervision and provides some suggestions for intervention with these therapists.

In this investigation, intermediate supervisees indeed experienced and expressed a fragile and fluctuating level of confidence, a generalized state of disillusionment, and demoralization with the efficacy of providing therapeutic interventions, and they were anxious and sensitive to supervisor evaluation. They felt that their anxiety level decreased when supervisors helped to "normalize" their struggles as part of their ongoing development, and this type of intervention was often communicated in the form of a personal self-disclosure. They also characterized the optimal supervisory relationship as one experienced as empathic, nonjudgmental, and validating, with encouragement to explore and experiment. These conditions appeared to set the stage for nondefensive analysis as their confidence strengthened. In addition, participants reported an increased perception of therapeutic complexity, and they expanded their ability for therapeutic conceptualizing and intervening, a positive anticipation to reengage in previous difficulties and issues they had struggled with, and a resultant strengthening of the supervisory alliance.

Normalizing the Level 2 Experience

Supervisors must exhibit skill and courage to address these issues as they arise. Although therapists may initially struggle with these issues, later they are often viewed as a "critical incident" important to their growth and therapeutic competence.[15] The style or manner in which a supervisor points out or confronts these issues may vary depending on the level of sensitivity or defensiveness of the supervisee and, in this sense, requires more advanced skills or experience on the part of the supervisor. This is perhaps analogous to the development of therapeutic timing and acumen by therapists.

SUPERVISORY MECHANISMS

It is during this stage of development that the therapist is likely to engage in the most pronounced resistance toward the supervisor. Supervisees may selectively present cases with which they feel successful and avoid those with which they have difficulties. This choice is often a manifestation of confusion, a premature sense of autonomy, or a lack of insightful self-awareness. In asserting their independence, therapists in some situations may avoid discussion of cases if they suspect the supervisor will challenge their choice of interventions. This growing desire for independence, however, may limit the therapist's awareness of what should be addressed in supervisory sessions, leading to avoidance of clients with whom the supervisee has become impatient or angry. At times the only way to assess therapist functioning fully is to require, at a minimum, audiotaping of all ongoing clients so that the supervisor can monitor a case at any time within the supervision session. In other words, identifying the difficult cases and issues that are impeding growth in the supervisee at this stage is paramount to the Level 2 therapist's overall development. It is also important, however, to remain sensitive to his or her uncertain confidence, motivation, and fear of negative evaluation.

Thus, it is extremely important to monitor the therapist's progress during this stage primarily through live supervision formats or reviewing session audiotapes or videotapes. In our experience, it is not uncommon for supervisors to back off these activities as advanced therapists are viewed as "knowing what they are doing." At this stage it is not adequate simply to respond to what supervisees may present in session or request direction on. Supervisors should not allow too much autonomy across cases by simply discussing clients, relying on therapists' self-reports of ongoing client interactions, or monitoring progress notes. Although audiotaping or videotaping of ongoing sessions is somewhat normal procedure within academic training settings, supervisors working in hospitals or agency settings may view taping of ongoing sessions as an unnecessary burden on experienced therapists as well as clients. In addition, many settings do not have the physical facilities necessary for videotaping or direct observation from anywhere other than within the therapy room.

In our experience, both supervisees and clients across settings for the most part do not view taping procedures as a burden or barrier when the issue and procedures are presented in a straightforward, ethical manner (for example, informed consent). Our preference is to conceptualize this issue as a balance between training considerations and client welfare through monitoring of therapist *and* client concerns and behaviors. That is, it is inappropriate to allow the Level 2 therapist a completely free hand in working with clients. Although we want to support trainees in their independence at this stage and encourage risk taking with clients, we still need to be very careful in how we protect clients while encouraging therapist growth. Providing this delicate balance of challenge, autonomy, and growth in the trainee, along with attention to issues of client welfare, is truly one of the most difficult in the practice of clinical supervision.

Group supervision in the form of ongoing case conferences utilizing the case conceptualization format (see Chapter Seven) for formal presentations by Level 2 supervisees also serves to augment and increase exposure to, and discussion of, a variety of client concerns, populations, and treatment approaches. It also provides for appropriate questioning and challenge from colleagues, peers, and other professional personnel. The written case conceptualization format in particular serves as an excellent formal conceptual intervention in which the Level 2 trainee is required to pull information from diverse sources (for example, client reports, objective psychological instruments, therapist perceptions) and integrate and synthesize this information into a coherent conceptualization of a client leading to a diagnosis and treatment plan (see Appendix A for a model format). A couple of relevant prescriptive, as well as conceptual, adjuncts to this exercise are the requirements of at least one objective instrument assessing personality functioning (for example, the *MMPI-2*), along with an article from the recent research literature that provides some empirical validation for the supervisee's proposed treatment goals and plans.

The goal of these assignments is to facilitate exposure to a wider array of information, treatment approaches, and procedures. This is intended to elicit a more broad perspective from the Level 2 therapist who is focusing too much on the client's view. Table 4.1 summarizes the important considerations in supervising Level 2 therapists.

TRANSITIONAL ISSUES

The primary objective of supervision with Level 2 trainees is to set the stage for the transition to Level 3 by promoting a sense of conditional autonomy and confidence in domains where they exhibit competence. We also want to stimulate a sense of responsibility and acceptance of the need to seek direction in less well-developed domains. By the end of Level 2, supervisees come to the realization that some fluctuations in motivation levels are a normal reaction to the realization of the complexities and confusion they are encountering. This results in a stabilization of motivation at a higher level as they enter into Level 3. Finally, the supervisee at this point is more open to self-exploration and able to consider perspectives other than the client's acknowledging personal reactions and countertransference manifestations. This therapist, however, may still find it difficult to identify and act on these reactions in a therapeutic manner within the here and now of a therapy session. Thus, the Level 2 therapist continues to build on these foundations toward an orientation to practice in Level 3 that includes elements of personal and professional development.

General considerations	Less structure provided; more autonomy encouraged, particularly during periods of "regression" or stress
Client assignment	More difficult clients with more severe presenting problems (for example, personality disorders), confidence shaken
Interventions	Facilitative
	Prescriptive: used only occasionally compared to Level 1
	Confrontational: now able to handle confrontation
	Conceptual: introduce more alternative views
	Catalytic: process comments, highlight countertransference, affective reactions to client or supervisor
Mechanisms	Observation (video or live)
	Role playing (although less important than at Level 1)
	Interpret dynamics (see catalytic above), parallel process
	Group supervision
	Broader clientele

Table 4.1.   Level 2 Supervision Environment.

The transition to Level 3 therapist, like the transition from Level 1 to Level 2, is extremely dependent on the quality of the supervision received. Lack of attention to the variety of issues characteristic of the Level 2 supervisee or laissez-faire supervision during this important stage leads to what we characterize as the Pseudo Level 3 therapist. This individual is able to talk a good game and perhaps write convincing reports. However, close examination of in-session behavior of this type of therapist indicates that he or she has avoided dealing with the necessary development of an intensive focus on the client. Insufficient understanding of the client's world and a lack of true empathy keep this therapist functioning more at an advanced Level 1 than either Level 2 or 3.

Developmental stages cannot be skipped. Therapists must pass through the levels of professional development to move on toward excellence. Those who attempt to bypass a stage will be left with insufficient structures to move on to higher levels. Although a significant knowledge of theory is critical to development as a therapist, it cannot fully replace the need to collect essential data from the client. This can be accomplished only by an intensive focus on the client's behavior in session. Without this information and perspective, the Pseudo Level 3 therapist merely provides canned diagnoses and conceptualizations, although they may be quite articulate and detailed. Nonetheless, we will find with close scrutiny that difficult clients do not progress and the therapist knows little about the idiosyncrasies of the case.

Supervision of the Level 2 therapist provides quite a contrast to that of the Level 1 supervisee, requiring considerable skill, flexibility, and perhaps a sense of humor to negotiate this difficult stage successfully. As a result, the Level 2 supervisee may provide too much of a challenge for inexperienced supervisors or as an initial supervisory assignment for supervisors-in-training. However, a successful transition by a Level 2 therapist to Level 3 can result in some of the most rewarding experiences we have as supervisors.

CHAPTER FIVE

The Level 3 Therapist

—⁓— Supervisors who have the opportunity to work with more advanced trainees are those most likely to encounter Level 3 therapists. We consistently note throughout this book that levels of therapist development are not synonymous with a particular number of practica, years of experience, or age. Trainees (old and young, highly experienced or inexperienced) move at their own speed through the developmental levels. We can, however, encourage this growth by providing appropriate supervision. Recall that Wiley and Ray found that supervised experience influences trainee growth, while unsupervised therapy experience is unrelated.[1] A stimulating environment and corrective feedback are necessary for therapists to continue to develop and improve at their trade.

Thus, we cannot say that all therapists will reach Level 3 at a particular point in their training or at some time after completion of formal training. Indeed, some therapists never fully integrate into Level 3 in many, if any, domains of practice. Nevertheless, most therapists enter Level 3 in at least one or two domains after a few years of supervised experience. In doctoral programs, this occurs with some regularity during the predoctoral internship year. In master's or educational specialist programs, we expect initial entry into Level 3 in some domains after two or three years of postdegree supervision. It is important to keep in mind, however, that the quality of the supervision provided, as well as the type of clinical experience, will have an impact on both the speed and extent of professional development. Thus, some therapists will not reach these benchmarks in the noted periods of time or may attain them even more quickly than others.

The format of this chapter is consistent with that of the prior two chapters. We examine typical characteristics of individuals just moving into Level 3 in an initial domain, as well as those who have functioned in Level 3 in one or more domains and are now moving into this level in additional domains of practice. The overriding structures and domains we have used thus far to evaluate development will be discussed for this level of therapist.

We also discuss therapists who, for various reasons, do not complete the work required in Level 2 or try to circumvent these developmental steps, and imitate Level 3 behaviors without achieving Level 3 in the overriding structures. These Pseudo Level 3 therapists present challenges for supervisors in both assessment and supervisory interventions.

Although the IDM assumes Level 3 as the highest point of development within any domain, there is still considerable room for growth in one's clinical practice. The task for the therapist who is predominantly functioning at Level 3 is to integrate this level of skill and understanding across domains of practice. Thus, the Level 3i (integrated) therapist becomes the goal of professional development.

Finally, we explore the notion of lifelong professional development. Earlier models of therapist development[2] suggested that development essentially stopped at the "master" therapist stage. Consistent with models of adult development,[3] we know that development never really stops. Biology, experience, and the environment continue to exert influences on us as long as we live.

CONSTRAINTS ON SUPERVISION

Stoltenberg and Delworth's description of Level 3 as "the calm after the storm" highlights the resolution of some of the turbulence associated with Level 2.[4] As we will see in examining the structures, this therapist is characterized by greater self-knowledge, an understanding of the nuances of clinical practice, skills in taking the perspective of the client, and therapeutic effectiveness. Although the utility of supervision remains, in implementation it becomes considerably more collegial, and less differentiation of expertise and power is apparent.

Due to real-world constraints (such as budget and time), many therapists who have reached or are approaching Level 3 are no longer rigorously supervised. (Indeed, some therapists may never have been rigorously supervised and are likely to never reach Level 3.) Therapists who are still in formal training programs as they enter Level 3—for example, predoctoral internship or residency programs—are more likely to receive intensive supervision that will continue to encourage growth and integration. Unfortunately, even some of these training environments are limited in the use of videotaping, or even audiotaping, of sessions, and live supervision may be nonexistent; these difficulties severely impair the supervisor's ability to evaluate and educate the supervisee, even at Level 3. Others who are limited to postdegree supervision may experience little or no guidance whatsoever. This may be a function of high expectations for clinical expertise or merely a function of the economic pressures to focus one's efforts on providing billable services.

Learning and Cognition

By the time a therapist reaches Level 3 in any given domain, the associated skills will have become familiar and a level of proficiency is attained that allows for nearly automatic performance under certain conditions. Relationship skills, the fundamentals of setting up a session, assessment procedures, exploratory probes, and so on have been learned, practiced, and are now implemented as the situation demands. Little energy is spent on mentally practicing a response or struggling with uncertainty concerning what to do when engaged in practice. Rather, the skills necessary to engage the client, collect essential information, encourage exploration and insight, and facilitate functional behavior will flow more naturally from the therapist.

Sets or patterns of characteristics of the client, environmental context, and personal reactions will be more readily recognized, leading to quicker, more accurate, and useful diagnoses and conceptualizations. The forward thinking concerning possible paths to problem resolution is more characteristic of this level of therapist than what would have been possible in Levels 1 or 2. Memory retrieval and pattern matching can result in insights and understandings of the therapeutic experience that would appear to be intuitive or prescient to less experienced therapists.

The Level 3 therapist is better able to make decisions fairly quickly concerning which avenues to explore and which to abandon. By efficiently assessing a number of factors that may initially seem unrelated to the client's presenting problem or issues relevant to the case, the therapist can move more quickly and effectively in pursuing avenues of assessment and treatment. This integration across domains of practice is characteristic of the Level 3i therapist. Integration of perceptions, information, and knowledge within a domain is the strength of the Level 3 therapist. Thus, it is not just the acquisition of more knowledge or discrete pieces of information that results in the effectiveness of the Level 3 therapist; rather, it is the developed schemata and the links between them that allow for the activation of related concepts in memory. The therapist can now identify what is and is not important in a situation and move toward productive interventions.

Supervised experience can be helpful in identifying misinformation or irrelevant connections, and it strengthens the links or relationships among concepts that form relevant schemata. These schemata can then be readily accessed by the skilled therapist, who is more likely to activate useful propositions that will lead to effective problem solving.

Intensive supervision over a period of time, in combination with extensive clinical experience, allows the therapist to learn to integrate information and skills relevant to the work of therapy. Therapeutic skills, information about personality theory, theories of therapy, and an understanding of the self become integrated in the therapist's memory. Linkages are developed that allow the therapist to accept quickly certain information and impressions as relevant, while discarding considerable information that is irrelevant or not directly related to the issues at hand. This is a fairly dramatic difference between the Level 3 therapist and less developed ones. Information collected from the client and related sources is combined with information about people in general and clinical processes. This is combined with insightful self-knowledge to yield a considerably greater array of data from which the skilled therapist can make decisions and pursue interventions.

More advanced therapists are able to use Level 3 structures developed in certain domains to move more quickly into Level 3 in other closely related domains. This is what Loevinger[5] referred to as the "ameboid" model of development. As always, however, it is important not to assume Level 3 development across domains but rather to focus on evaluating the therapist's level of development for each domain relevant to supervised practice at any given time.

LEVEL 3 STRUCTURES

The changes in the overriding structures we have examined over the prior two chapters will continue for Level 3. The nature of these changes differs for Level 3 as the increasing skills, focus on others, and knowledge of the field culminate in a more aware, consistently motivated, and conditionally autonomous therapist.

Self and Other Awareness

In moving from an anxious self-awareness of weaknesses and then strengths, through a focus on the client, the trainee has developed an ability to empathize and understand the client's perspective. His or her self-knowledge has grown considerably and is useful in augmenting the knowledge of the client gained through careful attention and empathic understanding. The therapist's ability to focus intently on the client, developed in Level 2, now yields important information that can be compared and contrasted with the therapist's growing knowledge of personality theory and theories of therapy.

In the latter phases of Level 2, the therapist learned to monitor his or her own reactions to the client and process this information. An emphasis on encouraging self-exploration and self-understanding has enabled the therapist to assess the impact the client is having on him or her, as well as the therapist's impact on the client. Exploration of personal reactions as well as countertransference issues has provided important perspectives regarding the interpersonal impact certain clients can have on others, as well as how the therapist's own history can influence perspectives and behavior.

In contrast to the uninsightful self-awareness of the Level 1 therapist and the primary focus on the client of the Level 2 therapist, the Level 3 therapist is able to focus intently on the client and collect important data and perspectives. He or she can pull back in session and reflect on his or her own prior experiences, personal reactions, and professional knowledge. A third important attribute of the Level 3 therapist is the ability to take a more objective third-person perspective on the therapeutic process. This allows the therapist to observe and reflect on the interaction between client and therapist, sorting out client perspectives from therapist reactions and engaging in an examination of the process.

Three general sources of information are available in some detail for the Level 3 therapist that were not adequately available to less developed therapists. The high level of therapy skills allows this supervisee to pursue and collect relevant information from the client at a level of understanding that was not possible earlier in the developmental process. The skills allow the client to feel free to explore important issues and the therapist to communicate caring and understanding. The second source of information for the therapist is based on his or her cognitive and emotional awareness of personal and therapeutic reactions to the client. These reactions are processed into an understanding of one's own inclinations based on an individual learning history and knowledge of one's own personality characteristics. Thus, the therapist's reactions to specific "pulls" from the client may be judged as consistent with how people in general respond to this individual or as idiosyncratic to the therapist. The third source of information is professional knowledge based on an understanding of human behavior, the therapeutic process, and other resources developed over the course of training in science and professional practice as well as experience. The highly functioning Level 3 therapist will access all of this information to inform decision making and selection and implementation of therapeutic interventions. An example is in order.

Jeremy was a predoctoral intern who was working at an outpatient clinic as a rotation in his clinical internship. During one of his supervision sessions, he discussed his impressions of a depressed woman whom he had seen for a couple of sessions. The client had complained, among a number of things, about her inability to maintain romantic relationships. Jeremy shared with his supervisor his sense of the pain and hopelessness his client was experiencing, and her strong desire for him to help her change her life. Jeremy explained how he felt a very strong pull by the client to "take charge" of her life, tell her what to do, and make things better. He remarked to his supervisor how similar this feeling was to a situation he had experienced a number of years ago in a relationship that had ended badly: "I recall feeling trapped in the relationship and unable to meet the needs of my female friend. She was a very nice person, but I found myself frustrated and angry with her neediness." Jeremy went on to discuss the similarities between the current client and another with whom he had worked and diagnosed with a Dependent Personality Disorder. The remainder of the supervision session was spent comparing and contrasting characteristics across these experiences and planning mechanisms to assess his current client further.

Motivation

The fluctuation in motivation that we saw with the Level 2 therapist has been replaced with more stable motivation in Level 3. The vacillations in feeling effective versus ineffective that characterized Level 2 have subsided. A more complex understanding of the therapeutic process allows the Level 3 therapist to tolerate temporary states of confusion or lack of direction. Past successes have developed greater confidence, and an acceptance of personal strengths and weaknesses makes occasional setbacks less threatening.

The motivation is high, but no longer as naive or based on anxiety. The Level 3 therapist remains interested in learning and in seeking out new experiences but is much less likely to become enthralled with "new and improved" or fad approaches to clinical practice. The motivation is to build on present knowledge and expand his or her repertoire of abilities. A focus in terms of professional practice is important at this stage, and considerable time and energy tends to be invested in decision making about professional goals and development. Motivation to learn new approaches or work with different populations is usually based on a sense of professional direction and the need to refine practice skills.

The therapist who has reached Level 3 in one or more domains is more likely to assess his or her developmental level in other domains accurately than are less experienced therapists. In other words, therapists who have reached Level 3 in certain domains are better able to recognize domains where they are functioning at Levels 1 or 2. Indeed, as part of the increased focus on professional direction, they may decide after reflection that certain domains of professional practice are less important to them, and so they may not be motivated to improve their skills and knowledge in these areas or pursue practice opportunities.

Anna was finishing her internship at a medical center and entertaining career options. In processing her interests and goals with one of her supervisors, she mentioned that a postdoctoral fellowship had been offered to her in the department of pediatrics. She had recently completed a rotation through that department and had received high marks for her work with parents and families. The fellowship was to be grant funded and would focus primarily on working with children who had experienced abuse and neglect. The training opportunity, she noted, was excellent and would provide her with skills and experience that would be quite marketable down the road. On the other hand, she really was not interested in working specifically with children, but preferred adults or working more within a family context. Anna concluded after much deliberation that she would pursue positions in either a department of family medicine or psychiatry and continue her focus on adults and family units.

Autonomy

The Level 3 therapist begins with an assumption of conditional autonomy and grows into increasingly autonomous functioning. In the early phases, a desire to integrate skills and understanding further while expanding one's experiential base elicits a sense of responsibility and level of self-understanding that supports autonomous functioning. At the same time, an awareness of the utility of additional perspectives, evaluation, and resources that supervision provides typically motivates this therapist to continue to seek input. Professional development issues also may come to be increasingly important, and opportunities to process these issues in supervision are valued.

The Level 3 therapist is more aware of areas where he or she is not functioning at Level 3 and typically seeks to bring these domains up to similar levels of performance with his or her areas of strength. Of course, supervision within these domains would necessitate working with Level 2, or sometimes Level 1, structures. The overall focus of supervision will tend to be on consolidating growth or integrating across domains. In addition, the degree of responsibility for clients assumed by the therapist will be consistently higher than what we would encounter with therapists primarily functioning at lower levels. This responsibility, however, is reflected in the conditional dependency, or seeking out of advice and direction when needed, in contrast to the occasional counterdependency seen in Level 2 therapists.

The focus of supervision here is often on fine-tuning existing knowledge and skills rather than breaking new ground. The comfortable autonomy of the Level 3 therapist allows him or her to consider input without either uncritically accepting it or being overly critical in rejecting it.

STRUCTURES ACROSS DOMAINS

The advanced nature of Level 3 seems to encourage development in other areas if sufficient attention is paid to them in the supervision context. The informed knowledge of one's strengths and weaknesses, characteristic of the Level 3 therapist, enables him or her to acknowledge more readily where additional growth is necessary. Thus, the supervisor of Level 3 therapists can use the structural development of the supervisee to push him or her to develop to this level in other domains where functioning remains at Level 2, or move more quickly from Level 1 to Level 2 in other domains.

Intervention Skills Competence

Within a particular focus of therapeutic practice, and perhaps across a range of practice, Level 3 therapists demonstrate well-developed skills. The therapeutic behaviors associated with the particular orientation being used will be performed in an effective and nonself-conscious manner. The skills are used as tools in the hands of a artisan, selected with sensitivity for appropriate timing and effect. The skills become less visible, in a way, because they are becoming integrated with the therapist's use of self in the session. Thus, rather than applying an intervention in a particular situation, interventions flow from the therapist's understanding of the client, self-knowledge, and the therapeutic process. This integration, which was not possible at earlier levels, here becomes increasingly blended across clientele and contexts.

Skills useful for building a therapeutic alliance with the client flow from the therapist in an idiosyncratic manner consistent with his or her personality characteristics. Indeed, the therapist may not even be aware of when "skills" are being used versus when he or she is simply being "therapeutic." The cognitive, interpersonal, and affective information yielded by the client is used to decide a direction for therapy and selection of subsequent interventions. Understanding and empathy are communicated to the client in a genuine manner. Here the astute supervisor will recognize the difference between making an educated guess at the client's thoughts and feelings, versus true understanding of the client's world and accurate empathy. This flow of therapy is consistent with research on common factors of therapy that appear to be constant across most successful therapists regardless of theoretical orientation.[6]

This use of therapeutic self will be evident even when standard protocols or treatment manuals are being implemented. Evidence exists that experienced therapists are able to adapt to the needs of the client and the therapeutic situation in ways that enhance the effects of standard procedures.[7] Here the Level 3 therapist is able to alter treatment in ways that satisfy the idiosyncrasies of needs and characteristics of a given client.

Assessment Techniques

The Level 3 therapist has a solid sense of the role of assessment, the strengths and limitations of various strategies and instruments, and a personal understanding of how to use this information to advance knowledge of the client. This therapist is past a cookbook approach to interpretation and is more likely to understand how various assessment devices yield a breadth of information about clients. In addition, observations and impressions of client behavior during the assessment period are used to validate or modify information provided by the devices themselves. This information is integrated into a comprehensive picture of client functioning appropriate to the assessment issues. Assessment conclusions, diagnostic classifications, and so on are influenced by the assessment setting and the client's environment.

Interpersonal Assessment

The Level 3 therapist does not rely on stereotypes, either positive or negative, as the Level 1 therapist might do. Becoming confused or engulfed in emotion or countertransference, as might occur with the Level 2 therapist, is also uncommon for the Level 3 therapist. This individual will more effectively use interpersonal assessment. The ability to focus on the client *and* the ability to reflect on personal reactions to the client enables this therapist to use the interpersonal nature of therapy to generate an in-depth understanding of the client's interpersonal world.

The self-understanding developed over time by this therapist, and his or her knowledge of the therapeutic self, allows for valid processing of reactions to the client. Minuchin has used the term *client pull* to identify the manner by which clients attempt to get needs met by the therapist or move the therapist toward a particular path.[8] Similarly, Cashdan has described how clients attempt to recapitulate interpersonal patterns, and responses from others, in therapy.[9] The Level 3 therapist is sensitive to this pull from the client and is able to assess how this expresses a client need or personality style, as well as acknowledge any countertransference issues that could, if unidentified, affect the path of therapy.

Supervisors of Level 3 therapists often find that the supervisee has a considerably more complete understanding of the client than does the supervisor. There is less need to seek help during supervision in understanding the effect the client is having on the therapist and more of a desire for an opportunity to process this information verbally with input from another.

Jay was a master's-level therapist who was finishing his third year as a staff therapist in a university counseling center. Jay's therapy experience was fairly extensive across late adolescent and adult populations, although he had not worked with more mature clients (sixty years of age and older). He came to supervision one day (collegial with another staff member and totally voluntary) wanting to discuss a recent session with an older female client who had returned to school for an advanced degree. Jay commented on his sense of reticence in confronting the client concerning some ill-advised decisions she had recently made that had negative implications for her continued success in school, as well as her relationships with her family. Jay's self-reflection suggested to him that he usually would have pointed out to other clients how these decisions were self-defeating and congruent with the distorted thinking that had produced problems for her in the past. Instead, Jay found himself merely being supportive and politely listening to her story. He commented to his colleague that toward the end of the session, he realized that he was tying his own hands with a desire to be courteous to the client. As he reflected on this situation, Jay came to the conclusion that his upbringing may have played a role in his inhibitions. He had been raised to be respectful of older women and not to disagree overtly with them, because this would communicate a lack of courtesy. This "courteous" behavior, Jay reasoned, was getting in the way of his ability to assist his client in reality checking her recent decision making. This insight in hand, Jay felt more comfortable in the next session and was able to move his client toward a more intensive examination of her behavior.

Client Conceptualization

The tendency to focus on discrete pieces of information or overaccommodating to the client, as less developed therapists might do, has given way to an understanding of how diverse client variables interact to yield a complex conceptualization of the whole person. Diagnostic categories are no longer viewed as a collection of criteria that, once they meet the critical number, yield a label. Instead, the focus is on the pattern of characteristics that are relevant for the particular client and the intervention they suggest. Diagnoses are compared against templates of understanding developed in professional growth. Thus, implications for prognosis and treatment are more readily apparent. In addition, communication of this conceptualization and implications to others become clearer and more meaningful.

Individual Differences

The Level 3 therapist has developed an understanding of the influences of culture, gender, sexual orientation, and environment on the individual. Stereotypic thinking has been replaced with a breadth of knowledge regarding how various factors can affect the behavior and development of the individual client. Knowing patterns of value structures and traditions for various cultures, and differences common between genders in terms of biological and social factors, enables this therapist to understand how circumstances serve as modifiers for diagnosis, treatment, and so on. In addition, therapists at this stage of development entertain more than one interpretation of clients' observed behavior and collect clinical data to test their cultural hypotheses.[10]

Randy was a psychologist who was asked to see a young American Indian boy, Chuck, who had been experiencing difficulties in school. The referral noted that Chuck had missed classes for a full week without a reason or permission slip provided by his parents. The school counselor had tried to contact the parents and found that neither was living at the address listed as Chuck's residence. It appeared that Chuck was living with his grandparents, who noted only that he had had their permission to go hunting for a week with his uncles and cousins. Chuck had also gotten into trouble recently when he and some other American Indian boys had walked out on a drug prevention presentation given by some representatives of the administration office for the school district.

Randy explored Chuck's view of these problem situations and learned that it was a custom of his tribe to take a hunting trip each year at this time. This was an important tribal function, which included a number of Chuck's extended family members. He also learned that it was not unusual for children in Chuck's tribe to be raised primarily by their grandparents. Indeed, even when the parents were readily available in the same household, primary responsibility for raising the children fell to the grandparents. Finally, Randy learned that the drug prevention program was a puppet show in which an owl (Mr. Wise Owl) was the primary character. In Chuck's tribe, the owl signifies death, and it is deeply offending to them to display owls or use them in this manner. Randy subsequently met with the school counselor and helped her understand how Chuck's behavior had been consistent with his tribal customs and consulted with her in educating other teachers and children about issues of cultural awareness.

Theoretical Orientation

The Level 3 therapist is knowledgeable and flexible in using theory to guide practice. Rather than being driven by theory and forcing clients to fit a given orientation, theory serves as a means of generating a perspective on the world of the client. It is understood that the role of a good theory is to reduce the amount of information one processes to that which is related to conceptualization and treatment. Thus, the intimate knowledge of theory allows the Level 3 therapist to ignore certain paths of inquiry or intervention and focus on avenues more likely to yield useful understandings and directions for treatment.

This therapist will also tend to enjoy exposure to other orientations and will weigh an evaluation of the general advantages and disadvantages against a solid understanding of a personalized therapeutic orientation. This personalized orientation can take many forms, ranging from a primary reliance on a particular complex theoretical model, to an informed eclecticism born of a diverse exploration of theory with subsequent validation in practice or research. This therapist may add theoretical constructs from other models or from empirical research to his or her working knowledge of therapy but will not abandon one for another. Indeed, the focus is on integration and developing an increasingly complex and useful understanding of human nature and the therapy process.

Treatment Plans and Goals

For this level of therapist, there is finally an articulate connection between assessment and conceptualizations, which leads to a comprehensive and effective treatment plan. Goals of therapy and treatment plans are more focused and coherent, and they may be appropriately altered in response to the level of effectiveness of interventions. Idiosyncrasies of the situation and the client are integrated into approaches to treatment. If formal or standardized treatments are used, they are nonetheless effectively modified in scope and intervention appropriate to the conditions and needs of the client.

Professional Ethics

The ethical behavior of the Level 3 therapist comes from a detailed knowledge of ethical guidelines, often reflecting more than one profession, married to a personalized professional code of ethics. Guidelines are not viewed as commandments or imposed limitations on practice; rather, they are seen as examples or implications of a broader perspective on the rights of individuals and the responsibility of the profession. Complex issues reflecting situations where little direct guidance is provided by ethical standards can be dealt with in a manner reflecting the professionalism of the therapist. In new areas or regarding issues with multiple implications, the therapist will seek input and process alternatives with colleagues who may have specialized knowledge or experience.

SUPERVISING THE LEVEL 3 THERAPIST

We have been careful not to suggest a particular point in time when therapists will be functioning primarily in Level 3. It is safe to assume, however, that professional development takes time, and many therapists will be in a position where clinical supervision is either more limited than earlier in their development or nonexistent in a formal manner. Hospitals, agencies, and private practitioners often find that insufficient time exists in their schedules to provide, or otherwise make available, supervision for therapists other than those who, by law or regulation, need formal supervision. Thus, many Level 3 therapists rely on collegial supervision or seek out other avenues for furthering their professional development. (Chapter Eight discusses some of the issues that impede professional development and other important aspects of the clinical supervision process.) Many Level 3 therapists will still be in formal supervision as part of required postdegree supervision, as pre- or postdoctoral supervision, or as participants in collegial group supervision.

Less research exists examining the needs of experienced supervisees than we have found for less developed therapists. Most studies have, for the sake of access to subject populations, limited the higher levels of experience to predoctoral interns. Few studies have examined post-doctoral master-level therapists with extensive experience in the field. Indications with this truncated range of experience, however, are that more advanced supervisees are likely to behave more autonomously and show greater conceptual understanding and more desire for consultation than instruction.[11] Results consistent with expectations for experienced therapists were reported by Hillerbrand and Claiborn, who found that expert clinicians considered themselves more knowledgeable and confident, and rated their presented cases as clearer than did novices.[12] In a series of studies, McNeill, Stoltenberg and colleagues found advanced trainees less in need of structure in supervision and exhibiting increased perceptions of self-awareness, autonomy, and motivation.[13]

In one of the few studies to include postdoctoral fellows in the sample, Olk and Friedlander found reduced levels of role ambiguity or uncertainty regarding expectations and evaluation in supervision for experienced therapists.[14] On the other hand, role conflict or expectations for trainee versus counselor versus colleague roles tended to increase with higher levels of experience. This suggests the increased focus on professional development and decisions about career direction one anticipates in more advanced therapists.

General Considerations

For the Level 3 therapist, most of the structure is typically provided by the supervisee rather than the supervisor. This level of therapist knows more accurately what he or she needs from supervision at any given time and can effectively use this consultation to advance his or her professional development.

We will experience an increasing focus on personal and professional integration for therapists who are functioning at Level 3 in at least a couple of domains. If the therapist is still in a training setting, considerable attention may be paid to career decisions, although seasoned therapists will also often experience a change in professional direction and may choose to process this issue in collegial supervision.

It is important, as always, not to assume that a therapist who is competent in one or more domains and functioning at Level 3 is necessarily functioning at that high level across other domains. Even when this high level is apparent across a number of domains, the work of integration and movement to Level 3i remains an important focus of supervision.

For the more experienced therapist, it becomes increasingly common to be involved in supervising other professionals. Thus, this introduces another domain of professional development that interacts with therapist development in a number of ways. (We examine this process in more detail in Chapter Nine.) Also, we need to be effective evaluators of supervisees who are expected to be functioning at Level 3 to be certain that they have indeed reached that plateau and are not stagnating in late Level 1 and masquerading as Level 3 while actually being Pseudo Level 3.

The Level 3 therapist is more inclined to view the supervisor as a senior colleague than as an unassailable expert or perfect role model. Supervision becomes more of a process of give and take, with the role of "expert" occasionally switching from the formal supervisor to the formal supervisee, depending on the issues being addressed. Many of our advanced supervisees have had extensive experience before we begin working with them, and some of this experience is likely to be in areas where our own skills and knowledge are limited.

Daniel was assigned as a supervisor-mentor to a new therapist at the agency. They spent the first few meetings getting to know one another and the extent of their respective clinical knowledge and experiences. Daniel took considerable time assisting his colleague in learning about agency procedures and "mapping the political climate." After a couple of months, Daniel brought up in discussion a child who had recently been assigned to him. He mentioned in passing some of the puzzling aspects of the case and noted that he suspected the possibility of some abuse, even though that was not part of the presenting problem or reason for referral. Most of the supervision session was spent in discussing this case, with considerable helpful input given by Daniel's supervisee who, he discovered, had had extensive training and experience in issues of child abuse and neglect.

When the opportunity is available, supervision of Level 3 therapists can productively reflect a mentoring relationship, characterized by a fairly nondirective consultative role for the supervisor, who is attentive and invested in the general professional development of the supervisee as well as assisting him or her to acclimate to the particular clinical environment. It is not uncommon for some regression to occur when even experienced therapists enter a new environment.

Support and availability of a supervisor or mentor can make this transition brief and allow the therapist to reestablish prior levels of functioning within the new environment.

Before we examine specific interventions and mechanisms for supervising Level 3 therapists, it is useful to recall some of the important characteristics of this level of supervisee. As we have previously noted in this chapter, the Level 3 therapist is able to build an effective therapeutic alliance with the client and gather extensive therapy-related information. The effortless use of therapy skills creates a facilitative environment and encourages candid client disclosures. The therapist's ability to focus intently on the client, first developed in Level 2, enables a deep understanding of the client's perceptual world, as well as an empathic awareness of the client's emotional experience. Unlike the Level 2 therapist, these data are more accessible to the Level 3 therapist because of his or her ability to pull back and reflect on information and assess his or her own reactions to the client. Thus, this therapist can take a personal inventory of his or her cognitive and affective reactions to the client and use this information therapeutically with an awareness of the possible influences of countertransference issues. Finally, the Level 3 therapist is able to take a more objective third-person perspective on the therapeutic process as well as access memory to retrieve relevant clinically related information learned over the years. This ability allows the therapist to integrate three important sources of information in his or her work: the client, the therapist reactions, and professional knowledge.

A word of caution is in order here. Recall the discussion of the Pseudo Level 3 therapist in the preceding two chapters. Only adequate assessment by the supervisor, or any other person administratively over this therapist, can effectively identify this individual. This therapist will often sound knowledgeable (they often are) and may appear to be an effective therapist if judged only on unsupervised descriptions of clients and therapy or case reports. It is when this individual's work is observed that the lack of congruence between description and action can be noted. It is best to take the opportunity to observe a supervisee's work before assuming the level of therapeutic development.

Client Assignment

Deciding which types of clients are most suitable for the continued development of Level 3 therapists becomes less of an issue than it was previously. This therapist, at least in the domains within which he or she is functioning at Level 3, will have considerable ability to work effectively with a range of clients. Still, if possible, selection of clients with whom the therapist has less experience, or who reflect different cultural backgrounds, diagnostic classifications, and so on, will help consolidate gains and set the stage for his or her movement into Level 3i.

Because Level 3 therapists are unlikely to be functioning at this level across all domains, including modalities of therapy and various types of clients, it is particularly important to be aware of areas where the therapist is functioning at lower levels and work to encourage growth to bring them up to Level 3. Thus, client assignment may focus on areas where Level 3 has not yet been attained.

Interventions

The types of interventions discussed in the preceding two chapters remain useful categories for examining how supervisors can most effectively work with Level 3 therapists. Facilitative interventions remain useful. We never really grow out of an appreciation for support and caring within the supervision environment. They are less crucial in terms of protecting fragile therapeutic egos, as the Level 3 therapist has developed considerable confidence based on understanding and abilities, but remain effective in moving the relationship along and promoting self-disclosure and self-examination.

Prescriptive interventions are rarely used in domains where the therapist has reached Level 3 but may be used with respect to other domains where this therapist has not yet developed to this degree. In general, however, this level of therapist is able to select among options and usually will seek consultation in determining alternatives rather than asking for specific directions.

Confrontational interventions are still occasionally necessary. We are all susceptible to making mistakes, being misguided, or putting our own needs first from time to time. The supervisor can feel free to confront this therapist across nearly any issue and expect that the confrontation will be met with a careful analysis. Recall that Level 3 therapists will be able to engage in central route processing regarding most issues in therapy, so a critical examination of recommendations or input will be the norm. Uncritical acceptance of advice will be rare, unless it is congruent with the therapist's primary orientation and understanding of the situation. On the other hand, defensiveness will usually be limited. Some Level 3 therapists may feel so confident or knowledgeable that they focus little on certain input, particularly if it is dramatically different from their own perspective, and thus they may be resistant to criticism or engage in biased processing. At these times, confrontation may be necessary to encourage the therapist to engage in central route processes, scan relevant schemata, and carefully examine alternatives.

Catalytic interpretations will most often be used in response to blocks or stagnation. As skilled as the Level 3 therapist is, he or she may still have issues that can interfere with effective therapy. These may be unresolved historical issues, or they may be a function of recent life events. It is more likely, however, that the Level 3 therapist will be aware of these and the need to address them in supervision or therapy than will either the Level 1 or Level 2 therapist.

Eduardo had just heard over the radio that there was a terrible explosion at the Murrah Federal Building in Oklahoma City. Reports were still vague, but it was clear that the workday had begun and there were a number of people in the building when the explosion occurred. He got in his car and headed downtown to see if he could be of assistance. He had had training, both as a psychologist and in the military, to work with trauma victims. As he approached downtown, he felt a strong feeling of fear and aversion. Images of Beirut flashed in his mind, and he remembered helping to clear debris and bodies from the military base after the terrorist bombing there years before. He tried to fight off the feelings but decided to turn the car around and head back to work. He was not yet ready to face those fears and that kind of tragedy again.

Supervisory Mechanisms

The careful reader will have noticed that the range and number of specific mechanisms used in supervision have been reduced as we moved from Level 1 to Level 2 and now to Level 3 therapists. A primary reason is that tricks or techniques are less necessary and specific instructional technology less important as the skill level increases and the information base expands. With Level 3 therapists, the most common approach to supervision is collegial, which relies less on monitoring the therapist's behavior with clients or engaging in direct observation. Many of the mechanisms we have discussed will remain useful but are less crucial at this point.

Therapists still benefit from observing their work on videotape and getting input from a colleague or supervisor concerning interventions. As skilled as the Level 3 therapist is at pulling back in the session and taking an objective view of the process, it is still helpful to augment that perspective by watching one work on video. Observing others can be helpful too, particularly as it relates to expanding one's repertoire of skills and orientations. In addition, using videotape or direct observation is crucial in identifying Pseudo Level 3 therapists who may be able to talk a good game but have not progressed beyond late Level 1 or early Level 2 structures.

A common form of supervision with experienced Level 3 therapists is informal, collegial group supervision. Here the opportunity exists for colleagues to consult and challenge each other, as well as provide support. The primary advantage to this continued supervision is to work toward integration across domains and to share clinical experiences, insights, and problems with colleagues. Unfortunately, what often passes for group supervision is such activities as grand rounds or in-service training seminars. Although these can be quite helpful in gaining new knowledge and keeping abreast of the field, a limitation is that the therapist rarely gets much of an opportunity to work on clinical issues directly related to his or her clientele or address personal and professional issues.

Some settings are not conducive to open sharing and self-disclosure. This is unfortunate as it sets up an adversarial relationship among the staff or a sense of isolation that inhibits growth and does little to make the work environment enjoyable. In addition, some settings are so concerned with bottom-line economic issues that supervision, either individual or group, consists of little more than checking the number of billable hours and advising on finding ways to increase them. Although we understand economic pressures, this has a negative impact on the quality of clinical services and professional development.

Striving for integration across domains to move toward Level 3i is the goal of supervision with Level 3 therapists and should be the goal of the supervisees as well. Therapists who reach this level within domains now focus on developing the ability to move seamlessly from one to another domain. The supervisor can benefit the therapist by eliciting this focus in supervision and pushing the therapist to build stronger linkages between the schemata developed in response to training and experience within given domains, to make them more accessible across domains. In other words, the goal is to reduce the compartmentalization of knowledge and information so that it becomes readily activated in numerous clinical situations. The Level 3i therapist is able to, for example, consider the assessment process and the information it yields—diagnostic impressions and data—develop useful conceptualizations, and effectively use these in a supervisory or consultation context.

The interpersonal power of the supervisor will rest on the therapist's perception of his or her therapeutic expertise and supervisory skills. Level 3 therapists will readily evaluate the skills of the supervisor, and should they fall short, will ignore, circumvent, or actively challenge this authority. Remember that central route processing encourages careful and effortful scrutiny. An ineffective supervisor may fool a Level 1 therapist much of the time, a Level 2 therapist some of the time, but rarely for very long will one fool a Level 3 therapist. Although the amount of structure to be provided, and the responsibility one needs to assume for active supervision, is reduced for this level of therapist, the knowledge base and the level of integration must be high for one to supervise effectively. Thus, a Level 3 therapist can be supervised effectively only by another Level 3 therapist, and it is done best by a Level 3 supervisor. Table 5.1 summarizes relevant issues and supervision interventions for the Level 3 therapist.

BEYOND LEVELS

In our earlier models of therapist development, we posited the existence of master therapists who have reached the pinnacle of development across the domains of clinical practice. Very few of us will ever reach this point. Indeed, we can safely say that no one will be able to

General considerations	Most structure provided by trainee, more focus on personal and professional integration and career decisions
Interventions	Facilitative
	Confrontational: occasionally necessary
	Conceptual: from personal orientation
	Catalytic: in response to blocks or stagnation
Mechanisms	Peer supervision
	Group supervision
	Strive for integration

Table 5.1.   Level 3 Supervision Environment.

function equally well across the domains and subdomains of clinical practice. Do any of us know therapists who are highly proficient with all populations and working from any and all orientations across practice issues and contexts?

An even more relevant issue is one of continued development. We know that development never stops. Life goes on, and the associated changes affect us and our environment. We have worked with a number of parents over the years who have lamented that by the time they learn how to parent their child effectively, he or she had matured to a new stage of childhood, requiring different perspectives and skills. Similarly, when we believe we have reached the point in our practice where we understand our clients, our work, and ourselves, we grow older, meet new challenges, and have to face the reality that we are no longer the same person. We have watched trainees become colleagues over the years and adjust to dealing with the effects of their age on the perceptions of their clients and their therapy. As they mature, the youthfulness fades, family status often alters, and life experiences affect their views of the world. These changes must be integrated on a professional as well as a personal level. Our therapeutic selves change as our physical and psychological selves change in response to experience and aging. Thus, the task of development is never complete. We constantly face new challenges, new frontiers, and new personal changes that pose new implications for our professional development.

We maintain that some form of supervision remains beneficial throughout professional life to assist us in integrating changes in the profession, changes in the society, and changes in ourselves. Indeed, this is one of the most inspiring and exciting aspects of the career we have chosen. We should not hope to maintain the status quo. In development, staying the same is regression. If we do not move ahead, we fall behind.

CHAPTER SIX

The Supervisory Relationship

——~m~——

Central to the master-apprentice approach to the training and supervision of psychotherapists is the supervisory relationship that develops and evolves over time between the participants. This relationship involves personal as well as professional aspects that encompass the roles of teaching, mentoring, consultation, and evaluation. The moment-to-moment interactions of the participants also have an important interpersonal relationship that contributes to the increased self-awareness of the supervisee and serves to encourage further learning of psychotherapeutic skills. In our view, the supervisory relationship serves as the base of all effective teaching and training. Indeed, as Loganbill and colleagues[1] suggest, the supervisory relationship is essential in supervision in much the same manner as the counseling relationship is in psychotherapy. Consequently, we believe that an updated examination of the supervisory relationship in theory and research is warranted.

This chapter briefly reviews some recent research regarding the supervisory relationship and provides some guidelines and examples in working with supervisory relationships across developmental levels. Additionally, with the increasing importance for supervisors to possess knowledge about individual differences, especially in responding to the increasing diversity of supervisees in terms of gender, ethnicity, and sexual orientation, we address the unique needs of diverse therapists within the context of the supervisory relationship. In this way we hope to make the case for a more central role for the relationship in building a theory of supervision.

THEORY AND RESEARCH IN SUPERVISORY RELATIONSHIPS

It appears that most past theory building in supervision has simply assumed and acknowledged the inherent importance of the supervisory relationship. Some theorists such as Eckstein and Wallerstein[2] and Mueller and Kell[3] have hypothesized stages in the supervisory relationship as it grows and develops. The beginning stages in these models emphasize the development of trust and familiarity with the expectations of the participants. Other issues, including more unconscious or unarticulated expectations, are proposed to come into play in the second or middle stage. The end phases deal with various aspects of termination. Mueller and Kell[4] also place primary emphasis on the inevitability and resolution of conflict within the supervisory relationship.

Research investigating satisfaction with supervision supports the idea that supervisees differ in their needs and expectations regarding supervisory tasks contributing to the relationship across developmental levels. Beginning trainees prefer more attention to be devoted to the development of intake skills,[5] didactic training in counseling,[6] and more time spent on developing self-awareness.[7] Intermediate supervisees desire assistance with developing alternative conceptualization skills,[8] more emphasis on personal development than technical skills, working within a cohesive theory, and clear communication about expectations.[9] Advanced therapists prefer to examine more complex issues of personal development, transference and countertransference, parallel processes, and client and counselor resistance and defensiveness.[10]

Across developmental levels, good supervisory relationships encompass warmth, acceptance, respect, understanding, and trust.[11] In addition, it appears that good supervisors self-disclose and create an atmosphere of experimentation and allowance for mistakes.[12] Nelson also found that trainees prefer supervisors who show interest in supervision, have experience as a therapist, or currently provide psychotherapeutic services and possess technical or theoretical knowledge.[13] Significantly, Rabinowitz and colleagues identified the clarification of the supervisory relationship in the first three weeks as a major issue across all levels of therapist experience.[14]

Bordin extrapolates from the therapeutic alliance in psychotherapy and has perhaps been the theoretician to focus most strongly on the development of the relationship or working alliance in supervision. In addition to the basic tasks and goals of supervision, Bordin stresses the process of building a strong working alliance, or "bonding," between the therapist and supervisor encompassing trust, liking, and caring. He believes that this alliance potentially counteracts the "inescapable" tension associated with status differences between supervisors and supervisees.[15]

Most recently, Efstation, Patton, and Kardash have attempted to develop an instrument designed to measure the strength of the working alliance based on the work of Bordin and others. They conceptualize the supervisory relationship as an interactive process by which supervisors influence and facilitate the learning of the therapist. The Supervisory Working Alliance Inventory (SWAI) demonstrates some initial reliability and validity as Efstation and colleagues identified a factor structure that both supervisees and supervisors perceived as involving a *Client Focus,* or working to understand the client, and *Rapport* as common dimensions of the supervisory relationship. Additionally, supervisors identified the dimension of *Trainee Identification* with the supervisor.[16]

This work focused on investigating the supervisory relationship and yielded a promising instrument to measure aspects of the relationship. However, only limited follow-up investigations have been conducted to develop the promise of the SWAI. There appears to be a lack of focus on the supervisory relationship in the supervision research literature. In addition, the study is limited to the sample of therapists at the advanced practicum and internship levels. As the authors acknowledge, the factor or subscale structure of the SWAI may differ developmentally with beginning and intermediate-level supervisees and may indeed vary over time.

A recent investigation by Worthen and McNeill illustrates the primacy of the supervisory relationship in the view of supervisees and serves to alert us to the lack of attention paid to the development and processes of the supervisory relationship by researchers. In this investigation, they deviated from traditional research design by utilizing a qualitative phenomenological research methodology in order to investigate the experience of "good" supervision from the perspective of therapists. They conducted in-depth interviews with eight intermediate to advanced-level therapists that were guided by only one research question. The initial statement made to participants was simply, "Please describe for me as completely, clearly, and concretely as you can an experience during this semester when you felt you received good psychotherapy supervision." Participants were then invited to elaborate on the comment, and the interviewer's role was limited to facilitating the articulation of the good supervision description by focusing on understanding the experience as the trainee related it.[17]

Qualitative analyses yielded a general meaning structure for the experience of good supervision events. Identification of the salient themes that reflected good supervision events within the general meaning structure resulted in four distinct supervision phases: the existential baseline, setting the stage, a good supervision experience, and outcomes of good supervision. The *existential baseline* reflected a fluctuating to grounded level of confidence and a sense of disillusionment to a sense of efficacy with the therapeutic process in intermediate to advanced trainees. There was also a strong desire for rewarding supervision, and in most cases a previous experience with unrewarding supervision, as well as an aversion to overt evaluation. *Setting the stage* involved a perceived needing and sensed inadequacy on the part of supervisees. The most pivotal and crucial component of the *good supervision experience* evident in every case studied was the quality of the supervisory relationship. Therapists described effective supervisors as conveying an attitude that manifested empathy, a nonjudgmental stance toward them, a sense of validation or affirmation, and encouragement to explore and experiment. These dynamics are illustrated by the comments of one participant:

> And what was so great, was that my supervisor was really affirming of and validating of my ability to speak clearly. I felt very much understood by her and I felt also like she appreciated those abilities that I had taken pride in the past and which I had felt, I just hadn't felt were being recognized at all, at any level.[18]

The findings also suggested that the desire and need for a supportive supervisory relationship are ever present in supervision.

Supervisees believed that their supervisors helped to normalize their struggle, often accomplished by a personal self-disclosure from their supervisor. Other themes at this stage included a sense of "freeing" consisting of reduced self-protectiveness and receptivity to supervisory input, nondefensive analysis, reexamination of assumptions, and acquisition of a metaperspective. Finally, the *outcomes of good supervision* included a strengthened supervisory alliance, along with strengthened confidence, refined professional identity, increased therapeutic perception, and an expanded ability to conceptualize and intervene.

Supervisees in various training settings experience numerous short-term supervisory relationships as they progress through the stages of development. Hence, their expectations regarding the supervisory relationship will vary given their developmental level and previous experience with the supervision process. Consequently, in our view, hypothesized stages of the supervisory relationship put forth by previous theorists applicable across all levels of training are somewhat problematic. For example, most academic settings value the assignment of trainees to a variety of supervisors over the duration of an academic career in order to expose supervisees to a diversity of training approaches and models. The result is that trainees experience many short-term supervisory relationships rarely lasting more than a quarter or a semester (four to six months) with the same supervisor. Internships and postmaster's and doctoral job settings may allow for more longer-term supervisory relationships to develop (six to twelve months).

The fact that supervisees experience numerous supervisory relationships affects the experience and expectations that they bring to the next relationship. In addition, the idea of a transition to the next supervisor may more accurately reflect most relationships than the concept of terminating relationships extrapolated from the psychotherapeutic domain. Our developmental conceptualization of supervision suggests that therapists at varying levels bring different expectations to the supervisory relationship, based in part on previous such experiences. Finally, although conflicts may occur in many supervisory relationships, according to the IDM, they may be more likely with Level 2 supervisees. Thus, an overemphasis or exclusive focus on perceived supervisory or interpersonal conflict in therapists is not always appropriate and detracts from the many elements that comprise good supervisory relationships.[19]

It appears for the supervisees in the Worthen and McNeill investigation that the supervisory relationship served as the base of all good therapeutic and professional training.[20] This conclusion suggests that the learning and acquisition of professional skills and identity may be delayed, hampered, or not fully developed outside the context of an effective supervisory relationship. As Allen and colleagues have suggested, the didactic and structural components of supervision are not as influential determinants of quality as are clear communication and respect.[21] In addition, Black has concluded that "the largest and most structurally similar factor found in both effective and ineffective supervision was that of the supervisory relationship."[22] Important differences between supervisory relationships in effective versus ineffective supervision were responsive and supportive versus insensitive and judgmental.

A surprising, as well as disturbing, aspect of the Worthen and McNeill study was that six of the eight participants, in expressing a desire for a qualitatively different supervisory relationship, indicated that they had experienced some previous supervisory relationships as less than fulfilling.[23] This result is consistent with Galante's finding that 47 percent of trainees reported that they had experienced at least one ineffective supervisory relationship.[24] Thus, it appears that supervisors may need much more extensive training in supervisory models and relationship processes, exclusive of therapeutic training and experience, to increase their effectiveness. As supervisors attend to supervisee needs and provide the appropriate supervisory environment corresponding to a given developmental level, the supervisory relationship is strengthened, and the potential for conflict is reduced.

The interpersonal styles of supervisors vary in the manner in which they choose to attend to the various supervisory tasks across developmental stages. Some prefer to take a primary role as mentor, expert, consultant, or teacher. What the research, as well as our experience as practicing supervisors, suggests is that these roles may vary and serve certain functions at certain times. What may be lacking as a priority, however, are the interpersonal characteristics and expressions of warmth, acceptance, understanding, respect, support, and empathy across developmental levels and supervisor styles. This is similar to the commonly accepted notion that the basis of all therapeutic intervention across varying theoretical orientations is a therapeutic relationship or alliance characterized by trust, warmth, respect, and understanding.

SUPERVISORY RELATIONSHIPS ACROSS LEVELS

Supervisees of varying developmental levels bring differing expectations to the supervisory relationship; thus, there are various ways to strengthen the supervisory relationship.

Level 1

Beginning Level 1 supervisees are experiencing supervision for the first time; thus, their previous experiences with faculty members within the educational environment may be limited to the formal student-professor relationship. As a result, the more informal and unstructured aspects of the supervisory relationship are novel to them. In addition to the anxiety reflective of the typical Level 1 therapist, beginning trainees may also experience anxiety related to engaging in a more interpersonally focused relationship with a supervisor. Also, their evaluation anxiety is high and may be manifested in a trepidation to reveal too much of themselves as individuals beyond the role of a supervisee's willingness to learn. In essence, the beginning Level 1 supervisee is not sure what to expect in the supervisory relationship.

It is important for the supervisor of the beginning supervisee to communicate empathy and understanding of the journey toward becoming a therapist. Recalling and sharing one's own experiences at this stage may help reduce the supervisee's anxiety and provide needed affirmation and validation. Clarifying expectations and slowly establishing trust are the primary initial relationship-building skills. Creating an atmosphere of support, acceptance, and acknowledgment of the inevitability of making mistakes helps to build trust. Recall that the Level 1 therapist demonstrates limited self and other awareness. Thus, interpersonal processing of relationship dynamics between the supervisor and supervisee, as well as commenting on personality characteristics of the therapist, is best limited to those with obvious implications through very concrete interventions. A more intense focus on these dynamics is best left for supervisees who are making the transition into Level 2.

Mark was a beginning trainee who possessed a bachelor's degree in psychology, performed at the top of his first-year class academically, and was highly motivated to be an effective psychotherapist. Like most other beginning-level trainees, Mark was extremely self-conscious regarding evaluation, the relatively unstructured format of the individual supervision session, and the subjectiveness of evaluation in supervision. Similar to many other early trainees, these dynamics appeared to be manifested in a reluctance and inability to secure an audible tape of his therapy sessions. He proffered the gamut of excuses: forgetting to turn the machine on, poor-quality tapes, and clients' reluctance to provide permission to tape. To confront, interpret, and process these dynamics would only have served to exacerbate Mark's high level of anxiety. Instead, his supervisor provided a clear, cogent rationale to Mark regarding the importance of taping in relation to client welfare and assessment, and he issued a simple directive to Mark to have a tape ready by the following week. This intervention, designed to clarify the expectations of the supervisor, was effective; Mark was then able to obtain taped sessions consistently. Later, as an advanced student enrolled in a course on clinical supervision, Mark was able to understand and place the experience within the context of his personal dynamics.

Level 2

Due to the trial and tribulation associated with the Level 2 supervisee, the therapist-supervisor relationship at this stage is perhaps the most likely to undergo significant conflict and stress. At this point, the supervisee has also experienced other supervisory relationships and thus brings a set of expectations to the current relationship. Prior expectations may also have evolved by previous contact with a supervisor in another capacity (for example, in a classroom setting).

In clarifying expectations for supervisory sessions at this level, the supervisor may find it helpful to assess the therapist's perception of the nature of previous supervisory relationships. The supervisee who has experienced an unsatisfying relationship may express a desire for a qualitatively different experience. In contrast, the therapist who has experienced a satisfying, facilitative relationship with a previous supervisor may have similar or high expectations for the current supervisor. Due to the high dependence on the supervisor at Level 1, the supervisee may have come to idolize a previous supervisor. But whatever the relationship was, the earlier supervisor may come to set the standard for reference or comparison to the current developing supervisory relationship.

In assessing the nature of a previous supervisory relationship, the supervisor should show respect for and understanding of the expectations that the supervisee brings to the new relationship. This intervention also sets the stage for clarification of expectations, discussion of differing supervisory styles, as well as anticipation of the potential impact of possible stylistic and procedural differences.

Recall that one of the primary tasks of the supervisor of the Level 2 therapist is to foster a sense of independence that, coupled with the supervisee's developing sense of competence but lack of experience, results in a dependency-autonomy conflict. As a result, Level 2 therapists may resist or resent supervisors' lack of direction in fostering the supervisee's autonomy or directives concerning client welfare. These may be viewed as "overmonitoring" by confident supervisees. Such resistance or resentment places a strain on the supervisory relationship that is all too often left unaddressed by both supervisors and therapists.

This covert conflict and struggle seethes below the surface, resulting in passive-aggressive behaviors on the part of supervisees, who may selectively present successful cases or actively avoid discussion of cases for which they suspect the supervisor will challenge their skills or choice of intervention. The supervisee may passively agree with supervisor directives but not carry them out. As a result, the supervisor becomes increasingly frustrated by the perceived lack of respect for his or her clinical skills or power differential. Supervisors may first need to normalize the struggle in the form of a personal self-disclosure or acknowledge the supervisee's strengths and weaknesses in terms of multiple levels of development across various domains in order to defuse the situation and reduce supervisee defensiveness.

Despite the conflicts that supervisees at Level 2 experience, research indicates that at this level they begin to demonstrate an increased readiness and openness to processing of personal issues of self-awareness, defensiveness, transference and countertransference, and the supervisory relationship. Thus, at this point it may be necessary for the supervisor to confront and process the dysfunctional aspects of the supervisory relationship in the here and now. This has the added benefit of demonstrating or modeling important aspects of process as applied to the psychotherapeutic arena.

The parallel process between the supervisory and counseling relationships may become evident as a function of the development of the Level 2 supervisee's self and other awareness. Thus, confronting and processing the immediate aspects of the supervisory relationship can resolve impasses in the relationship, and it has the added benefit of modeling the interpersonal process aspects of the therapeutic relationship.[25] Because the Level 2 therapist is fluctuating in terms of developing a consistent sense of self and other awareness, process-type interventions may not always break through and resolve relationship issues. At this time, however, the supervisor may be planting the seed or setting the stage for later processing of the supervisory relationship as the supervisee moves to Level 3.

Michelle had completed her master's degree in counseling and thus had a year of supervised counseling experience. In her doctoral program, she had identified strongly with a female faculty member and arranged for this individual to provide her individual supervision over the course of two semesters. Her evaluations had been generally positive, but they lacked specificity in terms of strengths and weaknesses. Thus, Michelle felt confident in her ability to function independently as a counselor in most therapeutic situations.

After Michelle had provided some tapes to her current male supervisor, she received some critical feedback highlighting some deficits in her skills and specific areas in need of improvement. During the feedback session, Michelle was visibly upset, cried, and expressed her shock and dismay at receiving such criticism. At this point the supervisor attempted to normalize the process by pointing out her strengths, which she initially accepted. In subsequent supervisory sessions, however, it became clear that Michelle presented her cases in a distant, detached manner and simply acquiesced to the supervisor's suggestions and feedback, even when it was positive. The supervisory sessions lacked a vitality and sense of engagement. The supervisor noted his perception of a problem or lack of engagement in the supervisory relationship and process by Michelle. In her defense, she cited an inability to identify with the supervisor as a male and indicated that he did not understand her and was too harsh in his presentation of feedback. Although this discussion resulted in an increased openness and involvement in supervision, the relationship improved only in the sense of a working relationship in which Michelle implemented the supervisor interventions but did not value them. Later Michelle did not view process-type interventions as relevant. Although she was able to improve steadily in her skills, this impasse and the distance in her relationship with the supervisor was not resolved during her graduate career.

Level 3

Level 3 or Level 3i therapists have experienced a number of supervisory relationships by the time they have progressed through training and various employment settings. It remains important for supervisors of Level 3 therapists to assess the impact of previous positive and negative supervisory relationships and the potential impact on the current relationship. Previously unrewarding supervision experiences appear to result in an aversion to overt evaluation and a strong desire for more rewarding supervision by higher-level therapists. These supervisees also view good supervision as characterized by an empathic, nonjudgmental relationship, with encouragement to experiment and explore, and they are satisfied when their struggles are normalized.[26]

Therapists who are entering Level 3 in initial domains are often making a transition to a new and unfamiliar setting, perhaps encountering unfamiliar personnel and policies. Although it is common for these therapists to experience temporary regression, their highly developed skills and sense of self-awareness usually allow for the transition to the new setting to occur quickly. This transition is aided by a supportive and safe environment where the supervisee is able to establish an effective supervisory alliance. It is at this stage that the supervisee is most willing to explore personal dynamics and issues as related to the impact on client work. Now the supervisor may use the therapeutic relationship to increase the insight of supervisees regarding the impact of personal characteristics and reactions toward clients on the therapeutic process. Use of parallel process interventions, or process checks, will attend to the therapist's needs and willingness to examine these issues.[27]

The mutual respect and collegial exploration of these issues that now characterize the supervisory relationship lead to new insights by the therapist and take on a special significance, depth, and satisfaction associated with mentoring and observing the progress of a competent supervisee. It is not unusual for these relationships to continue long past the supervisory experience. Additional time may be spent attending to the supervisee's professional development needs at this point, including job search and future goals. This process is apparent in the comments of one of the participants in the Worthen and McNeill study.

> When I talk about that process, when we play with these process pieces or when we would stop the tape at whatever times, that couldn't have happened, I don't think, if it didn't feel like a real collegial relationship, if I didn't feel like I was respected at a level that, I guess, I wanted to be respected at, or if I was going to move on as a professional.[28]

Damage to the supervisory alliance at this point primarily occurs through misassessment of the supervisee's developmental level or rigidity by supervisors who apply similar techniques to all levels of therapists by not attending to the Level 3 supervisee's needs. Although processing of relationship dynamics can be extremely valuable at this stage, a constant or overly intrusive focus on process or relationship dynamics to the exclusion of other tasks important to the development of the supervisee can result in high levels of anxiety and dissatisfaction for therapists.

Debbie, the top choice of the predoctoral internship site she had chosen to attend, clearly exhibited strong clinical skills in her first couple of months. However, her supervisor demonstrated a strong psychodynamic supervisory focus and chose to devote the majority of supervisory sessions attending to the relationship dynamics between himself and Debbie, searching for the implications of conflict and potential transference and countertransference reactions in both supervision and counseling environments. Debbie soon became weary of this exclusive focus that she felt was not attending to the further development of her overall clinical skills, but rather was overly concerned with her interpersonal dynamics, so she raised the issue with her supervisor. However, this impasse could not be resolved, and Debbie was assigned to another supervisor. Immediately, Debbie took the initiative to process with the new supervisor her previous difficulties and discuss the implications for their current relationship. She exhibited a continued openness to examining supervisory relationship dynamics, and she appreciated her current supervisor's balance in attending to client issues and clinical skills, while raising these issues, when relevant, within a supportive and open atmosphere. Thus, despite a negative supervisory experience, Debbie was able to value the supervisory relationship and benefit from the intense interpersonal nature of the relationship to improve both personally and professionally.

SUPERVISORY RELATIONSHIPS WITH DIVERSE THERAPISTS

In prior chapters we focused on the domain of individual differences as an area of training that supervisees must master. Indeed, in the past ten years, the fields of counseling, professional psychology, and social work have devoted increasing importance to the influence of race, ethnicity and culture, gender, sexual orientation, and other human differences on the counseling process.[29] As others have noted, there is an increasing literature within this domain of individual differences and training criteria to prepare white middle-class therapists to work with racial and ethnic minority clients.[30] Yet despite the increasing attention given to issues of diversity in graduate training programs, there is a dearth of information available on the unique training and supervisory needs and/or perceptions of diverse supervisees.

Therapist demographics within training programs have changed over the past ten years, and it is not unusual for graduate programs currently to comprise of about 70 percent women, with increasing numbers of ethnically diverse and gay and lesbian trainees. Indeed, in our doctoral programs we typically have between 30 percent and 40 percent ethnic and racial minority students. Faculty demographics have been slower to change, however, and still consist primarily of white male faculty.[31] This means, of course, that supervision dyads typically consist of white male supervisors with diverse trainees.

Most recently, McNeill, Hom, and Perez examined the sparse literature concerning the unique and common experiences of ethnic and racial minority students in professional psychology programs.[32] These experiences unfortunately included exposure to stereotypes about multicultural, affirmative action, and recruitment issues. Culturally diverse trainees often question the knowledge and flexibility of white faculty and peers when in case conferences, important moderator variables such as socioeconomic status, ethnic identification, and acculturation are not deemed as relevant as biological factors and models of pathology. In addition, Vasquez and McKinley suggest that racial and ethnic minority trainees may be struggling with their own ethnic identity development in attempting to reconcile the Eurocentrically based culture of psychology that may conflict with their own cultural background. These authors view this solidification of a bicultural identity as a crucial developmental task for ethnic minority trainees.[33]

As a result, culturally diverse therapists are often faced with struggles to assert their unique needs and make others aware of the multicultural implications of course material, counseling theories, and interventions, especially in response to notions of color blindness in psychological intervention and assessment. It also appears that many culturally diverse therapists experience varying degrees of discrimination, isolation, racism, and differential treatment, resulting in feelings of confusion, anger, outrage, and discouragement. These therapists may or may not choose to disclose these experiences and feelings, and program faculty, directors of training, and clinical supervisors may remain unaware of the problem.

In reviewing the literature in this area, McNeill and colleagues found that previous authors consistently recommended that the variety of issues that racial and ethnic minority therapists face should be addressed within the supervisory relationship.[34] Although we believe that program advisers, directors, or mentors could also serve this role in their relationships with culturally diverse students, it seems that the intensive, interpersonally focused nature of the supervisory relationship lends itself well to the personal developmental issues of the ethnic minority supervisee. As Vasquez and McKinley point out, these issues include supervisees' own struggles with their ethnic identity, issues of discrimination, pressure from their own community to "work in the trenches," and resultant feelings of confusion, frustration, and anger.[35] Hunt states that for African American supervisees, ethnic identity and expressions of anger and hostility as reactions to white theories and various other patterns of relating to white and black peers and clients are best dealt with in individual supervision.[36] Zuniga described a graduate social work program with Chicano students that emphasized a supervisory focus on ethnic identity, family history, acculturation, and the processing of experiences of racism, especially within the educational environment as crucial components in the development of clinical skills in therapists.[37] Cook suggests that supervisors who ignore racial issues in supervision may unknowingly develop negative reputations for being racially insensitive and providing inadequate supervision.[38]

Although there is also a lack of an extensive literature surrounding the training and supervisory needs of female and gay and lesbian trainees, it appears that issues similar to those of culturally diverse therapists may exist and manifest themselves within the supervisory relationship for other diverse supervisees. For example, potential conflicts in the supervisory relationship may depend on supervisors' and supervisees' sexual identification and attitudes toward homosexuality.[39]

One of the few early investigations into the effects of gender on the supervision relationship, by Worthington and Stern, indicated that male supervisees thought they had better relationships with their supervisors, regardless of gender.[40] For women, sexist attitudes that are manifested by male supervisors may result in some preference for female supervisors, although recent studies within the area of gender matching in the supervisory dyad are mixed.[41] Some studies support gender matching;[42] others do not.[43] Nelson and Holloway reported differences in the treatment of female versus male supervisees by both male and female supervisors. These supervisors failed to encourage or support their female supervisees' assumption of power in deference to a more powerful authority figure more often than male supervisees. The authors concluded that supervisors in the expert role, regardless of gender, may assume more power in interactions with their female supervisees than with their male supervisees, either by withholding support for the female trainees' attempts at exerting power or by simply exerting stronger influence with female supervisees.[44]

Drawing on the work of Gilligan regarding women's moral development, Stoltenberg and Delworth suggested that female supervisees may be more relationship oriented and bond more easily with supervisors, whereas males tend to be more task oriented.[45] Limited work with gender issues within the ELM suggests that females may be more susceptible to influence than males under certain conditions. Cacioppo and Petty found females to be more agreeable than males, but only under conditions of low prior knowledge (which affects ability to engage in central route processing).[46] Thus, due to gender roles and socialization, women may be more susceptible to influence attempts in the interest of maintaining a harmonious supervisory relationship than males at Level 1, where supervisees lack prior knowledge about the counseling process, despite being highly involved and motivated. Because both male and female therapists gain knowledge about therapy as they progress through Levels 2 and 3, we would not expect gender differences in persuasion to occur at these later stages. All of these possible differences, however, need to be validated empirically within the supervision context.[47]

Supervisees lack power in relationships with supervisors, so they may be reluctant to express their feelings in relation to these issues. For supervisors, discussions of race, culture, gender, and lifestyle may be unfamiliar and uncomfortable, and therefore they avoid them. Supervisors may also view these issues as personal in nature and outside the traditional purview of clinical supervision, which attends only to client issues and concerns. Thus, to address diverse therapists' needs, it is incumbent on supervisors to take the responsibility to create a supervisory relationship and environment in which these needs and issues are viewed as relevant to supervisees' personal and professional development and openly dealt with and met.

In many circumstances, supervisors who are simply willing to listen are able to create a conducive environment, as supervisees desire a confidential outlet to express their feelings and perceptions. In other scenarios, the supervisor may need to advocate on the part of the supervisee to address blatant examples of discrimination or address negative acts of prejudice that exist within academic departments or work settings. To provide this relationship, supervisors must be knowledgeable in both traditional counseling models, recognizing the Euro-centric influence on these models, and with minority theory and interventions.

We are all too aware of clinical supervisors who lack up-to-date knowledge of cultural intervention and depend on their diverse supervisees to educate them on multicultural issues. As Gutierrez stresses, supervisors also need to understand differences in therapists that stem from cultural background and values, language, and socioeconomic status.[48] From an interpersonal influence viewpoint, we have previously noted that cultural differences may result in ineffective communication due to difficulties in message comprehensibility and subsequent processing, and that the supervisory relationship is not immune to these potential difficulties.[49]

Lack of knowledge of individual differences due to culture, gender, and sexual orientation and lack of understanding of multicultural models and interventions and experience with culturally diverse clients negatively affects the credibility or quality of the message of the supervisor from the perspective of diverse supervisees. In addition, cultural differences in communication styles between supervisors and trainees may limit the ability of the supervisor to be influential. Failure to deal with these differences may negatively affect supervisors' credibility and ability to present messages of high quality to diverse supervisees, potentially resulting in lower motivation or involvement of diverse therapists at all developmental levels.

Mateo was a second-year trainee of Chicano ethnic background and was one of two minority trainees enrolled in the program's multicultural counseling course. In his weekly individual supervision, he seemed impatient and irritated. In taped excerpts, he appeared very unfocused in his clinical work, only going through the motions. When the supervisor commented on this lack of focus, as well as his current level of irritation within the supervision session, Mateo let loose with a tirade against his peers and their remarks in class regarding the issue of affirmative action and the perceptions of minorities in this country. He referred to a professor's comments on the "lack of validity" for multicultural counseling models and stereotypical role plays of ethnic counseling issues in class. He also expressed doubts that he had been recruited to the program for his skills but rather for his ethnic minority status. The supervisor listened carefully as Mateo ventilated and provided validation for his experience as one of the few culturally diverse trainees in the program. They explored ways of dealing with insensitive peer comments in class, as well as the possibility of connecting with student minority groups on campus for support. Subsequent supervision sessions addressed similar issues as they arose. A few weeks later, Mateo confided in his supervisor that he had come very close to dropping out of the program had he not found a formal outlet for his frustrations.

—⁓—

In this chapter we have focused on the importance of the interpersonal aspects of the supervisory relationship that underlie the process of effective clinical supervision and the ways in which it may vary across developmental levels of supervisees. Consequently, it appears that analogous to the therapeutic alliance, the supervisory relationship may be important to the professional development of all supervisees, and in particular it provides an outlet for the unique and sometimes unaddressed issues of female, gay and lesbian, and culturally diverse supervisees.

CHAPTER SEVEN

Nuts and Bolts of Supervision

T he previous chapters have explicated the structure and assumptions of the IDM, giving specific guidelines and recommendations for supervising therapists of different developmental levels. This chapter addresses a collection of issues that together make up some of the "nuts and bolts" of the supervision process. The focus is on elements of supervision that are somewhat separate from the overarching model, but nevertheless important to consider in facilitating the clinical supervision process: the importance of knowing the licensure and certification standards for a given field in mental health, the importance of documentation, the various foci of supervision, group supervision, and differential supervision responsibilities. In addition, we address setting up the initial supervision session, assessing the status of the supervisee, and other incidentals of the clinical supervision process.

SUPERVISION STANDARDS

Mental health services are provided by a broad (and growing) spectrum of professionals, each with its own specific requirements regarding who can provide prelicensure or precertification supervision, how many hours of supervision are required, what type of direct clinical services qualify, and necessary documentation. Summaries of these requirements for various professional groups are provided elsewhere, and we will not examine them in detail. We strongly recommend that clinical supervisors, or aspiring supervisors, remain in contact with the appropriate licensure board or professional organization so they can keep up to date on the relevant requirements and standards.

Who Can Supervise?

This is a different question from "Who *should* supervise?" which we address in more detail in Chapter Nine. All supervisors need to be aware of state and professional requirements before engaging in a supervision relationship. For example, states typically require pre- and postdoctoral supervision for professional psychologists to be provided by psychologists licensed within that state. The American Psychological Association accreditation guidelines note that practicum supervision should be provided by a licensed psychologist. Similarly, postdegree supervision of licensed professional counselors (LPC) is also typically provided by LPCs. An increasing number of states are requiring marriage and family therapists to be supervised by a certified clinical supervisor (an additional credential beyond licensure) to qualify for licensure. A similar requirement often exists for pastoral counselors.

Although some professions accept supervision by an individual with a degree in a counseling-related field (such as, a licensed professional counselor), it is becoming increasingly common for specific professional groups to accept prelicensure or precertification supervision provided only by individuals who are licensed or certified in that field. It is important to research the specific requirements for the particular professional association the supervisee is entering.

What Constitute Acceptable Activities?

Most mental health professions recognize a breadth of activities as appropriate for supervised clinical practice. However, increasingly states and associations are specifying what constitutes the direct service component of professional practice and how much is required for pre- and postdegree supervised experience. Thus, it is important to examine the guidelines for the specific field of practice to be certain that standards are being met and the supervised experience will be acceptable to the accrediting organizations. For example, internship experiences for individuals pursuing licensure as professional counselors are often less than full time for part of a year. Predoctoral internships for psychology trainees, however, are typically full-time experiences for a full year (although they may be half-time for two years). Postdegree supervised experience required for licensure or certification is typically established around guidelines based on a given number of client hours or related professional activity over a period of time that usually incorporates an intensive clinical practice.

The amount of clinical supervision required for various training experiences across disciplines varies. However, a supervisor can expect to provide a minimum of one hour of individual supervision per week and, usually, additional time for in-service training, professional development, grand rounds, or case conferences. It is important not only to focus on the minimum requirements but to examine the needs of the supervisee for a given setting. For example, there are usually considerable administrative activities required of supervisees and their supervisors to meet agency documentation, organizational procedures, or third-party payment requirements. It is desirable to allow additional time for supervision of administrative activities apart from clinical activities or to have these responsibilities divided among two or more supervisors.[1]

Managed care presents a challenge in accommodating this extra time investment in supervision. Managed care organizations are reluctant to reimburse for much (if any) supervision time, so funding can be a problem. Nonetheless, if training is the focus, as opposed to simply monitoring performance, this investment of time is necessary.

We have already discussed in considerable detail the importance of addressing a number of professional and personal issues within the context of clinical supervision. These issues must be explored for the supervisee to develop as a professional and to be able to provide the best possible clinical services to clients. Although administrative tasks such as reading and approving case notes, reports, assessments and so on are crucially important to the supervisory experience (in addition to liability concerns), conducting these tasks within the limited supervision session may result in little or no time available for dealing with important clinical, professional, or personal issues that may directly have an impact on the growth and peformance of the supervisee.

With full appreciation for the economic and time constraints, we believe that it is best for the supervisor to examine notes, reports, and documentation outside the supervision session and bring in issues related to these only when there is a problem or the information is helpful in discussing the supervisee's clinical work. We have observed a distressing number of situations where clinical supervision consists primarily of completing and reviewing paperwork, billable hours, or other instrumental aspects of professional practice. This focus does little for the growth of the supervisee or the quality of services provided to patients or clients.

Documentation and Formats

The supervisor should carefully attend to documentation requirements for approved supervised clinical experiences. Documentation of direct service hours provided by the supervisee is required by many licensure boards, as are the number of hours of direct supervision. Supervisors should also be aware of the types of activities considered acceptable as direct service and monitor the amount of time spent in each. The beginning and ending dates of the supervisory relationship are also usually required by licensing boards. Increasingly, greater precision and specificity of information concerning the numbers of what types of clients, assessments, and so on completed by students during practica are required by internship settings.

There has been a recent dramatic increase in the number of unplaced psychology internship applicants. As we write, numbers are far from precise, but estimates suggest that over four hundred psychology students will not receive a predoctoral internship offer. Of those who do find internship slots, some will be at sites not accredited by the American Psychological Association, a situation that can have a negative impact on these therapists' subsequent attempts to qualify for licensure in some states. Others will be offered internship positions with no stipend attached. Thus, they will spend a year without pay. This level of competition makes it very important to keep accurate records regarding supervised clinical experiences. Accurate records can make the difference between a successful and nonsuccessful internship application.

We recommend keeping supervision session notes for reasons similar to keeping therapy session notes. We have encountered situations in the past when accurate supervision session notes proved helpful in dealing with ethical concerns as well as evidence for the adequacy of supervision provided (see Chapter Ten for a detailed discussion of legal and ethical issues in supervision). Session notes should include the following information:

1. Date and session number.

2. Identification of cases discussed.

3. Clients' progress and problems.

4. Assessment data.

5. Suggestions for further treatment or adjustments to the established treatment plan(s).

6. Supervisee progress and problems.

7. Training or remediation objectives and plans for the supervisee.

Supervisors should also be aware of the nature of required supervision experiences. For example, is individual supervision the only acceptable modality, or is group supervision of a number of supervisees also acceptable? As we will examine later in this chapter, group supervision has some unique aspects that can significantly affect the growth of the psychotherapist or inhibit that growth.

Supervisor Responsibilities

Supervisors need sufficient knowledge and experience to supervise the therapist's work across clinical activities and clients effectively. For adequate supervision to occur, the supervisor must have expertise in the domains for which he or she is providing supervision. If this is not possible, supervision responsibilities should be divided among supervisors who do have sufficient expertise. Responsibilities in such arrangements must be clearly articulated to avoid conflicts between supervisors.

The supervisor also needs sufficient knowledge of each client with whom the therapist is working to assist in developing and monitoring the effectiveness of treatment plans. The supervisor will often need to cosign therapy progress notes and reports. This is not a perfunctory task; it necessitates sufficient information to evaluate the adequacy of this documentation.

The most recent Ethical Guidelines from the American Psychological Association call for students and interns to identify themselves as such to clients at the beginning of clinical activity.[2] In addition, the name of the supervisor should be provided so the client is aware of who is ultimately responsible for his or her care. Similar guidelines exist for other professions; for example, the California Association of Marriage and Family Therapists also requires students and interns to identify themselves as such.

This notion of ultimate responsibility necessitates that supervisors be available for emergency consultation with the supervisee. In addition, if the situation requires, the supervisor should be prepared to provide direct intervention with the supervisee's clients.

In certain settings, it is common for the supervisee to have more than one supervisor. We previously noted the advantages of having different supervisors for clinical as opposed to administrative responsibilities. Occasionally we encounter situations where more than one supervisor is assigned to a supervisee. For example, many predoctoral internships in psychology assign a primary supervisor to an intern for the entire training experience, while other supervisors have responsibilities for given rotations. It is important to determine who will assume specific supervisory responsibility for which aspects of the supervisee's practice in such arrangements. Similarly, in our own training clinic, we have doctoral students supervise master's-level students; group supervision, and the ultimate responsibility for client welfare, rests with a faculty supervisor.

Ethically, no one should engage in psychotherapy concerning a given issue with a client who is under the care of another professional examining the same issue. Similarly, there are ethical problems with two supervisors' providing supervision to a trainee for the same clinical activity. The likelihood is too great that the supervisee will be put into a bind by differing expectations or guidance provided by more than one supervisor. In addition, the lines of professional and legal responsibility can become blurred in such an arrangement.

We occasionally encounter other situations where more than one supervisor may be responsible for the services provided to clients. In our own clinic, it is common for trainees to engage in cotherapy with couples and families, usually a valuable learning experience. Here, it must be clarified who has supervisory responsibility for the therapy if each trainee has a different primary supervisor. Once lines of authority are established, it is important for the one supervisor to avoid assuming responsibility for this case and leave the supervision to the other supervisor.

Consistent with our focus on nuts and bolts in this chapter, it is important to examine certain instrumental aspects of clinical supervision. Various resources examining the practice of clinical supervision differ in regard to the amount of focus they have on specific procedural aspects of supervision versus an overall orientation or model of psychotherapist development and training. In this book, we have chosen to articulate a model of professional development and training while providing specific guidance for dealing with supervisees of various developmental levels for different domains of clinical activity. Other resources focus more on specific tools or mechanisms useful for learning particular skills, instrumental supervisory tasks, documentation of activities, and prototypical forms. Although we have chosen to limit our focus on these resources in this book, we recognize the utility of this approach, particularly for beginning supervisors. One excellent source for some of these materials is *Practicum and Internship: Textbook for Counseling and Psychotherapy* by Boylan, Malley, and Scott.[3]

SETTING THE STAGE IN INITIAL SESSIONS

The initial meetings between the supervisor and supervisee set the stage for a positive working relationship. Some authors have described this process as the development of the supervision alliance, similar in concept to the therapeutic alliance.[4] The importance of this relationship and its development is the primary focus of Chapter Six in this book.

It is important for both participants to gain an early understanding of the professional experience and background of the other. Although the primary focus will be on the training needs of the therapist, information on theoretical orientation(s), professional experience across domains, and approach to supervision should be provided by the supervisor. This information allows the supervisee to develop an initial sense for the expertise and credibility of the supervisor and an impression about the domains for which the supervisor will be able to provide effective supervision.

The supervisor should collect, either formally or informally, information from the therapist concerning the extent of prior therapy, assessment, consultation experience, and any other experiences relevant to the domains to be addressed in supervision. It is also important to assess the expectations of the supervisee regarding supervisor availability, how the sessions will be conducted, who is responsible for what level of structure, and so on. These expectations are generally subject to change as the supervision relationship develops, but clarifying them early on can help avoid disappointment or resentment should the experience differ from expectations.

Ethical guidelines note the importance of establishing an appropriate process for providing feedback to students and supervisees. They should be informed about the expectations for performance, how their work will be evaluated, how feedback will be provided, and the responsibilities associated with the clinical practice experience. It is important to attend carefully to the mechanisms for evaluation and feedback in supervision. Therapists should be evaluated on the basis of actual performance or established training requirements, not on subjective perceptions of personal characteristics or unsubstantiated negative impressions of the theoretical orientation implemented.

We have found it useful to share with the supervisee the specific criteria for evaluation. This usually takes the form of an evaluation instrument that is reviewed in supervision every couple of months and completed at the end of the supervision relationship or periodically during extended supervisory relationships. The instrument, or series of criteria, should reflect expectations and standards relevant to the goals and objectives of the training experience or job description.

No one form suffices across all settings, so it is important to take some time and develop criteria targeted for a particular supervisory experience. If possible, it can be useful to have the supervisee participate in the articulation of goals and objectives and the related performance criteria.

Supervision is not a one-way street. It should also be made clear that ongoing evaluation and feedback concerning the utility of the supervision provided will be collected. We recognize that there is an obvious power differential present in most supervisory relationships that can inhibit honest evaluation of the supervision or result in retribution by the supervisor. Still, it is difficult for supervisors to improve or effectively evaluate their own performance without detailed feedback from their supervisees.

It is most helpful if an organizational climate can be established within a mental health facility that values candid and regular feedback across roles. Although it is difficult to rule out negative fallout from supervision evaluation procedures completely, structural protections should be developed to allow all parties the opportunity to evaluate the experience without undue fear or apprehension.

Finally, a review of current cases and clinical responsibilities of the supervisee should be conducted. This will usually need to be quite brief, given the other issues to be addressed in the initial session. More extensive information regarding clients and activities can be acquired by an examination of relevant case notes, reports, and so on by the supervisor outside the supervision session. However, the stage should be set for the continuation of monitored treatment by the supervisee with informed input by the supervisor. Also, the schedule for subsequent supervision sessions, expectations for channeling paperwork, and so on should be established by the end of the session.

SUPERVISEE ASSESSMENT AND EVALUATION

Assessment and evaluation of therapists play an ongoing and fundamental role in the supervisory process. It is necessary to alter the approach to supervision to meet the changing needs of supervisees across developmental levels and to provide the appropriate supervision environment to encourage and facilitate growth. By exposing supervisees to an environment that is too advanced, we run the risk of inducing confusion and anxiety, as well as negatively affecting client welfare. If we expose therapists to an overly structured environment, their growth is frustrated, and they may become bored, inattentive, and resistant.

By identifying the eight domains of development across the three structures, we have stressed the need to examine a number of areas within a particular level of development in order to assess supervisees accurately. Also inherent within the IDM is the assumption that assessment is an ongoing process and intimately related to the process of evaluation. Consistent with this is the provision of timely feedback to developing therapists in which their strengths and areas of weakness or improvement are clearly articulated and discussed in the context of the supervisory relationship.

Across supervisory settings and developmental levels, therapists are understandably sensitive to evaluation. The implications of evaluation as related to grades, recommendations for internship, professional advancement and compensation, or licensure or certification information required by regulatory bodies are substantial. Consequently, the power differential that exists between supervisor and supervisee, as well as the threat to the personal and professional development of therapists, adds to the anxiety associated with the evaluative process.

Unfortunately, supervisors, because of concurrent trepidation, negative connotations, and anxiety associated with evaluative procedures, all too often avoid what they perceive as negative feedback or instead give only vague and overly general feedback to developing therapists. This sort of evaluation does little to strengthen supervisee skills. Indeed, it is often the failure in identifying areas of weakness during the evaluative process that inhibits the development of therapists, resulting in the Pseudo Level 3 therapist.

From our perspective, the process of assessment and evaluation need not be characterized by these difficulties. The IDM provides a conceptualization where identification of domains in which therapists demonstrate areas of strength and need for improvement is normalized. Referencing performance across levels according to supervisees' previous training and experience in various domains reduces the negative aspects of evaluation. The overriding structures also provide a context for normalizing the issues and struggles that supervisees can expect to encounter along the road toward development as a therapist.

QUALITATIVE ASSESSMENT ACROSS DOMAINS

In previous chapters we outlined in detail the characteristic thoughts, feelings, and behaviors associated with each of the developmental levels in terms of the overriding structures across the eight domains of therapist experience. Thus, the complexity of our model is such that evaluation of therapists encompasses accurate assessment across domains. Although this type of qualitative assessment involves the clinical judgment of the supervisor, it is necessary to move beyond global clinical impressions related to general developmental level. Figure 7.1 provides a method of organizing supervisor impressions according to developmental level and overriding structures across the eight domains of counselor development.

Methods of Assessment

Stoltenberg and Delworth reviewed and evaluated a number of methods used to quantify supervisee behaviors through various rating

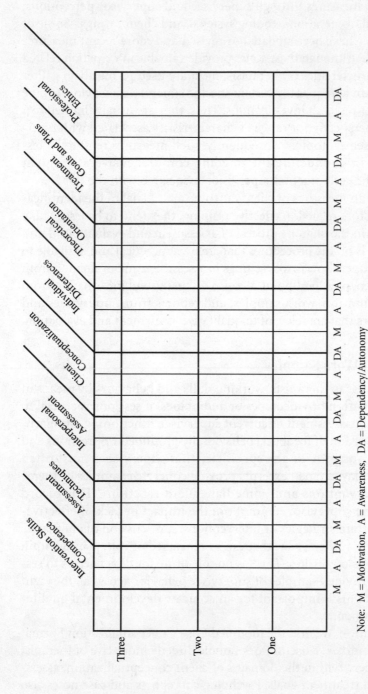

Figure 7.1. Counselor Development Profile.

Note: M = Motivation, A = Awareness, DA = Dependency/Autonomy

scales and measures through supervisee and supervisor perceptions, behavioral observations, coding systems, and client ratings.[5] Some of these scales have been updated or revised and more recent measures developed.[6] Although these scales provide valuable information related to the characteristics of therapists, most are used primarily to gather information and quantify certain specific supervisee behaviors for the purpose of research investigations. Thus, they are usually limited to a singular perspective or range of characteristics associated with a particular research topic. Consequently, such measures tend to be less practical in conducting the ongoing comprehensive assessment process of developmental supervision associated with the IDM.

Although measures of client outcome are crucial to the identification of factors related to effective training, they tend to be less readily accessible in the ongoing process of assessment and evaluation.[7] Thus, our focus is on the procedures that are most practical and available to working supervisors across settings in assessment and evaluation from a developmental standpoint. We also discuss useful information from instrumentation, work samples, and reports from supervisees and supervisors that are relevant to qualitative assessment and evaluation.

Work Samples

Direct access to therapists' working skills and behaviors by means of live observation or videotapes or audiotapes of sessions is crucial to an accurate assessment of current supervisee functioning. Similarly, in the provision of feedback, behaviorally grounded impressions and observations provide the specificity that supervisees most often desire. Replayed taped excerpts provide concrete examples of therapists' interventions and immediate client reactions. This record enables the supervisor to point out the impact or lack of effectiveness of certain strategies or interventions. A discussion of alternative strategies may then ensue that can be rehearsed or role-played within the supervision session. There is no substitute for direct access to sessions to provide examples of supervisee behavior across all the eight domains. This is important for an accurate developmental qualitative assessment.

In addition, we find the modified Case Conceptualization Format (see Appendix A) a useful work sample directly indicative of therapist development within the domains of client conceptualization, assessment, and treatment goals. Psychological reports and case notes also provide examples of therapist performance in various domains. It is very important, however, to assess a variety of work samples from supervisees. Certain samples may be selected based on perceived effectiveness, or they may be reflective of only limited skills. In addition, work samples for one client may not be indicative of a trainee's work with another client. For example, it is not unusual for supervisees to demonstrate skills in written activities (for example, diagnosis) but have trouble implementing other skills in therapy sessions. Work samples should not be limited to one modality or another if the goal is an accurate picture of a therapist across domains.

Supervisee Perceptions

When supervisors and supervisees initially discuss and clarify their expectations regarding the supervisory process, supervisees will elaborate on their perceived areas of strength and weaknesses across domains, along with previous supervised experiences with certain types of clientele and settings. This manner of information gathering, probably most often performed informally within the initial supervisory meetings, can be supplemented by more formal methods and procedures.

The Supervisee Information Form (Appendix B) can be completed by the supervisee and provides information regarding therapy and assessment experience, supervision, preferred theoretical orientation, and perceived areas of strengths and weaknesses. The completed form can be used with individual supervisees as a springboard for discussion and further information gathering. It can also be used as a quick assessment device in group supervision contexts to gather information from a number of supervisees.

The Supervisee Levels Questionnaire–Revised (SLQ–R)[8] (Appendix C) was developed to measure the general constructs associated with the IDM.[9] It consists of thirty items divided into three subscales intended to measure the overriding structures of Dependency-Autonomy, Self and Other Awareness, and Motivation. Cronbach alpha reliability coefficients for the three subscales have yielded reliability estimates of .83, .74, .64, and .88 for the Self and Other Awareness, Motivation, and Dependency-Autonomy subscales, and total scores, respectively. In addition, scores on the SLQ–R have been demonstrated to differ for trainees varying in global levels of counseling, supervision, and educational experience.

The response format for the SLQ–R is a seven-point Likert scale with Never and Always as polar anchors. Higher scores reflect higher levels of development as described in the IDM. Although the SLQ–R has been used primarily as a research tool, it can also serve as an assessment device to give a global indication of where supervisees fall within the three overriding structures. Examination of individual items with supervisees can also yield useful information for assessment of issues surrounding dependency-autonomy (for example, "At times I wish my supervisor could be in the counseling/therapy session to lend a hand"), motivation (for example, "Sometimes I question how suited I am to be a counselor/therapist"), and self and other awareness (for example, "I am able to assess my interpersonal impact on clients adequately and use that knowledge therapeutically").

As we have previously noted, supervisee perceptions and self-reports yield some of the richest and most important data regarding therapist attitudes, thoughts, feelings, and behaviors. Nevertheless, particularly during Level 1 and at times during Level 2, supervisees may not be sufficiently self-aware or resistance free to respond to questions in an accurate manner. At times, they may be subject to the demand characteristics of the supervision environment, resulting in responses that reflect more what the therapist believes he or she is supposed to think or feel or as a reaction against such a demand. Thus, supervisees' perceptions of their own development are valuable, but we must also consider the wide spectrum of information available to us as supervisors in conducting a thorough assessment.

Supervisor Perceptions

At the start of a supervisory relationship, supervisors often must rely on evaluations of supervisees provided by previous supervisors. These evaluations, in written and oral formats, are typically based primarily on the perceptions of a previous individual supervisor, although they may also include the perceptions of other staff members who have worked with the therapist in other activities. Often, however, these evaluations tend not to be based on systematic criteria and may provide only vague general assessments of overall positive and negative aspects of a therapist's current functioning in a limited number of domains.

As supervisors working from the IDM, we find that many times evaluations based primarily on supervisor perceptions are overinflated in terms of positive attributes or overly negative in terms of unrealistic expectations given a supervisee's expected and demonstrated level of development. In addition, supervisor impressions can be overly subjective and biased in favor of a particular theoretical orientation. Such a report does not provide a fair, objective evaluation of a supervisee working from a differing theoretical orientation.

Supervisor evaluations can also be somewhat limited depending on the focus of previous individual supervision. Evaluations of overall skills are somewhat suspect if a supervisor has not required taping of all ongoing clients and failed to review supervisee performance periodically by some form of direct access. If evaluations primarily rely on case notes or supervisee reports of client session, they are likely to be incomplete.

In order to gain more useful information from supervisor perceptions, we believe that it is necessary to obtain descriptions of therapist skills and characteristics that are based on actual behavior. By seeking and obtaining more behaviorally anchored descriptions of supervisees, we are better able to sort out what may have been an interpretation of a supervisee's behavior that we can then place into a developmental context. In this manner we can verify previous reports from supervisors as accurate, or place supervisee behaviors that may have been reported as overly positive or negative in the proper developmental context. This, combined with other sources of information, contributes to a more accurate overall assessment.

PROVIDING THERAPIST FEEDBACK

In order to set the context for ongoing assessment and feedback, supervisors need to conceptualize for supervisees the overall process of development, including expectations for developing skills within certain levels. For example, new supervisees typically are expected to begin developing basic facilitative listening and attending skills in the first semester of an organized practicum. The purposes of assessment should be presented at the beginning of the supervisory relationship so that the issue of evaluation is open and discussed before problems or misperceptions are formed. Supervisees need to understand that it is in their best interests for assessment and evaluation to occur on an ongoing basis.

Feedback to trainees concerning their performance should be provided in an ongoing manner during the supervisory process. The qualitative assessment process requires collecting information from a variety of sources. Once completed, it is extremely important to provide direct concrete feedback to the supervisee in the form of a written or oral evaluation of skills at least once or twice during the supervisory relationship. Typically, across training settings such formal evaluations all too often lack a systematic format and may be limited to global impressions or lack coverage of the various domains. In addition, the anxiety or discomfort that some supervisors feel in providing an evaluation of a supervisee and, in some cases, a grade or employment evaluation of therapeutic skills causes them to avoid this activity.

We believe that the use of the IDM provides a system of assessment and evaluation that helps to normalize the process of therapist development in a nonthreatening manner. By conceptualizing supervisee strengths and weaknesses in terms of levels of performance within various domains, the emphasis is on the growth of the developing therapist. Although there are skills associated with various approaches to therapy that must be learned in order to provide effective service to clients, the IDM places skills and techniques in a context of progressive movement toward a desired end state. Thus, being at a particular level of development need not be viewed as negative, but rather seen as the culmination of training to this point in time.

Consequently, there is nothing wrong with being a Level 1 or 2 therapist. Rather, it is a reflection of the individual's development to date given the growth-inducing experiences provided during the course of training and how they have been integrated. Supervisees will experience different rates of growth, and even with those who develop more slowly than others, the rate of development need not be considered a limiting factor in the degree of potential development. Thus, conceptualizing and communicating the process of evaluation and assessment to supervisees in this manner and remaining open to discussion of feedback and areas of clarification or disagreement from supervisees reduces the anxiety associated with evaluation. Feedback is presented within the context of the normal developmental process of becoming a therapist.

We can never entirely eliminate the anxiety associated with evaluation from the supervisee's perspective. However, normalizing the process through developmental assessment and placing strengths and weaknesses in the context of the normal progression provides less tension for the examination of therapist strengths and weaknesses.

Supervisors have the opportunity to model acceptance of and openness to the evaluative process by seeking ongoing feedback and evaluation regarding their own supervisory style. Evaluation of supervisors can also be performed on a formal basis and communicated to supervisors at the termination of a supervisory relationship.

GROUP SUPERVISION

The supervision of psychotherapists in a group context is widely used and has been a key component in training for a number of years.[10] This format allows for a focus on the interactions among trainees that is not possible in individual supervision.[11] Prieto has identified a number of possible advantages of using the group supervision format, among them the possibility of the supervisor's observing shifting coalitions among members, peer interactive learning, and various approaches to clinical (and interpersonal) problem solving.[12] In addition, group processes such as the development of goals, norms, roles, cohesiveness, and communication patterns and structures can be apparent. Changes across time in these factors may have a strong impact on the growth of the psychotherapist.

Our own experiences suggest that the relative advantages and disadvantages of this approach vary with the constellation of the therapists who participate in the group supervision context. For example, having therapists of varying developmental levels may have some advantages. Less developed therapists can learn by observation from their more advanced colleagues, and the more experienced therapists may benefit from the didactic role they play in working with their less advanced colleagues. On the other hand, frustration may develop when supervisees see others as considerably more advanced or, conversely, requiring more of a focus on fundamental skills.

The blend of personalities in the group may affect the nature of the process in positive and negative ways. Some of our group supervision seminars have been characterized by a warm and supportive environment and lighthearted challenges. Groups that stay together for a year or two, as is customary in some training programs, can benefit from knowing each other and each other's styles rather well and providing informed insights and observations. On the other hand, we have experienced groups where two or more therapists clashed on a regular basis. In the most potentially damaging of these instances, the process can become uncomfortably close to group therapy rather than group supervision.

In general, it appears that using more structured or didactic formats with beginning trainees can be effective.[13] However, we have little solid empirical evidence for establishing strong assertions for the effectiveness of group supervision, or reliable guidelines for conducting it.[14] Nonetheless, we believe that perceptive supervisors can facilitate the development of their supervisees by using the learning and group process possibilities of group supervision. They must carefully attend to ethical guidelines and use their clinical skills to keep the process functional and guard against damaging interactions.

It is also quite common for training sites (for example, internship settings) to arrange support groups for trainees. These experiences appear helpful in encouraging interactions, reducing stress, and increasing support for therapists-in-training. Of course, it is important to provide a leader for these support groups who is appropriately trained and credentialed and is not directly affiliated (in any evaluative role) with the training program.

CHAPTER EIGHT

Supervision Across Settings

In this chapter we describe a model of supervision across settings that was originally presented in our first book.[1] The Supervision-in-Context model (SIC) describes a way to conceptualize the differential influences of the training agency, the clinical supervisor, and (if the therapist is a student) the training program on the supervisee. This model has proved particularly helpful for participants when they discuss various influences, responsibilities, and interactions across these contexts.

THE SUPERVISION-IN-CONTEXT MODEL

Examining the role of supervision across contexts requires us to expand our view of supervision beyond the dyad of supervisor and supervisee or the triad of supervisor, supervisee, and client to an examination of the setting in which supervision occurs. We must consider at least four entities:

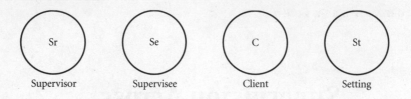

For student trainees, a fifth entity, the professional training program, is included:

Each of these elements is important in supervision, and all must function in the context of the setting, which is a mix of organizational policies, procedures, persons, and norms that allows the work to get done. The setting demands certain behaviors from the supervisor, the supervisee, and the client and, in return, (ideally) offers effective service and training. Although the setting is usually represented by one administrator, in reality it includes all those who develop, impart, and enforce its policies and norms. Generally this includes a number of personnel, especially support (clerical) staff. For students, the training program develops and enforces a set of expectations and norms regarding the process and outcome of the supervisory enterprise.

None of this is unfamiliar to the trainee or to the experienced supervisor. Supervisees often are aware of differences among settings that affect their experience in supervision, regardless of their supervisor. Beginning supervisors sometimes tell us stories of the ways in which the setting, often to their surprise, limits or contributes to the work they do with their supervisees. "War stories" abound, but in our experience, neither supervisees nor supervisors typically possess the understanding or conceptual framework that would allow them to make sense of the elements involved in supervision across contexts and to use them to produce optimal supervisory experiences. An important concept, we believe, is the realization that the supervisory setting and (often) the training program are key components. The next step is to conceptualize relationships among these and ways in which the relationships get played out, for better or for worse. The SIC provides one method of doing this.

The SIC is a perceptual instrument drawn by the supervisee or supervisor to indicate his or her perceptions of the wider supervisory context. It is composed of both components and functions.

Components

There are three components: circles representing elements in the process, contents within elements, and arrows indicating interactions or transactions among elements. We assume the five units or elements presented earlier:

1. Supervisor (Sr)

2. Supervisee (Se)

3. Client (C)

4. Setting (St)

5. Training (academic) program (TP) (may or may not be relevant)

Contents within units or elements vary according to theoretical framework and specific purpose in using the model. The following contents are generally relevant to our understanding:

For all units: Expectations, role, purpose

For units 1 and 2 (supervisor and supervisee): Competencies, developmental level (including ethics)

For unit 3 (client): Competencies, developmental level (for example, cognitive, ego, moral), specific problem

For units 4 and 5 (setting and training program): Structure, norms, facilities

Developmental level differs for units 1, 2, and 3. For unit 1 (supervisor), it refers to level of development as a supervisor. As we explain in Chapter Nine, supervisors appear to develop through stages in a manner similar to the development of therapists. Indeed, this constitutes another broad domain of professional development. For unit 2 (supervisee), it refers to the level of therapist development. For unit 3 (client), it refers to the level of development in cognitive, ego, or moral spheres as defined by relevant theory. Arrows indicate interactions by unidirectionality and transactions by dual directionality. Thus, an interaction by the agency to the supervisee focusing on role would look like this:

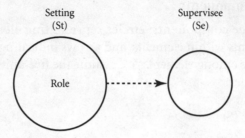

FUNCTION

Units, contents, and messages vary in saliency and relatedness. Saliency or perceived importance is indicated by the size of circles and arrows. The relationship of units is represented by relative position. Thus, an important unidirectional message regarding role from a distant and powerful setting would be drawn in this way:

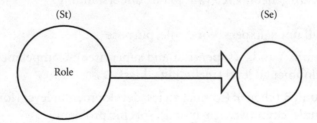

Utility

This visual model can be used in a number of ways to clarify issues of person-environment fit. One use is to have supervisees draw the units, relevant contents, and arrows describing their total supervisory context. In completing such an exercise, one student was able to understand and articulate his sense of frustration for the first time. His SIC looked like this:

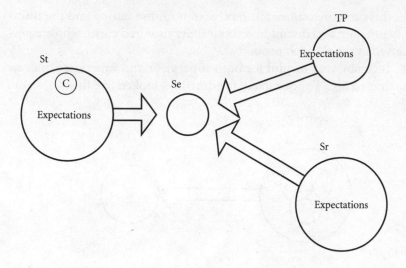

The trainee, who was a practicum student, perceived himself outside the agency in which the client was encapsulated. In addition, his supervisor had little contact with either the agency or the training program. Both the agency and the supervisor were powerful, and both were seen as sending strong messages regarding expectations. The training program, although more distant and less influential, was also perceived as sending unidirectional messages. It is no wonder that the student felt conflict and frustrated!

Another student depicted her situation as one in which she felt overwhelmed by united and strong forces:

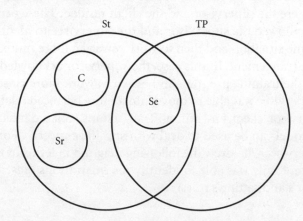

In this case, the trainee felt captive in both the setting and the training program and distant from both supervisor and client, who are perceived as the setting's property.

It can be very helpful for both supervisor and supervisee to draw their own SIC. For one dyad, the drawings looked like this:

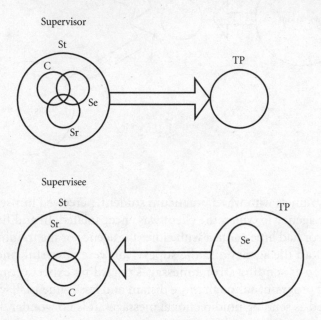

In this case, the supervisor felt connected to both the supervisee and client in a powerful setting, which was sending messages to a distant, smaller training program. The supervisee, however, felt encapsulated in a powerful training program that sent messages to the less salient setting where the supervisor and the client resided. These perceptual scenarios allowed the supervisor and the supervisee to identify how they saw the situation and then to work toward a more mutually satisfactory arrangement. In this case, the supervisor acknowledged the power of the training program and began to work more closely with it. The supervisee was able to move into a more balanced relationship with supervisor, client, and setting. Transactions replaced interactions.

The model can be used to deal with specific concerns. For example, a supervisee who drew the following diagram in terms of the purpose content only was able to identify his frustrations regarding the supervisor's and setting's roles:

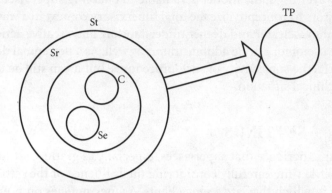

Although discussion was needed to clarify specific issues, it was clear that the trainee saw himself encapsulated by the setting and supervisory roles and as functioning as a small and insignificant part of the context.

This model can also be used to examine contents from differing theoretical constructs, such as perceived Holland types. (As many readers will be aware, Holland types are descriptions of categories of vocationally relevant interests that are useful in career decision making.) One such rendition—that of the "I" (Investigative) student, who is interested in research, in an "S" (Social) setting, in which interpersonal relationships are primarily valued—might look like this:

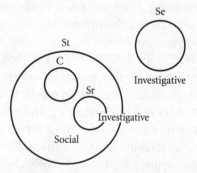

In this case, the student feels mismatched with an environment that exerts daily demands in one direction and quite distant from less salient allies—the training program and the clinical supervisor, which more clearly share the supervisee's interests.

However used, the model is valuable in enabling supervisees and supervisors to conceptualize the total supervisory context in a way that can lead to a clearer and deeper understanding and creative action. It may be useful for setting administrators as well. As a perceptual device, it inherits the subjectivity of such procedures, but it can still be useful in the clinical situation.

SETTINGS

It is our experience that supervisees, especially as graduate students, spend little time carefully considering the influence of the setting or agency in which they are seeing clients. Agency policies on numbers of sessions allowed, favored theoretical orientations or modalities of treatment, paperwork and documentation requirements, and the amount of time committed to various activities are some of the factors overlooked by supervisees in selecting training sites. They may complain about a specific procedure or facility, but rarely do they consider the setting in any organized way. Yet at another level, they are very aware of settings and the interactions among the units in the total supervisory context. Thus, they tend to be acted upon by the setting (interaction) and may react with confusion, withdrawal, or anger. Some of this affect is often transferred to the supervisor if he or she is a staff member in the setting or to the training program that placed the student in that setting. Rarely is an attempt made to conceptualize the setting in some organized and relevant fashion and thus enable the supervisee to understand the option of a transactional relationship between setting and supervisee.

A number of models look at settings. Barker's behavior-setting construct has been applied by Wicker to service settings.[2] As one part of the conceptual analysis, Wicker focuses on reactions of staff and clients to the common problem of understaffing and overpopulation. He notes that explanations for why the setting is not adequately staffed and populated help determine what actions individuals take to deal with their situations, Thus, a staff member who believes other workers are not doing their part may urge them to do more. A manager may use a variety of strategies to cope with the situation, including regulating clients' entrance into the setting or the time that clients may spend in the setting. Wicker notes that the duration of such a condition affects people's reactions. Wicker views Maslach's burned-out syndrome as the response of staff members to a prolonged situation of understaffing and overpopulation.[3]

Supervisees who enter such a setting may make a number of attributions based on staff behavior. That is, they may perceive staff as lacking empathy for clients and viewing clients in a stereotypical manner. A more careful analysis, such as Wicker proposes, would allow the supervisee to view the situation as a setting issue rather than as a problem of poorly motivated staff. This type of analysis fosters more potentially productive transactions with the setting.

In addition to using a model to understand settings, there are specific characteristics of settings that affect supervisees and that they should consider carefully. Among the most important are disciplinary mix, staff roles, ease of entrance and exit for clients, and amount of structure. Most often, in selecting a setting for field experience, supervisees focus on the types of clients served. This is certainly an important variable but is by no means a total indicator of fit. Some supervisees at some phases of training find a good match in settings that are relatively open and unstructured. Others, because of their individual characteristics or developmental level, are consistently frustrated and overwhelmed in such settings.

Given our developmental approach, we choose to place Level 1 supervisees in settings that are relatively structured, have a method to assign appropriate clients to the supervisee, and probably have a limited number of professional disciplines represented on the staff (for example, mostly psychologists, counselors, social workers, or psychiatrists, depending on the training program of the students). Appropriate and fairly close transactions with the training program are important here. A good fit for the Level 1 supervisee might look like this:

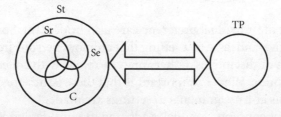

The supervisor is somewhat larger than the supervisee, and both fit closely together and with the client.

As the supervisee moves into Level 2, one or more of these components can be altered. Placing a supervisee who is entering Level 2 in a highly ambiguous, open, unstructured, and multidisciplinary setting will almost certainly exacerbate the conflicts and confusion characteristic of this level. The supervisee may be too overwhelmed to stick with it and may escape back to the certainty of Level 1. Or the supervisee may become disenchanted with counseling altogether. Thus, the training program should still be fairly influential, although somewhat more distant. The supervisor and supervisee become closer in size and overlap less, and the supervisor is less involved with the client. The scenario might look like this:

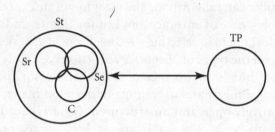

At Level 3, a good fit might involve both more distance from the training program and more separation between the supervisor and the supervisee:

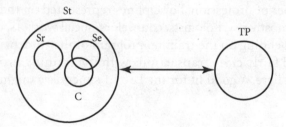

Matters of individual preference are also important. Some people enjoy the give-and-take of a setting that employs persons from diverse professions or disciplines. Others prefer to work with colleagues with similar training. What is important is that these issues are considered as selections and assignments to settings are made.

Whatever conceptual model is adhered to, consideration of context provides for a more comprehensive and accurate picture of supervision. In fields in which an intrapsychic focus is basic, such as professional psychology, looking beyond the individual supervisee and the supervisory dyad is very rewarding. As supervisors, we need to be aware that we do not constitute the total environment. Barker's behavior settings, the subcultural approach, Holland's types, and transactional constructs can each prove useful in looking at the total supervisory environment. We hope that these approaches used in a clinical context will lead to research specific to the context of supervision.

As supervisors, we can often be of most help to our supervisees by facilitating their understanding of the total context. With such understanding, we and they can formulate and implement transactions that are productive and rewarding. We can then, in Sarason's words, "venture forth with a sensitive grasp of social realities."[4]

CHALLENGES OF MANAGED CARE

The growth in influence of managed care organizations (MCO) has resulted in a number of changes in the economics and practice of mental health care. Although it is beyond the scope of this book to provide an assessment of the pros and cons of managed care on mental health services delivery—others have spoken to this issue at great length—the influence of MCOs is being felt across a number of contexts, and the implications for clinical supervision are becoming increasingly profound.[5] This discussion is based on our personal experiences with the changing economics of mental health care as well as the observations of a number of our colleagues across the nation.

A few years ago, third-party payment guidelines and their effects on psychotherapy trainees made it increasingly important for many training programs at the doctoral level to encourage students to earn a master's degree on their way to their doctoral degree. We discovered that a number of internship training programs strongly preferred having interns with a master's degree, as opposed to only a bachelor's degree, to enable them to bill third-party payers for the services these trainees provided. Although this arrangement still works in some settings, it is becoming increasingly common for third-party payers to require the service provider to hold an appropriate license for billable services. Indeed, some MCOs have instituted guidelines that require as many as five years of postdegree experience, in addition to the appropriate license, before a therapist can qualify to serve on the approved panel of service providers.

The negative implications for clinical supervision and training under these constraints are obvious. Hospitals and agencies that provide training opportunities for psychotherapists are being increasingly challenged to find alternative mechanisms for funding their training programs. Training agencies must be alert to have trainee services written into contracts with vendors. Of those MCOs that do allow billable services to be provided by interns or other trainees, increasingly they do not pay for the clinical supervision of these trainees. Indeed, some training sites have contracted with outside consultants to help them find a way to continue to fund their training programs in a managed care environment.

The fluidity of the current situation in mental health care can have a remarkably quick impact on agencies. A change in vendors for mental health reimbursement can result in the institution of new (and often more restrictive) guidelines from one day to the next, a situation that can have devastating implications for agencies and hospitals with a training component.

In addition to difficulties encountered with getting prelicensed therapists approved as reimbursable providers, the types of services covered by MCOs are becoming limited, in turn affecting the kinds of training that can be provided. New limitations in the number of therapy sessions that MCOs will reimburse has increased the need to train and supervise therapists in brief therapies or problem-solving approaches (critics would say symptom-focused therapies). Thus, experiences in longer-term approaches to treatment are becoming increasingly difficult to fund. Also, fewer MCOs are reimbursing for psychological (even neuropsychological) assessments. This situation, of course, can have a negative impact on the efficiency and effectiveness of therapy, as well as the difficulty in continuing to fund essential training experiences in assessment. Finally, certain modalities of therapy, for example, marital and family therapy, cannot be reimbursed if the decisions made by the MCO follow a medical model.

These policies have direct ethical implications for clinical supervisors as well as all therapists in general. Given a psychopathology-based model of reimbursement, there exists a strong incentive to find greater pathology (more severe diagnoses) and provide services (individual therapy) in situations where other diagnoses (marital or family disorders) and forms of treatment (for example, couples or family therapy) may be more appropriate. Additional concerns regarding problems with confidentiality in working with MCOs add to these challenges.[6]

Other changes necessitated in response to MCOs can have a negative impact on the quality of clinical supervision provided to therapists. We have already noted that the approaches to therapy that are reimbursable under these arrangements can be limited in addition to the acceptability of other clinical activities, such as psychological assessments and clinical supervision (at least in terms of receiving reimbursement for these activities). The danger of primarily focusing on completing forms and paperwork is greater still in this context.

In addition to supervising the therapist's documentation of case notes and traditional reports, the supervisor must now also invest considerable time in teaching supervisees how to fill out the forms required by the MCOs for reimbursement. Many of our colleagues view these forms as separate from (and not helpful to) the therapy process because the information requested appears to have little to do with treatment issues. The requested information often creates the potential of confidentiality issues for the therapist and the client.[7] Finally, supervisors increasingly are called on to teach therapists how to advocate for the client to the MCO for authorization of additional or continued services. This can be rather time-consuming and, of course, this time is not reimbursable.

Managed care is now a fact of life and will, in all likelihood, continue in some form or another into the foreseeable future.[8] In our opinion, the final chapter has yet to be written concerning the economics and practice of clinical supervision within this context. We cannot stress too greatly, however, the importance of finding and supporting mechanisms that allow for the continuation of effective forms of this most important aspect of training in the future. Any significant limitation of the effective practice of clinical supervision will have a strongly negative impact on the quality of mental health training and services provided by therapists both prior to and subsequent to licensure.

CHAPTER NINE

Supervisor Development and Training

~ I mplicit throughout this book and the IDM is that the training of supervisors is an area of professional development that requires focused and systematic procedures. It is no longer adequate to assume that skills used in therapy are sufficient for supervision or that one's experiences as a supervisee are viewed as adequate training to become a supervisor, which, as Loganbill and Hardy point out, have been the two basic approaches to supervisor training in the past.[1] Russell, Crimmings, and Lent have also noted that just as we require therapists to be proficient in therapeutic theory and intervention strategies, so too should we require training in clinical supervision and provide training opportunities to develop supervision skills.[2] Holloway has also recently proposed that the learning and teaching of supervision require specific knowledge of instructional methods appropriate for supervision.[3] Consequently, the process of supervision is increasingly becoming recognized as perhaps the most crucial of activities associated with the psychotherapeutic professions because the supervised training that developing therapists receive plays a formative role in establishing their therapeutic competency and represents the cornerstone of applied graduate education.[4] In addition, it appears that supervision of therapists will increase as managed care facilities expand in the use of subdoctoral applied personnel for direct service functions.[5] In anticipation of this growing demand for supervisory skills, the American Psychological Association recently added the area of consultation and supervision in its revised criteria for accreditation domains and standards.[6]

Consequently, in this chapter we focus on the development of the supervisor and related practicalities involved in the training of supervisors. We propose levels of supervisor development analogous to our levels of supervisee development and discuss issues of supervisor and supervisee match and supervisor assessment. We also provide some recommendations for the types of experiences necessary for the training of effective supervisors in educational and other applied training settings.

LEVELS OF SUPERVISOR DEVELOPMENT

Throughout this book, we have alluded to the various roles of the supervisor and the role flexibility required, depending on the developmental level of the therapist and the supervision environment. That is, the supervisor often starts out in the familiar roles of teacher, consultant, or evaluator and later develops the role of master supervisor for the supervisee. Our model of supervisor development assumes that the greater role flexibility required to meet the training environment needs of supervisees distinguishes more advanced supervisors from others. Less advanced supervisors tend to rely on one or two roles. Research regarding supervisor development suggests that supervisors indeed perceive themselves as varying the supervision environments for differing levels of trainees consistent with developmental theory and that actual supervisory behaviors change as counselors gain experience, although supervisees do not always perceive these differences in supervisor behavior.[7]

In our model of supervisor development, progression through the levels assumes prior progression through the levels of therapist development. For example, it does not appear possible for a therapist to be a Level 3 supervisor while still functioning as a Level 1 therapist in a domain in which he or she is providing supervision. This would be analogous to a Little League baseball player's coaching in the major leagues. However, Level 3 therapists in their early supervisory experiences are likely to be at Level 1 or 2 in our supervisor development model. Again, we propose that although supervision may at times be similar to psychotherapy, it is itself a new and unique domain for therapists. This is the case even for those who may possess highly developed therapeutic skills. The supervision process requires specific knowledge, skills, and training. As a result, we hypothesize a three-level model for supervisors similar to the IDM for therapists.

Level 1

Supervisors at this level tend to be either highly anxious or somewhat naive. Similar to Level 1 therapists, they are focused on doing the "right" thing and are usually highly motivated to be effective in their new role. They tend to apply a fairly mechanistic approach to supervisory tasks and may take a strong "expert" role with supervisees.

In early attempts to supervise others, Level 1 supervisors depend heavily on their perceptions of their own recent or current supervisors or their recollections of how they have been supervised in the past, and they are generally more aware of their own reactions than those of their supervisees. Level 1 supervisors take pride in providing their supervisees with appropriate conceptualizations or intervention strategies, and they provide moderate to high structure in exhibiting a high level of concern with the nurturance and success of their trainees. Additionally, depending on their own level of therapist development, they are often invested in getting the supervisee to adopt their therapeutic orientations and techniques.

Level 1 supervisors are often uncomfortable and anxious in regard to providing feedback and may avoid this function or tend to be overly positive or vague in their initial face-to-face evaluations. As a result, they may find it easier to follow a structured format for provision of feedback (for example, evaluation forms), such as a checklists, as opposed to written narratives. Because of this desire for structure, we have found Boylan and colleagues' collection of forms, observation sheets, and exercises useful for beginning supervisors to help them organize their early sessions.[8]

In general, it is desirable for Level 1 supervisors to be functioning at Level 3 in relevant domains, but a therapist who is well established in Level 2 can also adequately supervise Level 1 supervisees. In addition, the Level 2 therapist benefits from this experience. The necessary task of aiding the trainee with cognitive formulations is exceptionally helpful in inducing the supervisor to work through some of his or her own

Level 2 confusion. In addition, some Level 2 trainees are far better supervisors (if matched with Level 1 supervisees) than they are therapists. Level 2 therapists who are Level 1 supervisors often find that the need to provide basic structure for the beginning supervisee helps to resolve some of their own confusion and ambivalence.

Level 1 supervisors have great difficulty with Level 2 trainees, and thus this pairing should be avoided if at all possible. It is extremely difficult for the Level 1 supervisor to deal with the conflicts and confusion of the Level 2 supervisee. What often happens in this situation is that both parties wait out the period of supervision just to get the experience over with, and little progress occurs, resulting in negative experiences for both parties and inhibited therapist and supervisor development. Similarly, we do not recommend that Level 3 therapists be matched with Level 1 supervisors. In this scenario, there is a danger that therapists will regress to Level 2, especially in terms of motivation. Advanced supervisees often report losing their recently acquired consistent motivation when they are confronted with insecure, highly structured Level 1 supervisors. Again, the solution in this situation is often to wait it out to avoid political consequences within training agencies or seek additional informal supervision from other staff members.

Cathy was an experienced and well-respected therapist whose skills were reflective of late Level 2. However, she had received her only training in supervision theory and practice in a brief seminar format, and she was soon responsible for the supervision of Julie, an early Level 2 practicum trainee, who exhibited the common Level 2 characteristics of independence, fluctuating levels of motivation and confidence, and resultant confusion and conflict. Problems in supervision started when Julie administered a battery of psychological instruments to a client as part of her routine assessment procedure. Cathy was immediately taken aback and upset that Julie had proceeded without her direct permission. Cathy accused her supervisee of a potential ethical violation, viewing her as unqualified to administer assessment instruments and resistive toward any feedback or supervision. Julie, in turn, was shocked at her supervisor's reaction to what she viewed as a routine procedure. Their attempts to process this issue were unsuccessful, and it appeared that Cathy's direct supervisor was reluctant to intervene. Julie remained frustrated and viewed the supervisory relationship as suffering irreparable damage. Yet she felt that as a trainee, she lacked the power to request another supervisor, although she eventually communicated her difficulties to her practicum instructor. It was only through the intervention of Julie's practicum instructor, who spoke to the agency's director, that an alternative supervisory assignment was made, unfortunately well into the semester.

Level 2

The Level 2 supervisor resembles the Level 2 therapist in terms of confusion and conflict. This supervisor now views the process of supervision as more complex and multidimensional than he or she had initially perceived. As a result, motivation fluctuates, especially in settings where the supervisory function is not valued or rewarded. Level 2 supervisors may overfocus on the supervisee and lose the objectivity required to provide necessary confrontation and guidance. The supervisor attempts to assert his or her independence, with occasional lapses into dependency on a trusted supervisor or colleague. Level 2 supervisors may also tend to get angry or withdraw from their supervisees as a manifestation of their confusion and fluctuating levels of motivation. Thus, therapists may find it difficult to arrange sessions with supervisors, and a lack of investment by supervisors may be quite obvious. Frustration on the part of the Level 2 supervisor may also be manifested in evaluations and feedback focusing in on supervisees' global deficits and perceptions that the supervisee is either unable or resisting attempts to implement supervisor feedback.

Level 2 tends to be brief for most supervisors, as they are typically functioning at Level 3 as counselors and use their skills with the help of their own supervisors (if they have one) to work through and gain insight into the conflict and confusion they may be experiencing. On the other hand, for those who do not make the transition, the result may be withdrawal from the supervisory role, or they may not be assigned supervisees as they gain the reputation for not being sufficiently motivated and invested in the supervisory task. We have heard of far too many supervisors who were caught daydreaming or, worse, sleeping during supervision sessions. In such situations, the lack of motivation to conduct effective supervision should be recognized by the supervisor or others in the program or agency, and steps to increase involvement or remove one from supervisory responsibility should be taken.

Another risk for Level 2 supervisors is to deal with their frustration in their supervisory role by engaging in counseling or therapy with their supervisees. Therapy with supervisees is not ethical and is likely to result in more harm than good. It may occur when the frustrated Level 2 supervisor retreats to a domain where he or she feels more comfortable and effective, translating a supervisee's difficulty in conducting therapy into unresolved personal issues. Although these certainly do occur and need to be addressed when discovered, therapy with supervisees is best left to someone who can function solely in the therapist role and not someone who is the assigned clinical supervisor.

While the struggling Level 2 supervisor is a difficult match for any supervisee, the best assignment is with a Level 1 therapist, as this individual tends to elicit a protective, nurturing stance that results in more consistent behavior by the supervisor. Matches with a beginning Level 2 trainee are sometimes facilitative if the supervisor is aware of and consciously working through Level 2 supervisory issues. In this manner, a Level 2 supervisor may identify and empathize with the Level 2 therapist's struggles, facilitating their resolution.

Level 2 supervisors need ongoing and expert supervision to facilitate their own development and provide for the welfare of their supervisees and clients. Similar to the Level 2 therapist, this is not a time for laissez-faire supervision of the Level 2 supervisor, regardless of the Level 2 supervisor's level of therapeutic development. Without effective supervision of supervision, the Level 2 supervisor runs the risk of stagnation due to lack of feedback and observation of his or her work. It is too easy to fool oneself into thinking that one is effective and skilled without ongoing objective feedback from others.

The power differential in supervisory dyads can inhibit corrective feedback from coming from supervisees. For example, one of us remembers hearing about a male supervisor who regularly perceived his female supervisees as being sexually attracted to him. His view was apparently that little could be accomplished in supervision until his charges would admit to this attraction. It became a running joke among women supervisees that they needed to confess to being sexually attracted to this character early in the supervisory relationship so that other, more salient issues could be dealt with.

Another potential pitfall of Level 2 supervisors is to turn the focus of supervision to a domain or approach with which they feel comfortable. This can be good if a supervisee is interested in learning a different approach or orientation, but it can present real problems if there is not flexibility and some negotiation involved in setting up the supervisory relationship.

Karen was a new staff member at the agency who had had some supervisory experience prior to arriving. She was committed to a psychodynamic model of therapy and informed her supervisee, Lana, during their initial supervisory session that they would limit their focus to psychodynamic psychotherapy and related issues: "We will speak psychodynamically, interpret psychodynamically, and do therapy from a psychodynamic focus." Lana offered that she knew little about this approach and was having some success with a predominantly cognitive-behavioral orientation, which she had been studying for some time. She was also concerned that her current clients would become confused with a dramatic change in focus from the approach she had been using with them, to say nothing of the fact that she would have to renegotiate their treatment contracts to institute the new approach. Karen was unmovable, and the sparks began to fly. Lana complained to the agency director and asked for reassignment. Karen was not enjoying the experience either, complaining to the director that Lana was resistant to her feedback and recommendations and not valuing what Karen had to offer. Unfortunately, reassignment was not possible, and the supervisory relationship remained turbulent until Lana moved on to another agency.

Level 3

While some supervisors stagnate at Level 1 and others drop out at Level 2, in our experience the majority appear to go on to achieve the stable functioning characteristic of Level 3. At this level, motivation again becomes stable and consistent, as the supervisor is interested in improving his or her performance, while viewing supervision as a highly valued activity among the many that one experiences as a professional. The supervisor at this point is functionally autonomous but may seek consultation or regular supervision if needed. He or she is aware of the trainee, as well as of self, and is able to balance personal needs with those of both the trainee and the setting.

The supervisor at this level is able to make an honest self-appraisal of strengths and weaknesses as a supervisor and will articulate clear preferences for types of supervisees with whom he or she works best. Those who have difficulties with conflict, for example, may express preferences to work with either Level 1 or Level 3 supervisees. The Level 3 supervisor is also comfortable with the process of evaluation and makes a thorough, objective attempt to provide a balanced assessment of the supervisee's strengths and limitations.

Kelvin, a senior psychologist at the agency, was meeting with Kim for their last supervision session at the end of her advanced practicum experience. Kelvin had found Kim to be a sensitive, caring, and skilled therapist who was easy to supervise. He had enjoyed the experience and was sorry to see it end. After sharing his feedback with Kim concerning her work over the prior months, he asked if she wanted to share any perceptions of his supervision with him. He made it clear that he would carefully review the written evaluation she had prepared in addition, to see how the experience had been for her. Kim began describing her experience in supervision with Kelvin: "I found this experience very powerful in terms of my growth as a therapist. Sometimes I'd come in here not knowing exactly what I wanted, and you would somehow pick something out off a tape, or the way I would talk about a client, that would really hit a chord. You have this way of saying things in an unthreatening, low-key way, but with the force of a hammer. I learned more about myself as a therapist and, I think, as a person than at any other time in my training. I hate to see this end."

Level 3 Integrated

This level represents mastery of the supervisory domain as supervisors at this level are often referred to as master supervisors. What differentiates them from Level 3 supervisors is that they can work equally well with supervisees at any level and rarely have definitive preferences. These supervisors are especially adept in working with and helpful to Level 2 supervisees and supervisors, and they are often asked to provide supervision to less experienced supervisors. They are noted for their integration of ideas and skills, as is the 3i therapist. As such, the Level 3i supervisor must have attained Level 3i as a therapist and add to that the integration of supervision with the other domains. Clearly the number of such individuals is limited.

The Level 3i supervisor has developed the skills necessary to assess and monitor supervisee development across levels and domains while effectively communicating the expertise he or she has across domains to supervisees. This person can move with fluidity across domains in supervision, as well as across supervision relationships with assorted supervisees. We can only hope that these individuals are valued and well utilized in the settings in which they work.

RECOMMENDATIONS FOR SUPERVISOR TRAINING

In Chapter Six we suggested that the interpersonal characteristics of supervisors (warmth, acceptance, empathy, etc.) that comprise functional supervisory relationships serve as the basis for all effective supervision. In their recent review of the research regarding supervisor training, Russell and Petrie identify some general qualities of effective supervisors that may also be characterized as essential attitudes and behaviors, to be promoted and developed in the training of supervisors.[9] These include high levels of supervisor support, interest, and investment in (as well as commitment to) the supervisory process, flexibility in multiple roles and functions that effective supervision requires, therapeutic experience, and avoidance of certain negative attitudes and behaviors, such as disinterest in supervision, exploitation of supervisees, and unsupportiveness.

In terms of more specific components and experiences for training effective supervisors, our recommendations overlap with those put forth by other authors and reflect a growing consensus regarding the importance of systematic, focused training in the supervisory process.[10] Consequently, we recommend that training in supervision consist of two essential components: (1) formal course work comprising conceptual and didactic training in supervision and (2) experiential training in supervision consisting of practicum elements. We thoroughly agree with Russell and Petrie's recommendation that brief seminars or workshops, which may be successful in presenting basic elements of supervision theory or practice, do not allow aspiring or practicing supervisors time or exposure to develop a knowledge base or acquire applied skills.

Conceptual and Didactic Training

In terms of the conceptual and didactic component of training, supervisor development is related to development as a therapist. Thus, prospective supervisors enrolled in a course or seminar dealing with supervision theory and practice should have had adequate applied supervised experience and be functioning as a late Level 2 or Level 3 therapist in preparing to supervise Level 1 therapists. Thus, this type of course should be restricted to advanced graduate trainees.

As Russell and Petrie suggest, three critical areas of the conceptual foundation of any supervision course are examination of theoretical models of supervision, supervision research, and ethical and professional issues.[11] Coverage of these areas is accomplished through assigned readings, lectures, discussion, and demonstrations. Many of the references included in this book can serve as the basis for these activities. For example, Robiner and Schofield have compiled a supervision bibliography covering books, as well as theoretical articles and empirical investigations that may be supplemented by more recent articles.[12] Audiotapes and videotapes of actual supervision sessions presented by faculty and students, as well as the Goodyear tapes, are useful in demonstrating hands-on supervision behaviors and interventions across different supervisory theoretical approaches and stimulating class discussions.[13] In our own classes, one of us has developed videotapes demonstrating characteristics of the three levels of therapist development across structures within supervision sessions. These have proved quite helpful in stimulating discussion and making the issues of each level of therapist more salient for supervisors-in-training.

Russell and Petrie recommend a required research proposal as a written project for seminars in supervision in order to stimulate knowledge of the empirical literature and provide students an opportunity to explore an interest area in depth. We have also found it helpful to include other types of projects as requirements for students, such as training tapes (for example, intake demonstrations) or workshop proposals, providing students with opportunities to design projects related to career goals or future work settings.

As we note in Chapter Ten, the area of ethics and related professional issues is crucial to the training of supervisors, and it may be especially salient as beginning supervisors find themselves responsible for the welfare of both the client and supervisee for the first time. Examination of the implications for various ethical codes and guidelines for supervisory functions should be covered along with state guidelines and laws regulating the practice of supervision in various postgraduate training and work settings.

Supervisor training in the area of diversity lags. As we noted in Chapter Six, it is still common for trainees to encounter supervisors who remain uninformed regarding multicultural counseling models even while working with a diverse clientele and supervisees, and are not necessarily open to addressing these issues within the supervisory context. As Bernard and Goodyear acknowledge, multicultural supervisory issues are still approached with trepidation by supervisees and supervisors alike.[14] Certainly many current practicing supervisors may not have received such training in their graduate programs, but lack of exposure to or knowledge of issues of diversity due to gaps in previous training is not excusable. We certainly would not accept a lack of skills in assessment merely because certain instrumentation is periodically revised. In other words, the clear imperative exists that all practicing psychotherapists should be prepared to function in a multicultural, multiracial, and multiethnic society. In addition to these reasons for acquiring competencies, multicultural issues are increasingly linked to treatment efficacy.[15] To this imperative, we would add issues of gender and sexual orientation. Thus, within any conceptual and didactic component in supervision courses related to ethics and professional issues, we recommend coverage of the developing literature on multicultural training, including examples of training models, methods, and environments related to the development of cultural awareness and sensitivity and multicultural counseling competence.[16]

Although many training programs at the graduate level offer separate courses dealing with issues of multicultural counseling or working with diverse populations, if true unself-conscious integration of these issues into psychological theory and practice is to be achieved, multicultural content and issues of diversity must be infused into all existing graduate-level course work and training. The crucial components addressed in this so-called integration model are therapists' knowledge of diverse cultures and lifestyles, attitudes toward members of diverse groups, and acknowledgment of the role and influence of differing cultural values and worldviews on psychological practice.[17] Lefley, and Lefley and Bestmen, have reported increased cross-cultural knowledge, sensitivity, and skills, along with decreases in social, attitudinal, and cognitive distance associated with an intense eight-day cross-cultural training program for mental health clinicians and administrators.[18]

In applying the integration model within a developmental context, optimally Level 1 therapists are beginning to be exposed to issues of social and cultural diversity in beginning theories courses apart from idiosyncratic and, at times, limited exposure to diverse peoples. Required intercultural interactions as described by Mio, where trainees interacted with immigrant students, may serve as a useful adjunct for initial exposure to diversity at this developmental level.[19] Level 2 therapists again demonstrate a greater openness and increased readiness to understand diverse clientele and should be exposed at this time to more specific courses and fieldwork experiences dealing with issues of diversity. This type of exposure may be accomplished by cultural learning experiences and exercises described by Merta, Stringham, and Ponterotto.[20] Level 3 therapists depend on continued exposure to and work with ethnically and culturally diverse clients in order to develop their ability to integrate cultural knowledge and hypotheses into the diagnostic and treatment process. Training seminars that reinforce the importance of issues of diversity and allow for open discussion around these issues augment this process and may also provide a nonthreatening invitation and exposure to these issues for experienced supervisors who lack knowledge of multicultural theory and intervention.

Many courses in supervision are essentially constructed as surveys that skim across a number of models and issues, relying heavily on brief descriptions presented in single chapters of a book or theoretical articles. Although exposure to various approaches can be useful, if little or no time is invested in assisting the students to understand a particular model thoroughly, they will be left with insufficient knowledge and skills with which to practice clinical supervision. We do not expect students to be effective therapists after having only a survey course on therapy theories. Similarly, we should not assume scant attention is sufficient for supervision training. We have been clear throughout this book that we prefer a comprehensive model of supervision to guide our work. Naturally we think that the IDM is a good choice for intensive training in clinical supervision.

Experiential Training

The second critical component in the training of supervisors concerns opportunities to engage in supervision of less experienced therapists-in-training and receive supervision and guidance in relation to the actual supervisory function. If the scope of supervision training is limited to didactic presentations, the supervisor-in-training will be ill prepared to engage in the supervision process. Careful supervision of supervision is necessary for anyone to become familiar with the intricacies of a given model and effective implementation.

The conceptual and didactic component of training may serve as a prerequisite to experiential training components. However, our preference is to provide training in both concurrently. One format we apply is that advanced students enrolled in the didactic portion of a supervision seminar are also enrolled in an advanced practicum that provides opportunities for supervision of a therapist-in-training in which the developing supervisor trainee is paired with a supervisor (who is both a Level 3 therapist and supervisor) for both supervision of supervision as well as supervision of direct services provided by the trainee. The advantage of this format is that developing supervisors are exposed concurrently to supervision theory and research while engaging in actual supervisory practice. All supervisory sessions are audiotaped and videotaped for training purposes, and thus examples or descriptions and demonstrations of current supervisory issues and cases may be integrated into the seminar component. Having supervision case presentations, including write-ups, and showing portions of videotapes of supervision sessions give supervisors the opportunity to demonstrate what they have learned and to get useful feedback from colleagues.

Russell and Petrie describe another variation of the concurrent format, where trainees' experiential training requires them to supervise one or two therapists weekly, with one client per therapist.[21] Each therapy session is then observed by the supervisor, and a supervision session follows. The supervision session is videotaped and may be presented as part of a two-hour, weekly supervision of supervision class group meeting. This type of supervision case conference component, in which supervisors-in-training present cases and discuss their experiences as supervisors, provides an atmosphere of mutual support and trust that is particularly facilitative in the successful resolution of the challenges that take place as supervisors progress through the levels of supervisor development.

SUPERVISOR ASSESSMENT

Similar to our conceptual model of supervisee development, assessment of supervisors follows a format in which a variety of sources of information relevant to the structures of motivation, self-awareness, and autonomy are considered within the supervisory domain. This information is integrated into a holistic picture of the supervisor who is functioning at a particular level of supervisor development. As is true for therapist development, supervisors may vary in level depending on the level of the supervisee with whom they are working. For example, a supervisor who has attained a Level 3 mode of functioning with most supervisees may find himself or herself operating more at Level 2 when confronted with an especially difficult Level 2 therapist. Primary in this assessment is an informal evaluation of the level of supervisory development based on the attitudes and behaviors previously described. For example, one of us who has primarily been supervising Level 2 and Level 3 therapists over the past few years recently found himself less than optimally effective in supervising a Level 1 therapist. Again, videotaped or audiotaped supervision sessions are useful for review in supervision of supervision. They provide direct access to supervisory behaviors and should be a required activity. Of course, assessment of previous supervisory training experiences (both didactic and experiential), as well as previous experience as a supervisor (both amount and type), is essential information in assessing supervisor development. Finally, assessment of level of therapist development (see Chapter Seven) is also paramount to the complete assessment of the skills of the developing supervisor.

SUPERVISION IN FIELD SETTINGS

We have described a training format for clinical supervision that is close to ideal. We realize that this arrangement is not possible for all therapists who desire to learn to conduct clinical supervision or improve their skills in this domain. Until recently, course work on supervision was not required by many training programs for mental health professionals. Even now, the training provided is often limited, due to the amount of other course work and practicum experiences required by states and accreditation bodies.

Considerable opportunities can be created in nonacademic field settings if the desire and administrative support exist to improve supervision services. Unfortunately, funding for effective supervision and training is becoming a greater challenge. Nonetheless, it is clear that attention to supervision will have a positive effect on clinical service delivery, as well as add to the professional development of the staff.

Although in-service seminars and workshops are less than ideal in providing a sufficient informational and experiential background for therapists who have not been exposed to the supervision literature, periodic and ongoing in-service training and case conferences on supervisory issues can have a dramatic impact on the quality of supervision provided by the senior staff. We have found it imperative to have the opportunity to discuss supervisory issues with other supervisors in our programs. These arrangements need not be formalized, although setting aside time for an activity increases the perceived importance of it and the likelihood that it will actually occur.

These in-service seminars or ongoing case conferences can be facilitated by an external consultant, or an agency staff member can assume organizational responsibility. For therapists who invest much time in supervision, these continuing-education opportunities can be time well spent.

In addition to serving as a useful adjunct to didactic seminars in supervision theory, the group supervision case conference may be particularly useful as a training method in field, internship, or post-graduate supervision settings for supervisors. Although a long-term didactic component is very beneficial, supervision case conferences can serve as an effective adjunct to brief workshops or seminars offered in these settings.

—⁓—

The preparation and training of supervisors need to be both focused and extensive. In the best of all worlds, this training starts with conceptual and didactic course work in the graduate school setting concurrently with beginning experiential supervision practice, and later with more supervised experiences in providing supervision to therapists in internship, postgraduate, and employment settings. The importance of such training is fundamental to the training of psychotherapists and ultimately to the consumers of therapy who desire and deserve high-quality direct services.

CHAPTER TEN

Ethical and Legal Issues

~~~

Lamb, Cochran, and Jackson hold that supervisors are responsible for training in three broad areas of the supervisee's professional functioning: (1) ethical knowledge and behavior, (2) competency, and (3) personal functioning.[1] Although the areas clearly overlap, each deserves separate consideration.

ETHICAL KNOWLEDGE AND BEHAVIOR

Formal training in ethics is mandated in training programs in counseling, psychology, and related fields. Yet, as Welfel notes, research on the outcomes of this training is still meager and demonstrates inconsistent findings.[2] The interpersonal and immediate nature of the supervisory relationship provides a unique opportunity to address ethical and legal issues in depth and perhaps result in the central route processing discussed in this book.

To facilitate ethical knowledge and behavior in supervisees, supervisors at a minimum must possess a thorough knowledge of the ethical and regulatory codes in their professions and jurisdictions. This may sound simple, but these codes are subject to regular update, and it is not unheard of for supervisors who have completed their formal training and certification to neglect these essential updates. At this minimal level, then, the supervisor is responsible for the knowledge and behavior expected of all practitioners in the relevant setting.

Understanding of ethical codes is essential for all mental health practitioners. For psychologists, the main document is the 1992 *Ethical Principles of Psychologists and Code of Conduct* of the American Psychological Association (APA).[3] The 1987 *General Guidelines for Providers of Psychological Services* (APA) is also a relevant and informative document.[4] Counselors and social workers have ethical codes that mandate specific behaviors. In situations in which state licensing applies, the relevant codes are usually adopted as part of the statutory basis for regulating members of each profession. Thus, the ethical codes become part of the regulatory or legal process.

As professionals assume the role of supervisors, they are responsible for knowing and using the portions of the codes that deal with supervision. Beyond codes and standards, practitioners and supervisors alike should be familiar with at least several models that seek production of ethical behavior. Such models are especially useful in dealing with more complex issues and in cases in which the codes themselves are silent. For example, training issues and client welfare issues are often intertwined. Also, what constitutes professional competency—particularly in contexts in which referral options are limited—can present difficult challenges. In addition, the codes speak to the processes involved in making ethical choices.

One model that has demonstrated some efficacy in the research literature is that of James Rest.[5] This model, based on Kohlberg's model of moral development, identifies core abilities or competencies that the ethical person must possess:[6]

1. The ability to perceive, role-take, and imagine consequences of action and construct mental scenarios of probable causal chains of events

2. The ability to decide which of the options in a dilemma is morally fair, right, or closest to one's ideals

3. The ability to make a decision regarding a course of action by selecting among competing values

4. The ability to follow through on a course of action

Karen Kitchener's model is especially helpful in comparing and choosing options for action.[7] She identifies five critical ethical principles for the evaluation of ethical dilemmas in professional practice:

1. Autonomy—responsibility for one's behavior; freedom to choose that does not interfere with the freedom of others.

2. Nonmaleficence—prevent or minimize the infliction of harm.

3. Beneficence—attempt to contribute to the welfare of those with whom we work.

4. Justice—fairness and equity.

5. Fidelity—honest, genuine and consistent interaction.

Each of these principles can be examined in the context of a clinical issue and related to both ethical codes and the context of the immediate situation. For example, a white male intern supervisor found himself avoiding offering of challenging, but necessary, feedback to his female African American supervisee. He was concerned that the practicum student would view him as "racist, or trying to be superior." In discussing this problem with his own supervisor, the intern acknowledged the ethical demand of fidelity, that is, his obligation to provide honest and timely feedback to his supervisee. With the ethical issue clear, he and his supervisor were able to discuss possible approaches to convey the feedback.

In another case, a supervisor evaluated her practicum student supervisee as not providing the quality of treatment necessary for effective work with a particular client. At the same time, the supervisee was clearly learning a great deal in working with this client. Here the principles of beneficence and nonmaleficence required that the supervisor balance among competing positive goals to be achieved and between competing harms to be avoided. Thus the supervisor needed to assess both the possible and probable harm versus good to the client, as well as the potential growth of the therapist. Justice was also a concern here, that is, the client's right to treatment that meets acceptable standards of care. In this situation, it was possible for the supervisor to work as a cotherapist with the practicum student, a solution that allowed for effective treatment as well as development for the supervisee.

Hall notes that in malpractice actions, this responsibility is often called vicarious liability, stemming from the doctrine of "respondent superior," which holds the "master" responsible for the acts of his or her "servants."[8] Thus, the next area in the Lamb et al. model, competence, covers both the professional skills of supervisor and supervisee and supervisory abilities of the supervisor.[9]

COMPETENCE
Professional Competencies

An important ethical mandate is that services provided must be within the competence of the provider. This is an especially provocative issue in the case of supervisees who are near the beginning of their professional education in that they may have few competencies to offer. Supervisors are best advised to be involved in the selection of clients for such supervisees, in order to match client needs to counselor competencies as much as possible. Regardless, supervisors are often called on to teach and model specific techniques for such supervisees. Vigilant supervision is necessary to ensure client welfare in these situations, and supervisors often need to be involved in decisions regarding how many clients the supervisee should see at any one time. Saccuzzo reminds supervisors of the possible legal liability of supervisees' lack of competence in working with specific clients or client issues, and recommends a level of monitoring based on the level of education and experience of the supervisee.[10] With beginning trainees, it is important to review progress notes carefully, assess supervisees' work on a continual basis, and use videotapes or live observation. The amount of supervisor time that has to be devoted to such careful monitoring should be considered when deciding how many beginners a supervisor can or should supervise at one time.

Even experienced clinicians often revert to Level 1 processing when learning and implementing new techniques and dealing with unfamiliar client issues. Supervisors should be alert for such events and provide focused supervision until the new techniques or issues become more comfortable for the supervisee.

A related issue is that of supervisor competency in the indicated clinical competency or client issue. It is assumed that supervisors possess competencies in most of the areas for which they will be providing supervision. However, there will always be circumstances in which this is not the case. Additional training, reading, and consultation can all be appropriate solutions, depending on the specific context. In some instances, the supervisor may want to arrange supervision for the supervisee with a colleague who possesses the needed experience and expertise.

There are also specific client issues with which supervisees, especially advanced clinicians, may have more competency than the supervisor possesses. With confident and experienced supervisors, this situation can provide an opportunity to strengthen colleagueship and gain additional competency. But certain of these situations can be very problematic. An example would be the supervisee whose cultural background and identity is different from that of the supervisor. Such a supervisee may, even in the early stages of becoming a therapist, claim expertise in dealing with a client of his or her background and reject what the supervisor has to offer. This situation can be especially difficult with supervisees at Level 2. On the one hand, the supervisor needs to acknowledge the insight that the supervisee has gained by virtue of cultural similarity to the client. On the other hand, there may well be some universals that the supervisee is overlooking as a result of the similarities. Leong recently presented a model of multicultural counseling that identifies universal, cultural group centered, and individual levels of client functioning and concerns.[11] While traditional counseling approaches often neglected the cultural group issues, the danger now is that in some cases this area may be overemphasized. This may especially be true for therapists who share a similar group identification to that of the client.

The point we made earlier is again emphasized: All practitioners have an ethical mandate to increase their competencies in working with diverse populations. Supervisors are no exception, and learning from supervisees can be a valuable opportunity. At the same time, the role and experience of the supervisor must be acknowledged. We strongly advise consultation for the supervisor (and perhaps the supervisee as well) in such situations. Handled well, they can improve both communication between supervisor and supervisee and effective services for clients.

In one situation with which we are familiar, a Latino practicum student was convinced that his female white supervisor could not understand the concerns of the student's Latino client. The client, a highly acculturated medical student, was dealing with the death of his mother. The supervisee, somewhat less acculturated, insisted on focusing on the client's grief solely within the context of Hispanic culture. When the supervisor pointed out the more universal aspects of the grief process, the therapist listened to her words passively but then ignored them when working with the client. When asked about his response in the next supervision session, the therapist accused his supervisor of not comprehending the cultural context. The supervisor, after some initial defensiveness, consulted with a colleague, who was able to help her separate her admitted need for further understanding of some cultural variables from her supervisee's inability to grasp the entire picture of his client's distress. Although the Level 2 supervisee remained somewhat resistant, he made sufficient progress to provide the client with effective help in working through his grief process.

Competence to Supervise

New supervisors clearly need to attend to statements of ethics, professional standards, and guidelines such as those articulated in this and the previous chapter. For example, General Standard 1.04 of the *Ethical Principles of Psychologists and Code of Conduct* specifically addresses the need for training and supervision in new areas. The *Standards for Counseling Supervisors* of the Association for Counselor Education and Supervision addresses the need for both conceptual knowledge and skill in supervision.[12] Chapter Nine addresses the crucial importance and increased need for competence in supervision and discusses guidelines for such supervisor development.

There are a number of general legal theories of liability under which medical and mental health professionals have been held liable. Each of these deals specifically with supervisor competence. As listed by Saccuzzo, negligent supervision is a matter of direct liability, and three theories—respondent superior, the borrowed servant rule, and enterprise liability—cover cases of vicarious liability.[13]

In order to establish direct liability for negligent supervision, the plaintiff must demonstrate a direct link between his or her injuries and the actions of the supervisor. Although cases involving mental health supervisors have been relatively few thus far, there are a number of relevant cases in medical settings from which analogies can be drawn. Regulatory agencies are also aware of and utilizing tenets of direct liability. As one example, in *Masterson v. Board of Examiners of*

Psychologists, a psychologist's license was revoked for failure to "monitor and control" a supervisee.[14] The often-cited case of *Tarasoff v. Regents of the University of California* (in which a therapist and the police were cited for "failure to warn" a person that a threat had been made against her life) includes comments regarding supervisor negligence as well.[15]

The *respondent superior theory* holds those in positions of authority legally liable for damages caused by their subordinates. Supervisors may be held liable as either the "master" or as an employer. Under this doctrine, Saccuzzo notes that there is little doubt that where actions of an unlicensed supervisee negligently result in damages to a client or patient, the supervisor may be liable. Further, in the case of sexual misconduct, the supervisor may be liable even where the misconduct occurs outside the therapy office or after therapy has been terminated.[16]

The *borrowed servant rule* arises in the context of training programs that place students in mental health facilities outside the educational program. A critical factor in determining liability is who had control of the supervisee at the time of the negligent act. Professional training programs are thus well advised to arrange careful affiliation agreements with alternative training sites and to assure themselves that the quality and quantity of supervision at such sites are appropriate.

Enterprise liability theory views damages as part of doing business. That is, any profit the supervisor accrues from supervision involves the supervisor in the risk of damages to patients or clients.

Since there currently exists neither a consensus nor an explicit statement of the standard of care in psychotherapy supervision by relevant professional groups, it is essential that supervisors consult relevant ethical guidelines and related statements. The Kitchener principles cited earlier provide helpful standards.[17] The Association of State and Provincial Psychology Boards has published guidelines pertaining to supervision of unlicensed professionals.[18] Models such as this one that advocate an amount and type of supervision based on carefully assessed level of the therapist may be especially useful to the supervisor or agency in determining supervision practices.

Additional ethical and legal concerns must be addressed by supervisors as part of the mandate of competence. Chief among these are the following areas.

1.   *Confidentiality and informed consent.* Supervisors and supervisees need to discuss in advance, and then inform the client, the process by which supervision will be monitored. We suggest that patient or client agreement with this process be in written form, as part of the discussion regarding limits of confidentiality. The supervisee also needs to understand the expectations of and the process the supervisor will employ as part of the supervisory process.

2.   *Multiple relationships.* It is not difficult to understand the power differential between supervisors and supervisees, especially in situations in which the supervisee is a student. The APA Code speaks, as do others, to the necessity of avoiding conduct that is demeaning to supervisees, not engaging in sexual relationships with supervisees, and respecting the rights of others to hold values, attitudes, and opinions that are different from the supervisor's own.[19] Supervisors must also be alert to possible inappropriate relationships between supervisees and their patients or clients.

Supervisees may not be in a position to select their own supervisors, but every care must be taken to avoid multiple relationships in supervisory assignments as well as other areas. For example, we view it as unwise to assign students to their own academic adviser for clinical supervision, since this situation concentrates additional power in one person. Such a match should be made only with the fully informed consent of both parties, and then only if there is a well-founded belief that such a match will be more advantageous to the supervisees than other choices for supervision. The same guidelines would apply in an employer-employee situation.

3.   *Evaluation of supervisees.* Evaluation of all supervisees is crucial, both for supervisee development and ensuring the quality of professional services. It is essential that such processes be clear to all concerned and based on actual performance and established standards of practice. Possible impairment in the supervisee demands careful evaluation, feedback, and a clear plan of remediation.

4.   *Evaluation of patients/clients.* The supervisor must make initial and ongoing assessment of the patient/client, in order to assess an appropriate match with the supervisee. Especially with inexperienced trainees, this evaluation will surely include videotaping and possibly face-to-face interaction with the client.

5.   *Representation of credentials.* Supervisors practicing in jurisdictions in which practice is controlled by licensure or credentialing must be clear on the titles used by their supervisees. In some states,

the relationship of a licensed supervisor to an unlicensed supervisee could be constructed as "lending the license" unless such a relationship is made explicit. Such a practice would provide grounds for disciplinary action for the supervisor/licensee.

6. *Reimbursement for supervisee.* Insurance fraud may be charged if a supervisor signs as the provider for services actually provided by the supervisee. It is essential for the supervisor to understand and follow the billing practices of each entity with which a contractual agreement is negotiated. Principle 1.26 of the APA Code also specifically speaks to these issues.[20]

Competence then, becomes the heart and soul of the supervisory role. A competent and ethical professional who assumes the role of supervisor needs to realize that areas of competence in professional techniques and methods, ethics, and legal and regulatory areas must be expanded and sharpened. In addition, the supervisor assumes responsibilities for that third and often most ambiguous area of the Lamb et al. model, personal functioning.[21]

PERSONAL FUNCTIONING

Supervisors have a responsibility to monitor and assess the personal strengths and limitations and general well-being of their supervisees, for the benefit of the supervisees themselves and to protect client welfare. However, the supervisor must not become the supervisee's therapist. Knowing when to refer a supervisee to therapy is a challenging task.

Supervisees are individuals who, like others, will sometimes be in the midst of personal problems that have the potential for interfering with their clinical work. Most of these problems are ones that can be dealt with by supervisor and supervisee. However, some difficulties require additional attention. Lamb et al. offer a model for response to psychology intern impairment that can easily be adapted to fit other situations with other supervisees.[22] Their model consists of a four-step process: (1) identification of the problem, (2) explicit discussion and planning with training staff, (3) implementation and review of actions, and (4) addressing organizational reaction to the decisions and process.

Dealing with supervisee impairment is perhaps the most complex and demanding activity required of supervisors. The dual commitment to supervisee and client can be deeply tested. This is one of those times when the knowledge, commitment, and moral strength of the supervisor are on the line. Supervisors are strongly advised to seek support and consultation from relevant colleagues in such situations.

Surprisingly, at least to us, some supervisees are able to handle the early years of training, where they are typically working in a clinical setting only a few hours a week, without demonstrating impairment. In the intensive, full-time arena of internship, residency, or the first professional position, hiding difficulties that interfere with effective client treatment is far more difficult. Then, too, being away from familiar support systems and assuming many new responsibilities at one time is stressful to most people, and some advanced supervisees and newer professionals are unable to handle this stress productively.

IMPLICATIONS FOR SPECIFIC LEVELS

Each level of supervisee functioning in the IDM frames relevant issues. Level 1 supervisees are generally eager to learn and use appropriate ethical and regulatory codes. In their studies, however, they often encounter only client situations in which ethical and legal guidelines are clear and unequivocal. Supervisors in such cases can stretch supervisees' thinking a bit by introducing models of ethical and moral development and suggesting relevant reading on ethical issues in clinical practice. When complex issues arise for supervisees at this level, an extraordinary level of supervisor support is necessary. The supervisor will also usually need to help the supervisee move through the ethical decision making in careful detail.

Generally supervisees at Level 2 are very aware of and committed to the ethical demand of client welfare. They can on occasion avoid dealing with other ethical or legal issues that may conflict with their ideas regarding what is best for their client. This is the prime time for the use of models of ethical development. The developing need for autonomy on the part of the supervisee is well matched by models that require careful consideration of options and may pose conflicting interests. A real challenge for the supervisor is to encourage this autonomy while still monitoring ethical and legal basics. In other words, ethical decision making is a prime area in which the conflicts of Level 2 are acted out.

One of us worked with a trainee who, typical of Level 2, became almost totally encapsulated in his client's view of herself as an abused woman and chose to overlook the clearly abusive manner in which she was handling situations with her children. Only the supervisor's strong confrontation forced him to acknowledge the legal mandate to report the abuse, as well as deal with the very important clinical issues involved.

The broader personal and professional integration characteristic of Level 3 therapists presents opportunities for the supervisee to develop a personalized professional code of ethics. This person is now able to see guidelines and codes as part of a broader perspective on the rights of individuals and the responsibility of the profession. While possible at all levels, the relative calm and maturity of Level 3 provides an optimal opportunity for the integration of professional identity with salient issues of personal identity. As Vasquez and McKinley assert, "if we are to promote maximum growth in minority supervisees, we must attend to and stimulate their efforts to incorporate ethnic identity with professional identity."[23] Supervisors need to be aware of the possible gender and ethnic differences in supervisee development discussed throughout this book, and Level 3 provides a time to explore and integrate these more fully.

Each supervisee develops into his or her own professional person, bound to others by common competencies and ethics, but differing in style, beliefs, and areas of greatest expertise. The supervisor guides and facilitates, but Level 3 supervisees are ready and able to march to their own drummer. That is truly the reward of the ethical, competent, and committed supervisors who walked with supervisees on the journey.

—ᨊ— Epilogue

The role of clinical supervisor is broadly viewed as one of the more important training functions in the field of mental health. Unfortunately, the empirical support for the impact of supervision on client outcomes is still in its infancy.[1] Although models continue to proliferate, many of them appear to be reiterations of constructs and principles already articulated in prior models.[2] We have devoted much of our careers to the exploration of clinical supervision issues of practice, model building, and research, a field that has far too long languished in the shadow of clinical practice and, at times, has been identified as merely a subset of psychotherapy in general. We hope that our discussion of the IDM and related research has served to highlight the importance of clinical supervision as a unique enterprise, crucial to developing psychotherapy skills but a separate process.

In Chapter Eight we discussed some of the challenges facing mental health professionals who engage in clinical supervision that have emerged from the health care reform movement. We examined some of the potentially deleterious impacts of the economics of managed care on psychotherapist training and supervision. Other threats to progress in understanding and implementing effective clinical supervision involve apathy, lack of time, clinical naiveté, and professional burnout. Without a strong commitment to research and practice in clinical supervision by all of us who engage in it, we will do a disservice to our supervisees, our clients, and the profession.

We are confident that interest and investment in clinical supervision are continuing to grow. As we attend professional conferences, correspond with colleagues, read the literature, and present workshops, we are impressed with the commitment of mental health professionals to developing skills in and understanding the process of clinical supervision. We hope that this delineation of the IDM proves useful to everyone who sees the role of supervisor as an important part of professional identity.

Over the course of this book, we have addressed a number of issues relevant to the effective and ethical practice of clinical supervision. Although we believe this book to be the most comprehensive explication of a model of clinical supervision to date, we realize that we have probably overlooked some areas. Nevertheless, we hope that we have been sufficiently detailed in our discussion to enable you to understand the tenets of the IDM and how it is implemented. For those of you who engage, or plan to engage, in clinical or supervisory research, we hope that the level of detail we provided will allow you to investigate the model empirically.

Throughout this book, we have used scenarios and an occasional metaphor to exemplify supervisory issues. As we consider the importance of the role of clinical supervisor and the rewards associated with this process, another analogy comes to mind. All three of us have spent time at the University of Iowa in Iowa City. One of the more famous citizens there is Dan Gable, the university's wrestling coach whose success as an NCAA and Olympic wrestler preceded his success as a coach. A quotation that has been described as one of Coach Gable's favorites captures some of what we feel about working with supervisees in the clinical supervision process:

> To coach someone to be the best is a much higher honor than being the best.

Similarly, to assist psychotherapists to become as good as they can be, and be of assistance to the multitude of clients who will seek services from them, is for some of us an even higher calling than our own work as psychotherapists. We look forward to an ongoing dialogue on this issue as the practice of clinical supervision continues into the twenty-first century.

━ Appendix A
Case Presentation Format

This format is intended to help the therapist collect and integrate information relevant to case conceptualization, diagnosis, and treatment. It is not intended to serve as a concise summary of client attributes and treatment data but rather to organize a breadth of information and stimulate understanding and decision making.

1. Clinic Data
   a. Therapist name
   b. Status (first practicum, intern, staff, and so on)
   c. Agency/clinic site
   d. Number of sessions with client
   e. Type of sessions (individual, group, marital, family)
2. Client Demographic Data
   a. Name (initials or altered name for confidentiality)
   b. Date of birth/age
   c. Sex
   d. Marital status
   e. Children (in and out of home, ages, sex)
   f. Living situation
      (i) House, apartment, and so on
      (ii) People living in the home and relationship to client
3. SES Data
   a. Occupational status
      (i) Client
      (ii) Family members

b. Average family monthly income

c. Transportation status (drives own car, public transport)

d. Other economic resources (own house, savings, family support, and so on)

e. Economic stressors (debts, child support, and so on)

4. Presenting Problem(s)

This section should include a description of the problem areas (listed separately) from the client's perspective, particularly noting the client's view of their order of importance. Suggested items to focus on:

a. Were there precipitating factors?

b. How long have the problems persisted?

c. Have problems previously occurred? What were the circumstances?

d. In what way, if any, do the problems relate to each other?

5. Relevant History

This section will vary in comprehensiveness according to depth and length of treatment and in focus according to theoretical orientation and the specific nature of the problems. Suggested focuses include:

a. Family and relationship history

(i) Family of origin/developmental issues

(ii) Past marriages/significant relationships (duration, sexual functioning, dissolution factors, sexual preference, and so on)

(iii) Children (from current and prior relationships and current status)

(iv) Current family status and structure

b. Cultural history and identity

(i) Issues of ethnicity and race

(ii) Identification/acculturation

c. Educational history

(i) Childhood/developmental

(ii) Adulthood/current status

d. Vocational history (types, stability, satisfaction, and so on)

    e. Medical history (acute/chronic illness, hospitalizations, surgeries, major patterns of illness in family, accidents, injuries, with whom/where/how often receive medical care, and so on)

    f. Health practices (sleeping, eating patterns, tobacco use, exercise, and so on)

    g. Mental health history (prior problems, symptoms, diagnoses, evaluations, therapy experiences, past prescribed medications, current and family of origin mental health histories)

    h. Current medications (dosages, purposes, physician, compliance, effects, side effects, and so on)

    i. Legal history (arrests, driving under the influence, jail/prison, lawsuits, any pending legal actions)

    j. Use/abuse of alcohol or drugs (prescription or illegal)

    k. Family (current and origin) alcohol/drug history

6. Interpersonal Factors

This section should contain a description of the client's orientation toward others in his or her environment, including:

    a. Manner of dress

    b. Physical appearance

    c. General self-presentation

    d. Nature of typical relationships (dependent, submissive, aggressive, dominant, withdrawing, and so on)

    e. Behavior toward therapist (therapeutic alliance, and so on)

7. Environmental Factors

    a. Elements in the environment, not already mentioned, that function as stressors to the client—those centrally related to the presenting problems and more peripheral

    b. Elements in the environment, not previously mentioned, that function as support for the client (friends, family, recreational activities, and so on)

8. Personality Dynamics

    a. Cognitive factors: Data relevant to thinking and mental processes such as:

     (i)   Intelligence

     (ii) Mental alertness

     (iii) Persistence of negative cognitions

     (iv) Positive cognitions

     (v) Nature and content of fantasy life

     (vi) Level of insight (awareness of changes in feelings, behavior, reactions of others, understanding of the interplay, and so on)

     (vii) Capacity for judgment (ability to make decisions and carry out practical affairs of daily living)

  b. Emotional factors

     (i)   Typical or most common emotional states

     (ii) Predominant mood during interviews

     (iii) Appropriateness of affect

     (iv) Range of emotions client can display

     (v) Cyclical aspects of client's emotional life

  c. Behavioral factors

     (i)   Psychosomatic symptoms

     (ii) Existence of problematic habits or mannerisms

9. Testing (both past and recent)

  a. Methods or instruments

  b. Evaluator, location, dates, reasons for testing

  c. Results

10. Life Transition/Adaptation Skills

  a. Coping skills: Concrete efforts to deal with distressing situations (for example, anticipation, preparation, response)

  b. Social resources: Summary of supportive social networks

  c. Psychological resources: Adaptive personality characteristics (for example, self-efficacy, hardiness, optimism)

11. Formal Diagnosis

  a. *DSM-IV* diagnosis (all applicable axes)

  b. Checklist of symptoms/criteria showing how client meets diagnostic criteria

12. Therapist's Conceptualization of the Case

This section contains a summary of the therapist's view of the problems and their effects on the client. Include only the most central and core dynamics of the client's personality, relationships, and environmental influences. Note the interrelationships among the major factors. What are the common themes? What ties it all together? This is a synthesis of all the relevant data and the essence of the therapist's understanding of the client.

13. Treatment Plan

Based on the above information, describe the treatment plan you will follow to address the presenting and emerging problems. Make it consistent with your theoretical orientation and available empirical evidence. Estimate the number and types of sessions needed to address the issues.

14. Questions/Issues

Note the questions you have regarding this case and any issues you would like to address during the case conference.

—∿— Appendix B
Supervisee Information Form

This form can be used to collect relevant background information from supervisees for decision making in practicum, internship, and postdegree supervision. This information helps the supervisor to make an initial assessment of the developmental level of the supervisee.

Date _____

Name _____

Educational status (for example, year in program, years past degree, and so on) _____

_____

Highest degree earned _____

Hours of individual counseling or psychotherapy experience_____

Over how many years? _____

Hours of group counseling or psychotherapy experience_____

What types of groups?_____

_____

Hours of marital and family counseling or psychotherapy experience

_____

Over how many years? _____

Percentage of all counseling or psychotherapy experience that was supervised_____

Breadth of client populations (age, racial/ethnic/cultural, gender) including diagnostic classifications (please describe):

Professional environments in which you have worked (agencies, hospitals, private practice). Please describe and note how long you were there and what your duties included.

Hours of direct supervision received (total):

One-to-one _____

Group or peer _____

Theoretical orientations to which you have been exposed:

Preferred orientation:

What assessment techniques or instruments have you used (administered, scored, and interpreted)? Please estimate how many of each.

How many intake assessments? _____

How many written assessment reports? _____

For whom have these reports been written (courts, physicians, schools)?

Describe any special experiences not already covered.

What do you perceive as your professional strengths?

What do you perceive as your professional weaknesses?

Other comments?

━ Appendix C
Supervisee Levels
Questionnaire–Revised

SCORING KEY (PRELIMINARY)

Self and Other Awareness

1, 2, 3*, 5, 7*, 8*, 9, 11*, 15, 16, 17*, 21, 22*, 23*, 26*, 31*, 34*, 37, 41, 43, 44, 45, 46, 47

Motivation

12*, 13*, 18*, 20*, 24*, 27*, 29*, 33*, 36*, 38, 40, 42

Dependency-Autonomy

4, 6*, 10*, 13, 14, 19*, 20, 25, 28, 30, 32, 35*, 39

Note: *Indicates reverse scoring.

Note: The subscales are based on three developmental structures identified in the Integrated Developmental Model described in C. D. Stoltenberg & U. Delworth (1987). *Supervising counselors and therapists: A developmental approach*. San Francisco: Jossey-Bass.

━

The following instrument is designed to study the behaviors of counselors/therapists in training. The gaining of skills as a counselor/therapist is a learning process, and it is therefore necessary to gather new information continuously. Your total honesty will be greatly appreciated.

All information obtained will remain anonymous.

Thank you for your participation and cooperation!

PERSONAL DATA

Age: _____

Sex: _____

Current educational status:

Highest degree earned: _____

Previous supervision received (number of semesters or quarters; if less than one full term, number of hours: _____

Counseling/therapy experience (semesters, quarters, or hours): _____

Other relevant experiences:

Future career plans:

SUPERVISEE QUESTIONNAIRE

In terms of your own current behavior, please answer the items below according to the following scale.

1 = Never

2 = Rarely

3 = Sometimes

4 = Half the time

5 = Often

6 = Most of the time

7 = Always

1. Within supervisory and counseling/therapy relationships, I am sensitive to my *own* dynamics.

Never						Always
1	2	3	4	5	6	7

2. I feel genuinely relaxed and comfortable in my counseling/therapy sessions.

Never						Always
1	2	3	4	5	6	7

3. I find myself using the same specific techniques in most of my therapy sessions.

Never						Always
1	2	3	4	5	6	7

4. I am able to critique counseling tapes and gain insights with minimum help from my supervisor.

Never						Always
1	2	3	4	5	6	7

5. I am able to be spontaneous in counseling/therapy, yet my behavior is relevant.

Never						Always
1	2	3	4	5	6	7

6. I lack self-confidence in establishing counseling relationships with diverse client types.

Never						Always
1	2	3	4	5	6	7

7. I find it difficult to express my thoughts and feelings clearly in counseling/therapy.

Never   Always
1   2   3   4   5   6   7

8. My verbal behavior in counseling/therapy is pretty much the same with most clients.

Never   Always
1   2   3   4   5   6   7

9. I am able to apply a consistent personalized rationale of human behavior in working with my clients.

Never   Always
1   2   3   4   5   6   7

10. I tend to get confused when things don't go according to plan and lack confidence in my ability to handle the unexpected.

Never   Always
1   2   3   4   5   6   7

11. I find myself intellectualizing about my clients' problems without being in touch with their feeling states.

Never   Always
1   2   3   4   5   6   7

12. The overall quality of my work fluctuates; on some days I do well, and on other days, I do poorly.

Never   Always
1   2   3   4   5   6   7

13. I depend on my supervisor considerably in figuring out how to deal with my clients.

Never   Always
1   2   3   4   5   6   7

14. I find myself working with my clients as I think my supervisor, or some other counselor/therapist I know of, would.

Never   Always
1   2   3   4   5   6   7

15. During counseling/therapy sessions, I am able to focus completely on my client.

Never   Always
1   2   3   4   5   6   7

16. I feel comfortable in confronting my clients.

    Never   Always
      1   2   3   4   5   6   7

17. Much of the time in counseling/therapy, I find myself thinking about my next response instead of fitting my intervention into the overall picture.

    Never   Always
      1   2   3   4   5   6   7

18. My motivation fluctuates from day to day.

    Never   Always
      1   2   3   4   5   6   7

19. I feel most comfortable when my supervisor takes control of what we do in supervision.

    Never   Always
      1   2   3   4   5   6   7

20. At times, I wish my supervisor could be in the counseling/therapy session to lend a hand.

    Never   Always
      1   2   3   4   5   6   7

21. I find myself focusing less on learning new techniques and approaches to counseling/therapy and thinking more about my general professional development.

    Never   Always
      1   2   3   4   5   6   7

22. During counseling/therapy sessions, I find it difficult to concentrate because of my concern with my own performance.

    Never   Always
      1   2   3   4   5   6   7

23. In describing clients and/or viewing videotapes, I am very concerned about my supervisor's evaluation of my performance.

    Never   Always
      1   2   3   4   5   6   7

24. Because there is so much to learn, I am highly motivated to use my supervisor as an educational resource.

    Never   Always
      1   2   3   4   5   6   7

25. Although at times I really want advice/feedback from my supervisor, at other times I really want to do things my own way.

Never   Always
1   2   3   4   5   6   7

26. In counseling/therapy sessions, I am very concerned about my clients' evaluation of my skills.

Never   Always
1   2   3   4   5   6   7

27. The more I learn, the more impressed I am with the counseling process.

Never   Always
1   2   3   4   5   6   7

28. Sometimes my supervisor is too structured and too directive with me.

Never   Always
1   2   3   4   5   6   7

29. Sometimes the client's situation seems so hopeless that I just don't know what to do.

Never   Always
1   2   3   4   5   6   7

30. It is important that my supervisor allow me to make my own mistakes.

Never   Always
1   2   3   4   5   6   7

31. I find myself becoming so in touch with my clients' emotions that I find it difficult to regain my objectivity.

Never   Always
1   2   3   4   5   6   7

32. Given my current state of professional development, I believe I know when I need consultation from my supervisor and when I don't.

Never   Always
1   2   3   4   5   6   7

33. Sometimes I question how suited I am to be a counselor/therapist.

Never   Always
1   2   3   4   5   6   7

34. I find myself becoming so in touch with my clients' emotions that I find it difficult to help them see alternatives.

Never   Always
1   2   3   4   5   6   7

35. Regarding counseling/therapy, I view my supervisor as a teacher/mentor.

Never   Always
1   2   3   4   5   6   7

36. Sometimes I feel that counseling/therapy is so complex that I will never be able to learn it all.

Never   Always
1   2   3   4   5   6   7

37. I find myself more inclined to think about how to help clients solve their problems than to empathize with how they feel.

Never   Always
1   2   3   4   5   6   7

38. I believe I know my strengths and weaknesses as a counselor sufficiently well to understand my professional potential and limitations.

Never   Always
1   2   3   4   5   6   7

39. Regarding counseling/therapy, I view my supervisor as a peer/colleague.

Never   Always
1   2   3   4   5   6   7

40. I think I know myself well and am able to integrate that into my therapeutic style.

Never   Always
1   2   3   4   5   6   7

41. I find I am able to understand my clients' view of the world yet help them objectively evaluate alternatives.

Never   Always
1   2   3   4   5   6   7

42. At my current level of professional development, my confidence in my abilities is such that my desire to do counseling/therapy doesn't change much from day to day.

   Never   Always
    1   2   3   4   5   6   7

43. I find I am able to empathize with my clients' feeling states but still help them focus on problem resolution.

   Never   Always
    1   2   3   4   5   6   7

44. I am able to assess my interpersonal impact on clients adequately and use that knowledge therapeutically.

   Never   Always
    1   2   3   4   5   6   7

45. I am adequately able to assess the client's interpersonal impact on me and use that therapeutically.

   Never   Always
    1   2   3   4   5   6   7

46. I believe I exhibit a consistent professional objectivity and ability to work within my role as a counselor without undue overinvolvement with my clients.

   Never   Always
    1   2   3   4   5   6   7

47. I believe I exhibit a consistent professional objectivity and ability to work within my role as a counselor without excessive distance from my clients.

   Never   Always
    1   2   3   4   5   6   7

～ Appendix D
Empirical Studies of
Clinical Supervision

This table is reprinted, by permission, from Stoltenberg, C. D., McNeill, B. W., & Crethar, H. D. (1994). Changes in supervision as counselors and therapists gain experience: A review. *Professional Psychology: Research and Practice, 25*, 416–449. The table includes all of the empirical studies the authors could find between 1987 and the date of publication, 1994. For those readers interested in becoming familiar with the research literature on clinical supervision, this table should prove helpful.

～

Authors	Sample	Supervisors	Trainees	Design	Instrument	Theory	Selected Findings
Allen, Szollos, & Williams (1986)	National sample of 37 APA-accredited counseling and clinical psychology programs	None	142 counselor trainees (74 female, 68 male); mean of 4.4 years of graduate training	Chi-square, correlated t-tests, stepwise discriminant analysis	Questionnaire (this study)	Expanding the informational base on what differentiates trainees' perceptions of their best and worst supervision experiences	1. Quality supervision was best discriminated by perceived expertise and trustworthiness of the supervisor, duration of training in weeks, and an emphasis on personal growth issues over a focus on technical skills. 2. The most important discriminators of supervisor expertise were the specific ratings of "skill" and "reliability," which contributed to the summary evaluation of trustworthiness. 3. Authoritarian treatment and sexist behavior were considered detrimental to supervision.
Bahrick, Russel, & Salmi (1991)	One university counseling center, Midwest	None	Nineteen counselor trainees	Wilcoxon test of correlated samples	SEQ (this study,) SD (Osgood, Suci, & Tannenbaum, 1958), role induction audiotape (Bernard, 1979)	Measuring the effects of an audiotaped role-induction procedure on beginning counselor trainees	1. Over the ten-week period, trainees were less likely to view their supervisors as functioning in counselor or teacher roles and less likely to be open about revealing their worries or concerns about counseling to their supervisors, and the trainees' rating of supervision became more negative.

2. Following the role induction, trainees reported significantly clearer conceptualization of the supervisory process, viewing their supervisors as functioning in a more teacher-like role and being better able to recognize and express their needs, concerns, and worries in supervision.

Author	Setting		Design	Instruments	Purpose	Results
Blocher et al. (1985)	University counseling center, Northeast	None	Concurrent validity study: eight experienced Ph.D. counseling psychologists, ten first-year practicum students, Construct validity study: fourteen first-year master's students.	Development and validation of an instrument	CPQ (this study); PCM (Hunt, Butler, Noy, & Rosser, 1978), yielding differentiation score (D) and an integration (I) score; Crockett method (Crockett, Press, Delia, & Kennedy, 1973)	Development of an instrument for measurement of cognitive growth during supervision	1. Reliability coefficients of .97 for the D score and .94 for the I score. 2. Significant difference between Ph.D.s and first-year students in the D score. 3. I and D scores were unrelated to PCM scores. 4. I and D scores correlate .78 and .56, respectively, with the Crockett method. 5. I and D scores correlate .38 with each other.

Authors	Sample	Super-visors	Trainees	Design	Instrument	Theory	Selected Findings
Borders (1989b)	University counseling center, Midwest	None	Twenty-seven master's students, (twenty-three female, four male)	Correlational between one self-report and coded cognitions	SCT (Loevinger & Wessler, 1970); CRCS (Dole et al., 1982)	In-session cognitions of first-practicum trainees at various ego levels	1. Trainees at higher ego levels reported fewer negative thoughts about themselves or their clients, more objective retrospections, and fewer negative thoughts about their clients and themselves.
Borders (1990)	One university practicum course, Midwest	None	Forty-four master's students (thirty-seven female, seven male	ANCOVA	SLQ (McNeill, Stoltenberg, & Pierce, 1985)	Short-term longitudinal study of trainees' self-reported change along the dimensions of self-awareness, autonomy, and acquisition of theory and skills	1. Trainees reported significant increases in self-awareness, dependency/autonomy, and theory/skills acquisition across three supervisors.

| Borders (1991b) | One south-eastern university | Two Ph.D. (one male, one female), two Ph.D. students (two male) | Four second-year master's students (four females) | Frequency count and percentages | CVRMCS (Hill, 1985, 1986); supervisor cognition measure (Strozier, Thoreson, & Kivlighan, 1989); SSI (Friedlander & Ward, 1984) | Multiple case study | 1. At least half of the responses of all supervisors were directives; providing information was most frequent response type (40.5 percent); reported in-session cognitions that were on task; stated in the present tense; concerning out-of-session events, and focused on internal, psychological dynamics, most frequent intention was to give information; thoughts tended to be more cognitive than affective; described their styles as collegial and relationship and process oriented than didactic and practical. 2. Three of the trainees agreed with their supervisors' descriptions of supervisory style, while one trainee described style as primarily didactic. |

Authors	Sample	Supervisors	Trainees	Design	Instrument	Theory	Selected Findings
Borders & Fong (1989) Study 1	One introductory counseling skills class, southern university	None	Eighty first-semester Ed.S. students (sixty female, twenty male)	Correlation; multivariate multiple regression; post-hoc univariate multiple regression	SCT (Loevinger & Wessler, 1970); counseling skills exam; ratings of counseling effectiveness on session tapes; videotaped counseling skills exam	To explore the relationship of student ego development level to mastery of specific counseling skills	1. Significant relationship between ego level scores and ratings on the precounseling tape ($r = .24$; $p = .02$) 2. Counseling skills exam score and the posttraining counseling tape rating were correlated ($r = .39$, $p = .0003$). 3. Significant effect of pretraining counseling rating on counseling ability.
Study 2	One southern university, field-based practicum students	None	Forty-four beyond first-semester Ed.S. or doctoral students (twenty-nine female, fifteen male)	Multiple regression	SCT (Loevinger & Wessler, 1970); VPPS (Strupp, 1981)	To examine the relationship of ego development and counseling performance ratings in more advanced stages of training	1. No significant relationship between VPPS scores and ego development.

Borders, Fong, & Neimeyer (1986)	University of Florida's counselor education department	None	Sixty-three (twenty-seven first practicum counseling graduate students; ten second practicum students; 26 internship experience, 45 female, 18 male)	4 × 3 ANOVA, Friedman tests	Rep grid (Fransella & Bannister, 1977; Neimeyer & Neimeyer, 1981)	To examine level of ego development and level of experience as they relate to perceptions of clients	1. No significant differences in the structural complexity of client perceptions of counseling students at various levels of experience or levels of ego development.
Borders, Fong-Beyette, & Cron (1988)	One midwestern university student	None	One master's student (female)	Case study	CRCS (Dole et al., 1982)	Examination of the range of in-session cognitions of one first-practicum trainee	1. Participant focused more on events and feeling in the present than in the past or future, equivalently on in-session and out-of-session feelings and events. 2. In-session retrospections were focused more frequently on the counselor than the client or her supervisor, and they were negative. 3. More introspections had an internal locus.

Authors	Sample	Super-visors	Trainees	Design	Instrument	Theory	Selected Findings
Borders & Usher (1992)	Random sample of 729 nationally certified counselors	None	357 (62 percent master's-level prac-titioners; 38 percent Ph.D.; 66 percent female)	Survey response rate, 51.4 percent	Survey questionnaire (this study)	To document existing supervision practices; to determine the type of supervision that counselors in the field prefer	1. Trainees who received more supervision indicated a preference for more frequent supervision. 2. Respondents receiving no supervision preferred direct methods of supervision (live observation, cotherapy). 3. Respondents receiving the most supervision preferred self-report or audiotape and videotape review methods. 4. More experienced trainees preferred supervision less frequently. 5. Master's-level respondents wanted supervision for pro-fessional support; advanced trainees preferred it as a means of avoiding burnout. 6. Respondents tended to prefer supervision at the same frequency as current supervision.

| Carey, Williams, & Wells (1988) | Six Rocky Mountain region universities | Seven post-Ph.D., ten doctoral students | 31 master's students | Correlational; two self-report questionnaires | SRF (Heppner & Handley, 1982); CERS (Myrick & Kelly, 1971) | Examine relationships among supervisor expertness, attractiveness, trustworthiness, and supervision performance measures | 1. High SRF subtest correlations between expertness and attractiveness, expertness and trustworthiness, and attractiveness and trustworthiness. 2. Trainee performance ratings were significantly correlated to ratings of supervisor expertness ($r = .36$), attractiveness ($r = .39$), and trustworthiness ($r = .56$). 3. Supervisor trustworthiness was significantly correlated with CERS subscale scores, reflecting trainee competence in general counseling performance, professional attitude, counseling behavior, knowledge, supervision attitude, and behavior. |

Authors	Sample	Supervisors	Trainees	Design	Instrument	Theory	Selected Findings
Cook & Helms (1988)	National sample of clinical and counseling psychology students	None	225 minority students	Factor analysis, multiple regression, Tukey's honestly significant difference test	BLRI (Barrett-Lennard, 1962), SQ (Worthington & Roehlke, 1979)	Exploratory investigation of cross-cultural supervision satisfaction as predicted by trainee perceived relationship characteristics	1. Supervisor's liking and positive feelings toward the trainees accounted for 69.4 percent of the variance, and restrained involvement with the trainee accounted for 8.7 percent of the variance. 2. Trainees felt more liked than disliked and more emotionally close than distant. 3. Supervisor's liking and conditional interest predicted greater satisfaction in supervision. 4. Native Americans had a generally negative view of supervision, and Asian Americans had a generally positive view relative to the other groups.
Crane, Griffin, & Hill (1986)	Two marriage and family therapy counseling centers, mountain western and southwestern	None	Master's and Ph.D. students with one to five semesters of practicum experience	Stepwise multiple regression and ANOVA	Survey questionnaire (this study)	Evaluation of client perceptions of trainee skills and the relationships of these perceptions to therapy outcome	1. Client perception of fit of treatment predicted client-related outcome, and that trainee is "concerned" was the most important perceived trainee skill.

Study	Subjects		Sample	Design	Instrument	Purpose	Findings
Cummings, Hallberg, Martin, Slemon, Hiebert (1990)	Twenty-three counselors from one central and one western Canadian university	None	Two Ph.D. females; two master's level students (1 female, 1 male)	Proportions	CMT (Martin, 1985)	Content analysis of the conceptualizations of two novice and two experienced counselors	1. Experienced counselors displayed greater consistency in the concepts, employed a greater number of interactional concepts, used the concepts of family background and current relationships as a starting point for conceptualizing the client problem, and used more domain-specific concepts than the novice counselors.
Davis, Savicki, Cooley, & Firth (1989)	Members of the Oregon Personnel and Guidance Association	None	120 (49 school counselors, 16 community college counselors, 32 mental health counselors, 23 other [private practice and vocational rehabilitation])	Correlational between two self-report inventories	MBI (Maslach & Jackson, 1981); CSI (Davis, 1984)	Examination of the relationship between satisfaction with supervision and counselor burnout	1. Dissatisfaction with supervision was positively related to frequency and intensity of emotional exhaustion and intensity of depersonalization, and negatively related to frequency of feelings of personal accomplishment.

Authors	Sample	Supervisors	Trainees	Design	Instrument	Theory	Selected Findings
Efstation, Patton, & Kardash (1990)	National survey of internship supervisors, Ph.D. supervisors, interns, and advanced practicum students	185 Ph.D.s	178 pre-Ph.D. interns and advanced practicum students (103 female, 73 male, 2 gender unidentified)	Survey, return rate = 33 percent	SWAI (this study); SSI (Friedlander & Ward, 1984); SEI (Friedlander & Snyder, 1983)	Development of the SWAI; examination of the supervisory working alliance	1. Participants' experience of their working alliance in counselor supervision was multidimensional in nature. 2. Supervisors and trainees perceive that a focus on working to understand the client and rapport are common dimensions of their experience of the relationship.
Ellis (1991b)	One university counseling center, Northeast	Nine doctoral students (neophyte supervisors)	Nine doctoral students	One-way-ANOVA with a linear trend analysis for each supervision context; multivariate t-test; correlation; univariate t-tests	CIQ (Heppner & Roehlke, 1984); SSI (Friedlander & Ward, 1984); SER (Worthington & Roehlke, 1979); CESF (cited by Borders & Leddick, 1987)	Examination of supervisory issues as proposed by Loganbill, Hardy, & Delworth (1982) and Sansbury (1982); hierarchical versus nonhierarchical formulation of supervisory issues	1. Significant linear trend among hierarchically ordered supervisory issues confirming Sansbury's (1982) hierarchical formulation of supervisory issues and disconfirming Loganbill et al. (1982). 2. Critical incidences across both types of supervision were found to involve issues of relationship, competence, emotional awareness, autonomy, and personal issues but not theoretic identity issues.

Study	Setting	Sample		Theory	Method	Analysis	Findings
Ellis & Dell (1986)	Ohio State University's counseling psychology program	Nineteen (eight female, eleven male; six graduate-level students, 5 Ph.D. interns, 8 Ph.D.s)	None	Littrel, Lee-Boden, & Lorenz's (1979) developmental theory, Bernard's (1979) discrimination model of supervision	Questionnaire (this study)	Mann-Whitney U, Kruskal-Wallace, MDS analysis, multiple regression.	1. Three dimensions of a "cognitive map": process versus conceptualization, consultant versus counselor/teacher, and personalization versus teacher. 2. No evidence that experience level of trainee or supervisor affected the supervisor's description of supervision.

3. Disparity in supervisory issues between counselor-supervision and supervisor-supervision in purpose and direction and relationship issues.

Authors	Sample	Supervisors	Trainees	Design	Instrument	Theory	Selected Findings
Ellis, Dell, & Good (1988)							
Study 1	Ohio State University's counseling psychology program	Fifteen doctoral students (10 female, 5 male)	None	MDS analysis	Questionnaire from Ellis & Dell (1986)	Bernard's (1979) discrimination model of supervision, three-dimensional structure (cognitive map) (Ellis & Dell, 1986)	1. The "cognitive map" (Ellis & Dell, 1986) was supported and relabeled as Process versus Conceptual, Directive versus Nondirective, Challenging Cognitive-Behavioral versus Supportive Emotional.
Study 2	State University of New York at Albany's counseling psychology program	Forty-eight (twenty-three doctoral students, twenty-five master's level students; thirty-two female, sixteen male)	None	t-test to compare situations of trainees, constrained MDS analysis to qualify replication of study 1, unconstrained MDS analysis to include additional stimuli not used in study 1	Questionnaire from study 1 expanded by the addition of thirty pairs of role stimuli	To address alternative explanations for the results in study 1; developmental model of Littrel, Lee-Boden, & Lorenz, 1979	1. The "cognitive map" from study 1 was supported and found equally applicable to both the master's and doctoral trainees. 2. The trainees in study 2 were found to rely more on the third dimension than the other two.

Fenell, Hovestadt, & Harvey (1986)	East Texas State University's Department of Counseling and Guidance	None	Thirteen doctoral students	t-test	FTRS (Piercy, Laird, & Mohammed, 1983)	Comparison of a supervision approach based on a delayed feedback model of family therapist training and a live supervision model of training incorporating a supervision team	1. No statistically significant differences between the group trained using the delayed feedback supervision model and the group trained using the live supervision model.
Fisher (1989)	Colorado State University's Marriage and Family Therapy Clinic	Five AAMFT-approved supervisors (three Ph.D.; two master's; one female, four male)	One Ph.D., fifteen master's (seven female, nine male); "beginning" trainee was defined as having fewer than 500 clinical hours and 100 hours of supervision; and all others were considered "advanced" trainees	MANOVAs, chi-square, descriptive statistics	SFC (Fisher, 1982), RCC (Ericson and Rogers, 1973)	Hogan's (1964) developmental theory for "systems"-oriented supervisions	1. No significant differences between the supervision of "beginning" and "advanced" trainees regarding the focus of supervision. 2. No significant differences between the types of trainee relationships of "beginning" and "advanced" trainees.

Authors	Sample	Supervisors	Trainees	Design	Instrument	Theory	Selected Findings
Fong, Borders, & Neimeyer (1986)	University of Florida's counselor education specialist program	None	Forty-four first-semester counseling students (thirty-two female, twelve male)	2 (self-disclosure flexibility) × 2 (masculinity) × 2 (femininity) ANOVA; repeated measure ANOVA for effectiveness ratings on the counseling audiotapes; Tukey Studentized Range Test on mean sex role orientation scores, 4 (BSRI sex role typology) × 2 (self-disclosure flexibility) × 2 (time) repeated measures ANOVA	BSRI (Bem, 1981), SDSS (Chelune, 1976), Global Rating Scale (Gazda, Asbury, Balzea, Childers, & Walters, 1977) on a counseling skills examination and two audiotaped counseling sessions	To examine sex role orientation and self-disclosure flexibility as they relate to the acquisition and performance of counseling skills over one-semester counseling skills training course	1. High-flexibility trainees scored significantly higher (more effective) on the counseling skills examination than low-flexibility trainees. 2. Significant difference between masculinity and femininity in the BSRI sex role types. 3. Undifferentiated sex role (low masculinity, low femininity) trainees were significantly higher in response effectiveness ratings of the counseling tapes than were masculine sex role trainees. 4. Androgynous sex role trainees improved in response effectiveness at a slower rate than other types, although they were initially highest in response effectiveness.

| Friedlander, Keller, Peca-Baker, & Olk (1986) | State University of New York at Albany's counselor education, counseling psychology, clinical psychology, and social work students | None | Fifty-two graduate students (twenty-nine female, twenty-three male), with average prior counseling experience of twenty-two months | ANOVA, correlation MANCOVA | Self-Efficacy Inventory (Friedlander & Snyder, 1983), thought listing (Caciopopo & Petty, 1981), STAI (Speilberger, Gorusch, & Lushene, 1970), a performance measure of the trainees' upcoming session with a bogus client | To determine if and how one type of role conflict in the supervisory relationship affects trainees' self-statements, anxiety levels, and performance | 1. Inverse relation found between performance and anxiety and between anxiety and counselor self-efficacy. |

Authors	Sample	Super-visors	Trainees	Design	Instrument	Theory	Selected Findings
Friedlander, Siegel, & Brenock (1989)	State University of New York at Albany's Department of Counseling Psychology	One Ph.D. with nine years supervising experience (female)	One Ph.D. student, third year (female)	Case study, frequency count	BTC (Battle et al., 1966), CRF (Barak & LaCrosse, 1975), COQ (Loesch & McDavis, 1978), CPQ (Friedlander, 1982), HCVRCS-R (Friedlander, 1984), ICRS (Strong & Hills, 1984), I-E (Rotter, 1966), MMPI, SEQ (Stiles & Snow, 1984), SFRS (this study), SCL-90 (Derogatis, 1977), SSI (Friedlander & Ward, 1984), SPF (Heppner & Roehlke, 1984), RCCS (Ericson & Rogers, 1973; Rogers, 1979)	To explore to what degree parallel processes take place and identify behavioral features of an experienced supervisor	1. Trainee profile of the value of the supervisory sessions was similar to her profiled evaluations from the counseling sessions. 2. In verbal communication, the predominant self-presentational pattern in both dyads was complementary (leading and cooperating). 3. Little struggle for control (competitive symmetry) in either dyad.

| Guest & Beutler (1988) | Clinical psychology graduate students in a one-year training program in a medical school department of psychiatry | Nine Ph.D.s | Eight pre-Ph.D. interns, eight advanced pre-Ph.D. students | Multiple regression | TOQ (Sunland 1977a, 1977b); value survey (Rokeach, 1973, 1979); personality (Eysenck & Eysenck, 1969); locus of control (Rotter, 1966) | Longitudinal study of the relation between changes in theoretical orientations and values of trainees and the orientations and values of their supervisors | 1. None of the supervisory antecedent variables was found to contribute independently to changes in trainee orientation or values over training year. 2. At the end of the training year, factor relating to the belief that the therapist's personality is crucial to psychotherapy was significantly predicted by supervisors' scores on that factor; trainees became significantly more like the supervisors who had been rated as second and third most influential. 3. Supervisors' orientations were found to exert a reliable influence on trainees' theoretical orientations three to five years following conclusion of the training experience. |

Authors	Sample	Supervisors	Trainees	Design	Instrument	Theory	Selected Findings
Hillerbrand & Claiborn (1990)	Two midwestern universities and the Midwest region	None	Seventeen experts (over five years post-Ph.D. clinical experience and other criteria), fifteen novice (Ph.D. students with one to three semesters of practica experience)	2×3 repeated measures ANOVA on the primary and alternative diagnoses given for each case, 2×3 repeated measures MANOVA	Psychological report of case materials, five-point Likert scales examining the trainees' feelings and attitudes about the task: (a) accuracy of client diagnoses, (b) number of diagnoses, (c) rationale for the diagnoses, (d) predictions of future behavior (this study)	To explore differences in reasoning ability between expert and novice counselors engaging in different levels of cases within a diagnostic task	1. Experts rated themselves as significantly more knowledgeable; indicated that they felt significantly more confident about their responses and rated the cases as significantly clearer.

| Holloway, Freund, Gardner, Nelson, & Walker (1989) | Goodyear (1982) videotape series | Norman Kagan, Erving Polster, Carl Rogers, Albert Ellis, and Rudolph Ekstein | Harold Hackney | Sequential analysis; Z-score | Penman (1980) classification system | Multiple case study: a functional analysis of the supervision interviews | 1. All supervisors depended on a teacher-like role to communicate their observations regarding the client.
2. Each supervisor used the above pattern of discourse in combination with others in manners that were unique to each other.
3. Kagan promoted a more egalitarian supervisory relationship than the other supervisors. The highest proportion of his messages were in the form of exchange rather than advice. |

Authors	Sample	Supervisors	Trainees	Design	Instrument	Theory	Selected Findings
Kennard, Stewart, & Gluck (1987)	Two southwestern universities' clinical psychology programs	Forty-seven of ninety-four supervisors identified as providing extremely positive or extremely negative supervision experiences; sixty-eight supervision dyads, with 10 percent of the supervisors identified as both negative and positive	Twenty-six Ph.D. students (12 female, 14 male)	ANOVAs adjusted with $p = .01$ to minimize error, chi-square	Six-point Likert scale ratings on the frequencies of supervisory behaviors as recalled by the trainees; six-point Likert scale ratings on the perceptions of trainee dimensions; six-point Likert scale ratings by all participants, giving an overall rating of the quality of the supervisory experience (this study)	To explore variables influencing supervisor-trainee interactions that may contribute to positive or negative experiences in psychotherapy supervision	1. The positive experience group received significantly higher overall ratings by the supervisor and were significantly different in two dimensions: the trainee's interest in the supervisor's suggestions regarding professional development and the trainee's interest in the supervisor's feedback. The group also rated their supervisors significantly higher on the behavioral style dimensions of "supportive," "instructional," and "interpretive." 2. Positive pair members were more likely to have similar theoretical orientation and interpretive style.

| Kivlighan (1989) | One midwestern university, master's-level counseling program | None | Twenty-six (thirteen in a counseling methods class, thirteen not enrolled but with equivalent experience; twenty-six volunteer student clients (eighteen female, eight male) | Pretest, posttest nonequivalent design, MANOVAs | Intentions list (Hill & O'Grady, 1985), client reaction system (Hill, Helms, Spiegel, & Tichenor, 1988), HCVRCS (Hill et al., 1981), SEQ (Stiles & Snow, 1984) | To assess changes in counselor intentions and client reactions as a function of training in interpersonal dynamic training methods | 1. Student clients seen by trained trainees saw their post-semester session as deeper. 2. Trained trainees decreased their use of assessment intentions and increased their use of explore intentions and decreased their use of questions and increased their use of minimal encouragers relative to untrained trainees. |

Authors	Sample	Supervisors	Trainees	Design	Instrument	Theory	Selected Findings
Kivlighan, Angelone, & Swafford (1991)	One large midwestern university	One Ph.D., eight advanced doctoral counseling psychology students (novice supervisors)	Forty-eight master's level counseling students (twenty-nine female, nineteen male); forty-eight volunteer students receiving course credit, (between 78 percent and 82 percent female)	Chi-square, MANOVAs, ANOVAs, ANCOVAs multivariate t-test	WAI (Horvath & Greenberg, 1989), SEQ (Stiles & Snow, 1984), intentions list (Hill & O'Grady, 1985)	To compare the effects of live supervision to those of supervision using videotape	1. Clients of beginning trainees receiving live supervision perceived their sessions as rougher and perceived stronger working alliances than did clients of trainees receiving videotaped supervision. 2. Beginning trainees receiving live supervision used more relationship, set limits, and support intentions than trainees receiving videotaped supervision.

| Krause & Allen (1988) | Thirty-one university counseling centers | Eighty-seven post-Ph.D. supervisors | Seventy-seven doctoral students, mean counseling experience = 2.7 years | MANOVAs between correlated self-report question-naires | Supervision questionnaire (this study) | Empirical analysis of perceived supervisor behaviors | 1. Supervisors perceived themselves as varying their behavior with trainees of different developmental levels in a manner that accorded with Stoltenberg's (1981) model. 2. Trainees did not perceive differences in supervisor behavior. 3. Trainees, but not supervisors, in congruent dyads (rating trainee level) reported significantly more satisfaction. 4. All levels of trainees preferred a more collegial, self-reflexive, and mutually respectful interaction, with elements of counseling analogue. |

Authors	Sample	Supervisors	Trainees	Design	Instrument	Theory	Selected Findings
Martin, Goodyear, & Newton (1987)	One midwestern university counseling center	One Ph.D. counseling psychologist (male)	One Ph.D. student (female, thirty-three years old, with master's degree, and seven years of counseling experience)	Case study	SEQ (Stiles & Snow 1984), SSI (Friedlander & Ward, 1984), IMI (Kiesler, 1985), CIQ (Heppner & Roehlke, 1984), Penman Observation Coding System (Penman, 1980), MBTI (Myers-Briggs, 1962)	To follow a supervisory dyad through a semester, using multiple measures of process and outcome and both quantitative and qualitative data	1. Supervisor-trainee relation appeared to coalesce during the second session, the one that both parties identified as better. 2. Similarities and differences in MBTI score between both parties appeared consistent with their styles and the focus of their work together. 3. Differences in activity level between best and worst sessions were consistent with other findings. 4. Relatively small proportion of support statements by the supervisor was consistent with observations of actual supervisor statements and at variance with studies of trainee's perceptions of what the supervisor offered.

Study		Sample		Analysis	Instrument	Purpose	Findings
Martin, Slemon, Hiebert, Hallberg, & Cummings (1989)	None	Twenty-three counselors from one central and one western Canadian university	Twenty-three: eleven experienced counselors (eight Ph.D., three master's; six male, five female); twelve novice counselors (in second year of master's program)	$2 \times 2 \times 3$ MANOVA, ANOVAs on pooled CMT responses	CMT (Hiebert, 1987)	To examine the effect of level of experience on counselors' conceptualizations of general counseling process and specific client problems in nonanalogue settings	1. Novice counselors required more additional client-specific concepts to conceptualize individual clients and their problems than did experienced counselors.
McNeill, Stoltenberg, & Pierce (1985)	None	Eight counseling or clinical training programs, East, Midwest, South, and West	Ninety-one Ph.D. students (fifty female, forty-one male)	ANOVAs	SLQ (this study)	Stoltenberg's (1981) developmental theory	1. Expected significant differences for beginning versus intermediate trainees in Self-Awareness and Dependency-Autonomy, for intermediate versus advanced trainees in Dependency-Autonomy and Theory/Skills Acquisition, for beginning versus advanced trainees in Self-Awareness, Dependency-Autonomy and Theory/Skills Acquisition

Authors	Sample	Supervisors	Trainees	Design	Instrument	Theory	Selected Findings
McNeill, Stoltenberg, & Romans (1992)	Eight counseling or clinical training programs (East, Midwest, South, West)	None	104 Ph.D. students (66 female, 39 male)	Correlation, MANOVA, ANOVA, one-tailed t-tests	SLQ-R (this study)	Stoltenberg & Delworth's (1987) developmental theory	1. Significant differences found between the beginning and advanced trainees and the intermediate and advanced trainees in the expected direction. 2. Evidence of a lack of ceiling effects on the SLQ-R, suggesting higher possible range for scores of counselors who possess higher levels of experience.
Nelson & Holloway (1992)	Four counselor education programs in Oregon	Thirty-nine with graduate degrees, one no graduate degree (twenty female, twenty male)	Forty graduate students, mean practicum experience = eight credit hours (twenty female, twenty male)	MANOVAs; ANOVAs	Penman (1980) classification scheme	To investigate the dimensions of power and involvement as they relate to trainee and supervisor gender	1. Male and female supervisors reinforced their female trainees' high-power messages with low-power, encouraging messages significantly less often than they did with male trainees. 2. Female trainees were found to be significantly less likely to assume an expert role in response to supervisor low power then were male trainees.

| Nichols, Nichols, & Hardy (1990) | AAMFT-approved supervisors | 276 supervisors (224 Track 1, 52 Track 2) | None | Survey of approved AAMFT supervisors, 72.4 percent return rate | Replication of Everett (1980) survey | To compare supervisors and supervision between 1980 and 1990 | 1. More supervisors in 1990 study were female, younger than age forty-five, divorced, and were experienced clinical practitioners having ten or more years of MFT experience. 2. Major shift in clinical orientation was toward a systems orientation (36.4 percent) and in methods of supervision was from audio recordings to live supervision. 3. The use of video recordings nearly doubled, from 32.2 to 62.7 percent. 4. Fewer supervisors reported having participated in personal therapy. |

Authors	Sample	Super-visors	Trainees	Design	Instrument	Theory	Selected Findings
Olk & Fried-lander (1992) Study 1	Psychology training centers, hospital outpatient clinics and inpatient units, community mental health centers, and other mental health agencies	Six super-visors (four male, two female)	Nine trainees (five female, four male; three Ph.D. practicum, three interns, three post-doctoral)	Seventy-five items con-structed from inter-views with the sample; nineteen role ambiguity (RA) items and ten role conflict (RC) items were retained by a panel of ten experts	Role Conflict and Role Ambiguity Inventory (RCRAI)	Construction of the RCRAI	1. A twenty-nine-item scale for measuring role conflict and role ambiguity was constructed.

Study 2	National sample of counseling and clinical psychology practicum, advanced practicum, internship, and post-doctoral training sites	None	240 trainees (137 female, 97 male, and 6 who declined to indicate their gender), 80 practicum students, 126 interns, 33 postinterns	Item-scale correlations, internal consistency alpha coefficients, factor analysis, t-test, reduced model tests, univariate F tests	TPRS-R (Holloway & Wampold, 1984), JDI (Smith, Kendall, & Hullin, 1969), STAI (Spielberger, Gorusch, Lushene, Vagg, & Jacobs, 1983), demographic questionnaire	Test validity and reliability of the RCRAI and to evaluate role ambiguity and role conflict at different levels of counselor experience	1. Final version of the RCRAI is a sixteen-item RC scale and a thirteen-item RA scale, which was found to be both a reliable and valid measure of its constructs. 2. Role difficulties were predictive of more work-related anxiety, general work dissatisfaction, and dissatisfaction with supervision. 3. When role conflict was held constant, more role ambiguity was associated with less counseling experience.

Authors	Sample	Super-visors	Trainees	Design	Instrument	Theory	Selected Findings
Putney, Worthington, & McCullough (1992)	Thirty-one APA-approved training sites, nationwide (17 clinical psychology, 14 counseling psychology)	Eighty-four Ph.D.s (thirty-two female, fifty-two male)	Eighty-four Ph.D. interns (forty-eight female, thirty-six male)	Three 2×2 ANOVAs, stepwise multiple regression to predict perceived supervisor effectiveness	Personal data sheet (this study), supervisor data sheet (this study), SQ-R (Worthington, 1984), supervisor role questionnaire (Goodyear, Abadie, & Efros, 1984), supervisor focus questionnaire (Goodyear et al., 1984), supervisor effectiveness questionnaire (Cross & Brown, 1983)	To examine the effects of supervisor and trainee theoretical orientation on the trainees' perceptions of supervisors' models, roles, and foci; also to investigate variables influencing quality of supervision and trainee autonomy	1. Humanistic-psychodynamic supervisors were perceived to emphasize the supervisory relationship more than were cognitive-behavioral supervisors. 2. Cognitive-behavioral supervisors were perceived to assume the consultant role and to focus on trainees' mastery of skills and strategies more than humanistic-psychodynamic supervisors. 3. Humanistic-psychodynamic supervisors were perceived to focus on trainees' conceptualization of client dynamics more than cognitive-behavioral supervisors. 4. Greater perceived theoretical similarity, greater degree of theoretical match, and supervisor gender (female supervisors were perceived as more effective) were found to predict supervisor effectiveness individually and as a three-variable model. 5. Lack of gender match, perceived similarity of theoretical orientation, and less supervisor strength of adherence to theory.

| Rabinowitz, Heppner, & Roehlke (1986) | Large midwestern university, counseling center, APA-accredited internship | For the beginning trainees, doctoral interns; for the advanced trainees, licensed psychologists on counseling center staff | Forty-five: twenty-two beginning practicum students (twelve female, ten male), nine advanced practicum students (six female, three male), fourteen doctoral interns (eight female, six male) | Chi-square, ANOVAs | Two-part supervision checklist (this study): Part 1, the most important supervisory issues that week; Part 2, the most important supervisory intervention made that week | To examine trainees' perceptions of important issues and supervisor interventions on a weekly basis over one semester | 1. Most important issues and interventions across all levels of experience were related to supervisory support, treatment planning, and advice and direction from the supervisor. 2. The major issue across all levels of experience in the first three weeks of the semester was the clarification of the supervisory relationship. 3. More experienced trainees were likely to be concerned with personal issues' interfering with counseling. 4. Beginning trainees in the middle phase of the study were more concerned with their supervisors' believing that they have sufficient skills to be competent, the development of a treatment plan, and receiving support from their supervisor. 5. Advanced trainees were more concerned during the middle phase with "confronting a personal blind spot" and having confidence to make interventions independent of their supervisor's guidance. |

Authors	Sample	Supervisors	Trainees	Design	Instrument	Theory	Selected Findings
Robinson & Kinner (1988) Study 1	One university counseling center, Southwest	None	Twenty-two first-semester master's-level counseling students (fourteen female, eight male)	Multivariate t-test	CTRL (Delaney & Eisenberg, 1977)	Comparison of the effectiveness of self-instructional training (SI) to traditional training (TT) and handout-only training (HO)	1. No difference between trainees who receive SI and those who received TT. 2. The combined SI and TT group outperformed the HO group on dependent variables (DVs) of quantity, content, and type, but not on delivery.
Study 2	Same	None	Thirty first-semester master's-level counseling students (twenty female, ten male)	Multivariate t-test	Written responses to videotaped vignettes	Same	1. No difference between trainees who received SI and those who received TT, or those who received HO.

Study						
Study 3	Same	None	Twenty first-semester master's-level counseling students (fourteen female, six male)	Hotelling T	Oral responses to videotaped vignettes	Comparison of the effects of TT and SI on orally produced paraphrases	1. No difference between trainees who received SI and those who received TT.
Robyak, Goodyear, & Prange (1987)	Eleven counseling center training agencies, nationwide	Fifty-six supervisors from these agencies (twenty female, thirty-six male)	None	ANCOVA, IV: supervisor sex, supervisory focus, amount of supervisor experience; covariate: amount of direct service counseling experience	Power base scale (this study)	Investigation of the extent to which sex, amount of supervisory experience, and supervisory focus affect supervisors' preferences for the use of referent, expert, and legitimate power base	1. Male supervisors reported greater preference for the referent power base. 2. Less experienced supervisors preferred the referent power base. 3. Supervisors who focused on self-awareness preferred the expert power base.

Authors	Sample	Supervisors	Trainees	Design	Instrument	Theory	Selected Findings
Robyak, Goodyear, Prange, & Donham (1986)	Seven counseling psychology and nine counseling programs	None	102 participants (64 female, 38 male)	ANOVA	Power base scale (this study)	Test of preference for power base of the trainee in a hypothetical therapeutic situation	1. Preference for legitimate and referent power bases were found to increase as a function of supervised experience. 2. Neither gender nor type of presenting problem had a significant effect on trainees' preferences for any of the power bases.
Schiavone & Jessell (1988)	Eight university counseling centers, East and Midwest	None	Eighty-six master's-level counselor education students (forty-four female, forty-two male)	2 × 2 factorial design with three treatment dimensions	CRF (Barak & LaCrosse, 1975); CRF (adapted from Aubrey, 1978)	Examination of the effects of counselor and supervisor status and gender on trainees' perceptions of the supervisory characteristics of expertness and competence	1. Perceptions of supervisor expertness not affected by any interaction of supervisor gender, trainee gender, or attributed supervisor expertness. 2. Supervisor-ascribed expertness was rated significantly more favorably than was ascribed non-expertness.

| Stoltenberg, Pierce, & McNeill (1987) | Six counseling and two clinical programs, East, Midwest, South, and West | None | Ninety-one Ph.D. students (50 female, 41 male) | ANOVA, preplanned multiple comparisons | SNQ (this study); demographic questionnaire (this study) | Stoltenberg's (1981) proposition that counselor trainees' needs change as a function of developmental level | 1. Based on level of education, significant differences in the predicted direction between levels 2 and 3 for structure and overall needs, as well as between levels 1 and 3 for structure, feedback, and overall needs.
 2. Based on semesters of previous counseling experience, significant differences were found in the predicted direction between levels 1 and 2 for feedback, and between levels 1 and 3 for structure, feedback, and overall needs.
 3. Based on number of semesters of previous supervision, significant differences were found in the predicted direction between levels 1 and 3 for structure feedback, and overall needs, and between levels 2 and 3 for feedback. |

Authors	Sample	Supervisors	Trainees	Design	Instrument	Theory	Selected Findings
Stone & Amundson (1989)	Community crisis center, North Vancouver, Canada	Five counseling professionals (two female, five male)	Seven clinical Ph.D. students (two female, five male)	Hoyt Estimate of Reality and Chronbach's alpha for item analysis, correlation between trainee and supervisor scores for all six scales, Six 2 (Ss/Tr ratings) × 3(groups) × 3 (conditions) ANOVAs	Evaluation questionnaire: thirty-nine items requiring the trainees to rate the effects of the two case presentation methods (this study)	To compare metaphoric case drawing (MCD) and verbal case debriefing (VCD) methods of supervision	1. Scales were found to be highly internally consistent. 2. Both supervisors and trainees recorded similar ratings for VCD and MCD. 3. MCD method appears to increase trainee understanding on five target areas of client dynamics, counselor's role, client-counselor relationship, counseling goals, and case presentation effectiveness, and specifically in relation to themes of relationship problems, manipulative clients, depression, and suicide.

| Strozier, Kivlighan, & Thoreson (1993) | University of Missouri–Columbia, University counseling center internship site | One Ph.D. (male) | One Ph.D. intern (female) | Case study, frequency distribution, sequential analysis (cluster analysis; Hill, Helms, Tichenor, Spiegel, O'Grady, & Perry, 1988), chi-square to assess the use of intentions clusters across the samples | SEQ (Stiles & Snow, 1984), Supervisor Intentions List (this study), Trainee Reactions System (this study), Helpfulness Rating Scale (Elliot, 1985) | To examine the supervision process through evaluation of supervisor intentions and trainee reactions | 1. Supervisors use of the Assessment intention cluster significantly reduces the likelihood of the trainee's feeling supported. 2. Positive circuits of clusters were Relationship-Support-Relationship, Restructure-Challenged/Therapeutic Work-Restructure, Support-No Reaction-Support, Set Limits-No Reaction-Set Limits. 3. Both the supervisor and the trainee indicated that Relationship, Change, Explore, and Restructure were the most helpful intention clusters. 4. Both supervisor and trainee indicated that the supervisor's interventions were more helpful when the trainee used the supported reaction cluster. |

Authors	Sample	Supervisors	Trainees	Design	Instrument	Theory	Selected Findings
Thompson (1986)	Western Australian Institute of Technology	None	Thirteen first-year counseling graduate students (eleven female, two male), thirteen third-year undergraduate psychology students (ten female, three male)	Kappa statistic, 2 × 2 repeated measures ANOVA (group × interview), 2 × 2 repeated measures MANOVA (group × interview)	HCVRS (Hill, 1978; Hill et al., 1981), POI (Shostrum, 1963), quality ratings (this study; seven-point Likert, used by two experienced raters), student counselor ratings (this study; ten-minute interview)	To compare graduate counseling students with undergraduates who received relevant psychology training but nonspecific counselor training over a one-year period	1. Graduate students increased their use of open questions, closed questions, restatements, information, and confrontation responses and decreased their use of interpretations, minimal encouragers, and other responses (those related to the client's problems). 2. Undergraduates increased their use of self-disclosure, other, information, closed questions, and restatement responses and decreased their use of minimal encouragers. 3. Graduates became more inner directed and increased their self-acceptance. 4. Undergraduates became less inner directed and decreased their self-acceptance.

Author	Setting		Subjects	Instruments	Analysis	Purpose	Results
Tracey, Ellickson, & Sherry (1989)	Two APA-approved counseling psychology programs	None	Seventy-eight: forty beginning practicum counselors (up to one completed semester of counseling practicum), thirty-eight advanced practicum counselors (two or more completed semesters of completed practicum and not yet enrolled in practicum internship)	TRS (Dowd, Milne, & Wise, 1984), SES (this study), CRF-S (Corrigan & Schmidt, 1983), CDQ (Reising & Daniels, 1983)	Two-way (Experience Level × Reactance Level) MANOVA, MANOVAs on the high-structure versus low-structure suicide content tapes, the relationship between content tapes, t-test on levels of perceived realism between the above two tapes, three-way MANOVA (Experience Level × Reactance Potential Level × Structure)	To examine reactions of trainees of differing experience levels to different supervisory environments	1. In the crisis content condition, all trainees preferred structured supervision regardless of their reactance or experience level. 2. In noncrisis content supervision, beginning trainees preferred structured supervision, in the form of directive teaching and prescription, while more experienced trainees preferred less structure. 3. Advanced trainees with high reactance preferred supervision with less structure than did advanced trainees with low reactance.

Authors	Sample	Super-visors	Trainees	Design	Instrument	Theory	Selected Findings
Tracey & Sherry (1993)	One eastern university counseling center	Six: three Ph.D. and three Ph.D. interns	Eleven with at least one semester of previous practicum experience (six female, five male)	Loglinear analysis	SOQ (this study), inter-personal circumplex quadrant codes using the descrip-tions provided by Leary (1957) and LaForge & Suczek (1955)	To study the difference in the supervi-sion process by outcome, controlling for specific supervisor style differ-ences, focusing on only super-visors who had a good outcome and a poor out-come case	1. Given submissive-hostile trainee behavior, the supervisor in successful supervision (SS) did not demonstrate a predictable pattern of responding, and the supervisor in less successful supervision (LS) was more likely to respond with dominant-friendly behavior and less likely to respond with dominant-hostile behavior. 2. Given dominant-hostile trainee behavior, the SS were least likely to respond in a sub-missive-friendly manner, and the LS were most likely to respond in a dominant-hostile manner. 3. The LS were more likely to match the trainee in both power and affiliation, whereas this pattern was not true for the SS.

Study	Sample			Analysis	Instrument	Purpose/Model	Findings
Wetchler (1988)	AAMFT-approved supervisors, national sample	318 (122 female, 193 male), 213 Ph.D.s, 104 master's level	None	Survey, frequency count; response rate = 44.6 percent	Forced-choice questionnaire (this study)	To examine primary and secondary influential theories of AAMFT-approved supervisors in the United States	1. The most influential primary theory was structural family therapy (21 percent), and the second was intergenerational (16.4 percent). 2. The most influential secondary theory was intergenerational (19.2 percent), with structural (15.4 percent) following.
Wiley & Ray (1986)	Nine university counseling centers, East, Midwest, Southwest	71: 45 percent full-time counseling center staff, 28 percent counseling center interns, 18 percent part-time counseling center staff/faculty, 8 percent other; 65 percent Ph.D.	107: 72 percent Ph.D. students, 28 percent master's students; mean counseling experience 3.8 semesters	ANOVA and chi-square	SLS (this study); outcome instrument (this study)	Stoltenberg's (1981) Counselor Complexity Model	1. Most trainees were in supervision environments congruent to their developmental level. 2. Significant differences were found for mean number of semesters of supervised counseling experience grouped by developmental level. 3. No significant differences were found for number of years of nonsupervised counseling experience by developmental level. 4. Satisfaction and learning as perceived by both trainees and supervisors were not related to the degree of congruency between the person and the environment.

Authors	Sample	Supervisors	Trainees	Design	Instrument	Theory	Selected Findings
Winter & Holloway (1992)	Three western university counseling centers	None	Twenty-six doctoral students, thirty master's students (thirty-eight female, eighteen male)	Multiple regression analysis	A measure of counselor experience; PCM (Hunt, Butler, Noy, & Rosser, 1978); videotape of supervision approaches (Goodyear, 1982)	Trainee experience (trainee development), trainee conceptual level, supervisor approach	1. Less experienced trainees preferred focus on client conceptualization, while more experienced trainees preferred to focus on their personal growth. 2. Trainees with higher conceptual levels were more likely to prefer to focus on development of counseling skills. 3. Supports developmental supervision models suggesting that as trainees increase in experience, they prefer to focus increasingly on personal issues. 4. More experienced trainees were less fearful of negative evaluation.

ABBREVIATIONS KEY

AAMFT	American Association of Marriage and Family Therapists
APA	American Psychological Association
BLRI	Barrett-Lennard Relationship Inventory
BSRI	Bem Sex-Role Inventory
BTC	Behavioral Target Complaints
CDQ	Counselor Development Questionnaire
CERS	Counselor Evaluation Rating Scale
CIQ	Critical Incidents Questionnaire
CMT	Cognitive Mapping Task
COQ	Counseling-Orientation Questionnaire
CPQ	Counselor Perception Questionnaire
CRCS	Counselor Retrospective Coding System
CRF	Counselor Rating Form
CRF-S	Counselor Rating Form–Short Version
CTRL	Counselor Tacting Response Lead
CVRMCS	Counselor Verbal Response Modes Category System
FTRS	Family Therapist Rating Scale
HCVRCS-R	Hill Counselor Verbal Response Category System–Revised
ICRS	Interpersonal Communication Rating Scale
I-E	Internal-External Locus of Control Scale
IMI	Impact Message Inventory
JDI	Job Description Index
MBI	Maslach Burnout Inventory
MBTI	Myers-Briggs Type Inventory
MDS	Multidimensional Scaling
MFT	Marriage and Family Therapy
MMPI	Minnesota Multiphasic Personality Inventory
PCM	Paragraph Completion Method
POI	Personal Orientation Inventory
RCRAI	Role Conflict and Role Ambiguity Inventory
RCC/RCCCS	Relational Communication Control Coding System

SCL-90	Symptom Checklist
SCT	Sentence Completion Test of Ego Development
SD	Sematic Differential
SDSS	Self-Disclosure Situations Survey
SEI	Self-Efficacy Inventory
SEQ (Bahrick et al.)	Supervision Expectations Questionnaire
SEQ (Stiles & Snow)	Session Evaluation Questionnaire
SER	Supervisor Evaluation Ratings
SLQ	Supervisee Levels Questionnaire
SLQ-R	Supervisee Levels Questionnaire–Revised
SLS	Supervisee Level Scale
SNQ	Supervisee Needs Questionnaire
SOQ	Supervision Outcome Questionnaire
SPF	Supervisor Perception Form
SQ	Supervision Questionnaire
SQ-R	Supervision Questionnaire–Revised
SFC	Supervision Focus Coding System
SFRS	Supervisory Feedback Rating System
SRF	Supervisor Rating Form
SSI	Supervisor Style Inventory
STAI	State-Trait Anxiety Inventory
SWAI	Supervisory Working Alliance Inventory
TOQ	Theoretical Orientation Questionnaire
TPRS	Trainee Personal Reaction Scale
TRS	Therapeutic Reactance Scale
VPPS	Vanderbilt Psychotherapy Process Scales
WAI	Working Alliance Inventory

─⁓─ Notes

Introduction

1. Stoltenberg, C. D., & Delworth, U. (1987). *Supervising counselors and therapists: A developmental approach*. San Francisco: Jossey-Bass.
2. Stoltenberg, C. D. (1981). Approaching supervision from a developmental perspective: The counselor complexity model. *Journal of Counseling Psychology, 28*(1), 59–65.
3. Worthington, E. L., Jr. (1987). Changes in supervision as counselors and supervisors gain experience. *Professional Psychology: Research and Practice, 18*(3), 189–208.
4. Loganbill, C., Hardy, E., & Delworth, U. (1982). Supervision: A conceptual model. *Counseling Psychologist, 10*(1), 3–42.
5. Holloway, E. L. (1987). Developmental models of supervision: Is it development? *Professional Psychology: Research and Practice, 18*(3), 209–216.
6. Bernard, J. M., & Goodyear, R. K. (1992). *Fundamentals of clinical supervision*. Boston: Allyn and Bacon.
7. McNeill, B. W., Hom, K. L., & Perez, J. A. (1995). The training and supervisory needs of racial/ethnic minority students. *Journal of Multicultural Counseling and Development, 23*, 246–258.
8. Stoltenberg, C. D., McNeill, B. W., & Crethar, H. C. (1994). Changes in supervision as counseling and therapists gain experience: A review. *Professional Psychology: Research and Practice, 25*, 416–449.
9. Eichenfield, G., & Stoltenberg, C. D. (1996). The sub-level 1 trainee: Some developmental difficulties encountered with counselor training. *Clinical Supervisor, 14*, 25–37.
10. Stoltenberg, C. D., McNeill, B. W., & Crethar, H. C. (1995). Persuasion and development in counselor supervision. *Counseling Psychologist, 23*, 633–648.

Chapter One

1. Stoltenberg, C. D., McNeill, B. W., & Crethar, H. C. (1994). Changes in supervision as counselors and therapists gain experience: A review. *Professional Psychology: Research and Practice, 25,* 416–449.

2. Anderson, J. R. (1985). *Cognitive psychology and its implications* (2nd ed.). San Francisco: Freeman. Anderson, J. R. (1996). ACT: A simple theory of complex cognition. *American Psychologist, 51,* 355–365.

3. Anderson (1985, 1996). *ibid.*

4. Anderson (1996). *ibid.* Anderson, J. R. (1983). *The architecture of cognition.* Cambridge, MA: Harvard University Press.

5. Gagné, E. D., Yekovich, C. W., & Yekovich, F. R. (1993). *The cognitive psychology of school learning* (2nd ed.). New York: HarperCollins.

6. Stoltenberg, C. D., McNeill, B. W., & Crethar, H. C. (1995). Persuasion and development in counselor supervision. *Counseling Psychologist, 23,* 633–648.

7. Strong, S. R. (1968). Counseling: An interpersonal influence process. *Journal of Counseling Psychology, 15,* 215–224. Strong, S. R., & Matross, R. P. (1973). Change processes in counseling and psychotherapy. *Journal of Counseling Psychology, 20,* 28–37.

8. Dixon, D. N., & Claiborn, C. D. (1987). A social influence approach to counselor supervision. In J. E. Maddux, C. D. Stoltenberg, & R. Rosenwein (Eds.), *Social processes in clinical and counseling psychology* (pp. 83–93). New York: Springer-Verlag.

9. Petty, R. E., & Cacioppo, J. T. (1986). *Communication and persuasion: Central and peripheral routes to attitude change.* New York: Springer-Verlag.

10. Lerner, R. M. (1986). *Concepts and theories of human development* (2nd ed.). New York: Random House.

11. Harris, D. B. (1957). *The concept of development.* Minneapolis: University of Minnesota Press. Schneirla, T. C. (1957). The concept of development in comparative psychology. In D. B. Harris (Ed.), *The concept of development.* Minneapolis: University of Minnesota Press.

12. Werner, H., & Kaplan, B. (1956). The developmental approach to cognition: Its relevance to the psychological interpretation of anthropological and ethnolinguistic data. *American Anthropologist, 58,* 866–880. Kaplan, B. (1983). A trio of trials. In R. M. Lerner (Ed.), *Developmental psychology: Historical and philosophical perspectives.* Hillsdale, NJ: Erlbaum.

13. Baltes, P. B., Reese, H. W., & Nesselroade, J. R. (1977). *Life-span developmental psychology: Introduction to research methods.* Monterey, CA: Brooks/Cole.

14. Lerner (1986). *ibid.*

15. Baltes, Reese, & Nesselroade (1977). *ibid.*
16. Lerner (1986). *ibid.*
17. Lerner (1986). *ibid.*
18. Stoltenberg, C. D., & Delworth, U. (1987). *Supervising counselors and therapists.* San Francisco: Jossey-Bass.
19. Lerner (1986). *ibid.*
20. Worthington, E. L., Jr. (1987). Changes in supervision as counselors and supervisors gain experience. *Professional Psychology: Research and Practice, 18*(3), 189–208.
21. Stoltenberg, McNeill, & Crethar (1994). *ibid.*

Chapter Two

1. Watkins, C. E., Jr. (1996, August). *Developmental approaches to psychotherapy supervision: Translating theory into practice.* Paper presented at the annual meeting of the American Psychological Association, Toronto, Canada.
2. Stoltenberg, C. D. (1981). Approaching supervision from a developmental perspective: The counselor complexity model. *Journal of Counseling Psychology, 28*(1), 59–65. Loganbill, C., Hardy, E., & Delworth, U. (1982). Supervision: A conceptual model. *Counseling Psychologist, 10*(1), 3–42.
3. Jacobson, N. S., & Christensen, A. (1996). *Integrative couple therapy: Promoting acceptance and change.* New York: Norton.
4. Leach, M. M., Stoltenberg, C. D., McNeill, B. W., & Eichenfield, G. A. (in press). Self-efficacy and counselor development: Testing the Integrated Developmental Model. *Counselor Education and Supervision.*
5. Tracey, T. J., Ellickson, J. L., & Sherry, P. (1989). Reactance in relation to different supervisory environments and counselor development. *Journal of Counseling Psychology, 36,* 336–344.
6. Finkelstein, H., & Tuckman, A. (1997). Supervision of psychological assessment: A developmental model. *Professional Psychology: Research and Practice, 28,* 92–95.
7. Beutler, L. E., & Clarkin, J. (1990). *Systematic treatment selection: Toward targeted therapeutic interventions.* New York: Brunner/Mazel.
8. Hale, K., & Stoltenberg, C. D. (1988). The effects of self-awareness and evaluation apprehension on counselor trainee anxiety. *Clinical Supervisor, 6,* 49–69. Stoltenberg, C. D., McNeill, B. W., & Crethar, H. C. (1994). Changes in supervision as counselors and therapists gain experience: A review. *Professional Psychology: Research and Practice, 25,* 416–449.

9. Gilligan, C. (1982). *In a different voice: Psychological theory and women's development*. Cambridge, MA: Harvard University Press.

Chapter Three

1. Eichenfield, G., & Stoltenberg, C. D. (1996). The sub-level 1 trainee: Some developmental difficulties encountered with counselor training. *Clinical Supervisor, 14*, 25–37.
2. Stoltenberg, C. D., McNeill, B. W., & Crethar, H. C. (1994). Changes in supervision as counselors and therapists gain experience: A review. *Professional Psychology: Research and Practice, 25*, 416–449.
3. Hale, K., & Stoltenberg, C. D. (1988). The effects of self-awareness and evaluation apprehension on counselor trainee anxiety. *Clinical Supervisor, 6*, 49–69.
4. Duval, S., & Wicklund, R. A. (1972). *A theory of objective self-awareness*. Orlando, FL: Academic Press.
5. Stoltenberg, C. D., & Delworth, U. (1987). *Supervising counselors and therapists*. San Francisco: Jossey-Bass.
6. Beutler, L. E., & Clarkin, J. (1990). *Systematic treatment selection: Toward targeted therapeutic interventions*. New York: Brunner/Mazel.
7. Schneider, S. F. (1990). Psychology at a crossroads. *American Psychologist, 45*, 521–529.
8. Kagan, H. (1975). Influencing human interaction—Eleven years with IPR. *Canadian Counselor, 9*, 74–97. Ivey, A. E. (1971). *Microcounseling: Innovations in interviewing training*. Springfield, IL: Thomas.
9. Boylan, J. D., Malley, P. B., & Scott, J. (1995). *Practicum and internship: Textbook for counseling and psychotherapy* (2nd ed.). Washington, DC: Accelerated Development.
10. Guest, P. D., & Beutler, L. E. (1988). Impact of psychotherapy supervision on therapist orientation and values. *Journal of Consulting and Clinical Psychology, 56*, 653–658.
11. Krause, A. A., & Allen, G. J. (1988). Perceptions of counselor supervision: An examination of Stoltenberg's model from the perspectives of supervisor and supervisee. *Journal of Counseling Psychology, 35*, 77–80. Stoltenberg, C. D. (1981). Approaching supervision from a developmental perspective: The counselor complexity model. *Journal of Counseling Psychology, 28*(1), 59–65.
12. Wiley, M. O., & Ray, P. B. (1986). Counseling supervision by developmental level. *Journal of Counseling Psychology, 33*, 439–445. Ellis, M. V., & Dell,

D. M. (1986). Dimensionality of supervisor roles: Supervisors' perceptions of supervision. *Journal of Counseling Psychology, 33*, 315–324. Stoltenberg, C. D., Pierce, R. A., & McNeill, B. W. (1987). Effects of experience on counselor trainee's needs. *Clinical Supervisor, 5*, 23–32.

13. Stoltenberg, Pierce, & McNeill (1987). *ibid.* McNeill, B. W., Stoltenberg, C. D., & Pierce, R. A. (1985). Supervisees' perceptions of their development: A test of the counselor complexity model. *Journal of Counseling Psychology, 32*, 630–633. McNeill, B. W., Stoltenberg, C. D., & Romans, J. S. (1992). The integrated developmental model of supervision: Scale development and validation procedures. *Professional Psychology: Research and Practice, 23*, 504–508. Tracey, T. J., Ellickson, J. L., & Sherry, P. (1989). Reactance in relation to different supervisory environments and counselor development. *Journal of Counseling Psychology, 36*, 336–344.

14. McNeill, Stoltenberg, & Pierce (1985). *ibid.* McNeill, Stoltenberg, & Romans (1992). *ibid.*

15. Olk, M. E., & Friedlander, M. L. (1992). Trainees' experiences of role conflict and role ambiguity in supervisory relationships. *Journal of Counseling Psychology, 39*, 389–397. Winter, M., & Holloway, E. L. (1991). Relation of trainee experience, conceptual level, and supervisor approach to selection of audiotaped counseling passages. *Clinical Supervisor, 9*, 87–103.

16. Loganbill, C., Hardy, E., & Delworth, U. (1982). Supervision: A conceptual model. *Counseling Psychologist, 10*(1), 3–42.

17. Romans, J. S. C., Boswell, D. L., Carlozzi, A. F., & Ferguson, D. B. (1995). Training and supervision practices in clinical, counseling, and school psychology programs. *Professional Psychology: Research and Practice, 26*, 407–412.

18. Korzybski, A. (1948). *Science and sanity: An introduction to non-Aristotelian systems and general semantics* (3rd ed.). Lakeville, CT: International Non-Aristotelian Library.

19. Stoltenberg & Delworth (1987). *ibid.*

20. Eichenfield & Stoltenberg (1996). *ibid.*

21. Cummings, N. (1996). Now we're facing the consequences. *Scientist Practitioner, 6*, 9–13.

22. Maddux, J. E., Stoltenberg, C. D., & Rosenwein, R. (Eds.). (1987). *Social processes in clinical and counseling psychology*. New York: Springer-Verlag. Snyder, C. R., & Forsyth, D. R. (1991). *Handbook of social and clinical psychology: The health perspective*. New York: Pergamon Press.

23. Stoltenberg, C. D., McNeill, B. W., & Crethar, H. C. (1995). Persuasion and development in counselor supervision. *Counseling Psychologist, 23*,

633–648. Strong, S. R. (1968). Counseling: An interpersonal influence process. *Journal of Counseling Psychology, 15,* 215–224. Strong, S. R., & Matross, R. P. (1973). Change processes in counseling and psychotherapy. *Journal of Counseling Psychology, 20,* 28–37. Dixon, D. N., & Claiborn, C. D. (1987). A social influence approach to counselor supervision. In J. E. Maddux, C. D. Stoltenberg, & R. Rosenwein (Eds.), *Social processes in clinical and counseling psychology* (pp. 83–93). New York: Springer-Verlag. Petty, R. E., & Cacioppo, J. T. (1986). *Communication and persuasion: Central and peripheral routes to attitude change.* New York: Springer-Verlag.

24. Lopez, S. R., Gover, K. P., Holland, D., Johnson, M. J., Kain, C. D., Kanel, K., Mellins, C. A., & Rhyne, M. C. (1989). Development of culturally sensitive psychotherapists. *Professional Psychology: Research and Practice, 20,* 369–376.

Chapter Four

1. Gilligan, C. (1982). *In a different voice: Psychological theory and women's development.* Cambridge, MA: Harvard University Press.

2. Tracey, T. J., Ellickson, J. L., & Sherry, P. (1989). Reactance in relation to different supervisory environments and counselor development. *Journal of Counseling Psychology, 36,* 336–344.

3. Lopez, S. R., Gover, K. P., Holland, D., Johnson, M. J., Kain, C. D., Kanel, K., Mellins, C. A., & Rhyne, M. C. (1989). Development of culturally sensitive psychotherapists. *Professional Psychology: Research and Practice, 20,* 369–376.

4. Stoltenberg, C. D., Pierce, R. A., & McNeill, B. W. (1987). Effects of experience on counselor trainee's needs. *Clinical Supervisor, 5,* 23–32. Wiley, M. O., & Ray, P. B. (1986). Counseling supervision by developmental level. *Journal of Counseling Psychology, 33,* 439–445.

5. Rabinowitz, F. E., Heppner, P. P., & Roehlke, H. J. (1986). Descriptive study of process outcome variables of supervision over time. *Journal of Counseling Psychology, 33,* 292–300. McNeill, B. W., Stoltenberg, C. D., & Romans, J. S. (1992). The integrated developmental model of supervision: Scale development and validation procedures. *Professional Psychology: Research and Practice, 23,* 504–508.

6. Tracey et al. (1989). McNeill et al. (1992). McNeill, B. W., Stoltenberg, C. D., & Pierce, R. A. (1985). Supervisees' perceptions of their development: A test of the counselor complexity model. *Journal of Counseling Psychology, 32,* 630–633.

7. Worthington, E. L., Jr. (1987). Changes in supervision as counselors and supervisors gain experience. *Professional Psychology: Research and Practice, 18,* 189–208. Stoltenberg, C. D., McNeill, B. W., & Crethar, H. C. (1994). Changes in supervision as counselors and therapists gain experience: A review. *Professional Psychology: Research and Practice, 25,* 416–449.

8. Stoltenberg, C. D., & Delworth, U. (1987). *Supervising counselors and therapists.* San Francisco: Jossey-Bass.

9. Rabinowitz et al. (1986). Kennard, B. D., Stewart, S. M., & Gluck, M. R. (1987). The supervision relationship: Variables contributing to positive versus negative experiences. *Professional Psychology: Research and Practice, 18,* 172–175. Worthen, J., & McNeill, B. W. (1994). A phenomenological investigation of "good" supervision events. *Journal of Counseling Psychology, 43,* 25–34.

10. Petty, R. E., & Cacioppo, J. T. (1986). *Communication and persuasion: Central and peripheral routes to attitude change.* New York: Springer-Verlag.

11. Stoltenberg, C. D., McNeill, B. W., & Crethar, H. C. (1995). Persuasion and development in counselor supervision. *Counseling Psychologist, 23,* 633–648.

12. Stoltenberg & Delworth (1987). *ibid.*

13. Heppner, P. P., & Roelhke, H. J. (1984). Differences among supervisees at different levels of training: Implications for a developmental model of supervision. *Journal of Counseling Psychology, 31,* 76–90. McNeill, B. W., & Worthen, J. (1989). The parallel process in psychotherapy supervision. *Professional Psychotherapy: Research and Practice, 20,* 329–333.

14. Heppner & Roelhke (1984). *ibid.*

15. Heppner & Roelhke (1984). *ibid.*

Chapter Five

1. Wiley, M. O., & Ray, P. B. (1986). Counseling supervision by developmental level. *Journal of Counseling Psychology, 33,* 439–445.

2. Stoltenberg, C. D. (1981). Approaching supervision from a developmental perspective: The counselor complexity model. *Journal of Counseling Psychology, 28*(1), 59–65.

3. Smolak, L. (1993). *Adult development.* Englewood Cliffs, NJ: Prentice Hall.

4. Stoltenberg, C. D., & Delworth, U. (1987). *Supervising counselors and therapists.* San Francisco: Jossey-Bass.

5. Loevinger, J. (1976). *Ego development: Conceptions and theories.* San Francisco: Jossey-Bass.

6. Goldfried, M. R. (1980). Toward the delineation of therapeutic change principles. *American Psychologist, 35,* 991–999. Beutler, L. E., & Clarkin, J. (1990). *Systematic treatment selection: Toward targeted therapeutic interventions.* New York: Brunner/Mazel.

7. Jacobson, N. S. (1991). Toward enhancing the efficacy of marital therapy and marital therapy research. *Journal of Family Psychology, 4,* 373–393.

8. Minuchin, S., & Fishman, H. C. (1981). *Family therapy techniques.* Cambridge, MA: Harvard University Press.

9. Cashdan, S. (1988). *Object relations therapy: Using the relationship.* New York: Norton.

10. Lopez, S. R., Gover, K. P., Holland, D., Johnson, M. J., Kain, C. D., Kanel, K., Mellins, C. A., & Rhyne, M. C. (1989). Development of culturally sensitive psychotherapists. *Professional Psychology: Research and Practice, 20,* 369–376.

11. Rabinowitz, F. E., Heppner, P. P., & Roehlke, H. J. (1986). Descriptive study of process outcome variables of supervision over time. *Journal of Counseling Psychology, 33,* 292–300. Ellis, M. V., & Dell, D. M. (1986). Dimensionality of supervisor roles: Supervisors' perceptions of supervision. *Journal of Counseling Psychology, 33,* 315–324.

12. Hillerbrand, E., & Claiborn, C. D. (1990). Examining reasoning skill differences between expert and novice counselors. *Journal of Counseling and Development, 68,* 684–691.

13. McNeill, B. W., Stoltenberg, C. D., & Pierce, R. A. (1985). Supervisees' perceptions of their development: A test of the counselor complexity model. *Journal of Counseling Psychology, 32,* 630–633. Stoltenberg, C. D., Pierce, R. A., & McNeill, B. W. (1987). Effects of experience on counselor trainee's needs. *Clinical Supervisor, 5,* 23–32. McNeill, B. W., Stoltenberg, C. D., & Romans, J. S. (1992). The integrated developmental model of supervision: Scale development and validation procedures. *Professional Psychology: Research and Practice, 23,* 504–508.

14. Olk, M. E., & Friedlander, M. L. (1992). Trainees' experiences of role conflict and role ambiguity in supervisory relationships. *Journal of Counseling Psychology, 39,* 389–397.

Chapter Six

1. Loganbill, C., Hardy, E., & Delworth, U. (1982). Supervision: A conceptual model. *Counseling Psychologist, 10*(1), 3–42.

2. Eckstein, R., & Wallerstein, R. (1972). *The teaching and learning of psychotherapy* (2nd ed.). New York: International Universities Press.

3. Mueller, W. J., & Kell, B. L. (1972). *Coping with the conflict: Supervising counselors and psychotherapists*. Englewood Cliffs, NJ: Prentice Hall.

4. Mueller & Kell (1972). *ibid.*

5. Heppner, P. P., & Roelhke, H. J. (1984). Differences among supervisees at different levels of training: Implications for a developmental model of supervision. *Journal of Counseling Psychology, 31,* 76–90.

6. Worthington, E. L., Jr., & Roehlke, H. J. (1979). Effective supervision as perceived by beginning counselors-in-training. *Journal of Counseling Psychology, 26,* 64–73.

7. Nelson, G. H. (1978). Psychotherapy supervision from the trainee's point of view: A survey of preferences. *Professional Psychology, 9,* 539–550.

8. Mueller and Kell (1972). *ibid.*

9. Allen, G. J., Szollos, S. J., & Williams, B. E. (1986). Doctoral students' comparative evaluations of best and worst psychotherapy supervision. *Professional Psychology: Research and Practice, 17,* 91–99.

10. McNeill, B. W., & Worthen, J. (1989). The parallel process in psychotherapy supervision. *Professional Psychotherapy: Research and Practice, 20,* 329–333.

11. Hutt, C. H., Scott, J., & King, M. (1983). A phenomenological study of supervisees' positive and negative experiences in supervision. *Psychotherapy: Theory, Research, and Practice, 20,* 118–123. Martin, J. S., Goodyear, R. K., & Newton, F. B. (1987). Clinical supervision: An intensive case study. *Professional Psychology: Research and Practice, 18,* 225–235.

12. Nelson (1978). *ibid.* Hutt, Scott, & King (1983). *ibid.* Black, B. (1988). Components of effective and ineffective psychotherapy supervision as perceived by supervisees with different levels of clinical experience (Doctoral dissertation, Columbia University, 1987). *Dissertation Abstracts International, 48,* 3105B.

13. Nelson (1978). *ibid.*

14. Rabinowitz, F. E., Heppner, P. P., & Roehke, H. J. (1986). Descriptive study of process outcome variables of supervision over time. *Journal of Counseling Psychology, 33,* 292–300.

15. Bordin, E. S. (1983). A working alliance based model of supervision. *Counseling Psychologist, 11,* 35–42.

16. Efstation, J. F., Patton, M. J., & Kardash, C. M. (1990). Measuring the working alliance in counselor supervision. *Journal of Counseling Psychology, 37,* 322–329.

17. Worthen, V., & McNeill, B. W. (1996). A phenomenological investigation of "good" supervision events. *Journal of Counseling Psychology, 43,* 25–34.

18. Worthen & McNeill (1996, p. 30). *ibid.*

19. Mueller & Kell (1972). *ibid.*

20. Worthen & McNeill (1996). *ibid.*

21. Allen, Szollos, & Williams (1986). *ibid.*

22. Black (1988, p. 167). *ibid.*

23. Worthen & McNeill (1996). *ibid.*

24. Galante, M. (l988). Trainees' and supervisors' perceptions of effective and ineffective supervisory relationships. (Doctoral dissertation, Memphis State University, 1987) *Dissertation Abstracts International, 49,* 933B.

25. Teyber, E. (1997). *Interpersonal process in psychotherapy: A relational approach* (3rd ed.). Pacific Grove, CA: Brooks/Cole.

26. Worthen & McNeill (1996). *ibid.*

27. Teyber (1997). *ibid.*

28. Worthen & McNeill (1996, p. 30). *ibid.*

29. Atkinson, D. R., & Thompson, C. E. (1992). Racial, ethnic and cultural variables in counseling. In S. D. Brown & R. W. Lent (Eds.), *Handbook of counseling psychology* (2nd ed., pp. 349–382). New York: Wiley. Gilbert, L. A. (1992). Gender and counseling psychology: Current knowledge and directions for research and social action. In S. D. Brown & R. W. Lent (Eds.), *Handbook of counseling psychology* (2nd ed., pp. 383–418). New York: Wiley. Fassinger, R. E. (1991). The hidden minority: Issues and challenges in working with lesbian women and gay men. *Counseling Psychologist, 19,* 157–161.

30. Bernard, J. M., & Goodyear, R. K. (1992). *Fundamentals of clinical supervision.* Needham Heights, MA: Allyn & Bacon.

31. Kivlighan, D. M. (1996). *Council of Counseling Psychology training programs 1996 survey of doctoral training programs.* Unpublished manuscript, University of Missouri, Columbia.

32. McNeill, B. W., Hom, K. L., & Perez, J. A. (1995). The training and supervisory needs of social/ethnic minority students. *Journal of Multicultural Counseling and Development, 23,* 246–258.

33. Vasquez, M. J., & McKinley, D. (1982). A conceptual model—Reactions and extension. *Counseling Psychologist, 10,* 59–63.

34. McNeill, Hom, & Perez (1995). *ibid.*

35. Vasquez & McKinley (1982). *ibid.*

36. Hunt, P. (1987). Black clients: Implications for supervision of trainees. *Psychotherapy: Theory, Research, and Practice, 24,* 114–119.

37. Zuniga, M. E. (1987). Mexican-American clinical training: A pilot project. *Journal of Social Work Education, 23,* 11–20.

38. Cook, D. A., & Helms, J. E. (1988). Visible racial/ethnic group supervisees' satisfaction with cross-cultural supervision as predicted by relationship characteristics. *Journal of Counseling Psychology, 35,* 268–274.

39. Burhke, R. A. (1989). Lesbian-related issues in counseling supervision. *Women and Therapy, 8,* 195–206.

40. Worthington, E. L., & Stern, A. (1985). Effects of supervisor and supervisee degree level and gender on the supervisory relationship. *Journal of Counseling Psychology, 32,* 252–262.

41. Behling, J. C., & Foster, S. A. (1988). Impact of sex-role combinations on student performance in field instruction. *Journal of Education for Social Work, 18,* 93–97.

42. Behling & Foster (1988). *ibid.* Thyer, B. A., Sowers-Hoag, K., & Love, J. P. (1988). The influence of field instructor-student gender combinations on student perceptions of field instruction quality. *Clinical Supervisor, 6,* 169–179.

43. Nelson, M. L., & Holloway, E. L. (1990). Relation of gender to power and involvement in supervision. *Journal of Counseling Psychology, 37,* 473–481. Putney, M. W., Worthington, E. L., Jr., & McCullough, M. E. (1992). Effects of supervisor and supervisee theoretical orientation and supervisor-supervisee matching on interns' perceptions of supervision. *Journal of Counseling Psychology, 39,* 258–265.

44. Nelson & Holloway (1990). *ibid.*

45. Gilligan, C. (1982). *In a different voice.* Cambridge, MA: Harvard University Press. Stoltenberg, C. D., & Delworth, U. (1987). *Supervising counselors and therapists.* San Francisco: Jossey-Bass.

46. Cacioppo, J. T., & Petty, R. E. (1980). Sex differences in influenceability: Toward specifying the underlying processes. *Personality and Social Psychology Bulletin, 6,* 651–656.

47. Stoltenberg, C. D., McNeill, B. W., & Crethar, H. C. (1995). Persuasion and development in counselor supervision. *Counseling Psychologist, 23,* 633–648.

48. Gutierrez, F. J. (1982). Working with minority counselor education students. *Counselor Education and Supervision, 21,* 218–226.

49. McNeill, B. W., & Stoltenberg, C. D. (1989). Reconceptualizing social influence in counseling: The elaboration likelihood model. *Journal of Counseling Psychology, 36,* 24–33.

Chapter Seven

1. Falvey, J. E. (1987). *Handbook of administrative supervision.* Alexandria, VA: Association for Counselor Education and Supervision.

2. American Psychological Association. (1992). *Ethical principles of psychologists and code of conduct.* Washington, D.C.: Author.

3. Boylan, J. C., Malley, P. B., & Scott, J. (1995). *Practicum and internship:*

Textbook for counseling and psychotherapy (2nd ed.). Washington, DC: Accelerated Development.

4. Bordin, E. S. (1983). A working alliance based model of supervision. *Counseling Psychologist, 11,* 35–42. Efstation, J. F., Patton, M. J., & Kardash, C. M. (1990). Measuring the working alliance in counselor supervision. *Journal of Counseling Psychology, 37,* 322–329.

5. Stoltenberg, C. D., & Delworth, U. (1987). *Supervising counselors and therapists.* San Francisco: Jossey-Bass.

6. Stoltenberg, C. D., McNeill, B. W., & Crethar, H. C. (1994). Changes in supervision as counselors and therapists gain experience: A review. *Professional Psychology: Research and Practice, 25,* 416–449.

7. Stein, D. M., & Lambert, M. J. (1995). Graduate training in psychotherapy: Are therapy outcomes enhanced? *Journal of Consulting and Clinical Psychology, 63,* 182–196.

8. McNeill, B. W., Stoltenberg, C. D., & Pierce, R. A. (1985). Supervisees' perceptions of their development: A test of the counselor complexity model. *Journal of Counseling Psychology, 32,* 630–633.

9. McNeill, B. W., Stoltenberg, C. D., & Romans, J. S. (1992). The integrated developmental model of supervision: Scale development and validation procedures. *Professional Psychology: Research and Practice, 23,* 504–508.

10. Bradley, L., & Richardson, B. (1987). Trends in practicum and internship requirements: A national study. *Clinical Supervisor, 4,* 57–67. Prieto, L. R. (1996). Group supervision: Still widely practiced but poorly understood. *Counselor Education and Supervision, 35,* 295–307.

11. Rosenberg, E., Medini, G., & Lomranz, J. (1982). Factorial dimensions of supervisor-student evaluation. *Journal of Social Psychology, 118,* 105–111.

12. Prieto (1996). *ibid.*

13. Savickas, M., Marquart, C., & Supinski, C. (1986). Effective supervision in groups. *Counselor Education and Supervision, 26,* 17–25. Wilbur, M., Roberts-Wilbur, J., Morris, J., Betz, R., & Hart, G. (1991). Structured group supervision: Theory and practice. *Journal for Specialists in Group Work, 16,* 91–100.

14. Prieto (1996). *ibid.*

Chapter Eight

1. Stoltenberg, C. D., & Delworth, U. (1987). *Supervising counselors and therapists.* San Francisco: Jossey-Bass.

2. Barker, R. G., and Associates (1978). *Habitats, environments, and human*

behavior: Studies in ecological psychology and eco-behavioral science. San Francisco: Jossey-Bass. Wicker, A. W. (1979). *An introduction to ecological psychology.* Monterey, CA: Brooks/Cole.

3. Maslach, C. (1978). Job burnout: How people cope. *Public Welfare, 36,* 56–58.

4. Sarason, S. B. (1972). *The creation of settings and the future societies.* San Francisco: Jossey-Bass.

5. Anonymous (1995). Hidden benefits of managed care. *Professional Psychology: Research and Practice, 26,* 235–237. Cummings, N. A. (1995). Impact of managed care on employment and training: A primer for survival. *Professional Psychology: Research and Practice, 26,* 10–15. Hersch, L. (1995). Adapting to health care reform and managed care: Three strategies for survival and growth. *Professional Psychology: Research and Practice, 26,* 16–26. Sullivan, M. J. (1995). Medicaid's quiet revolution: Merging the public and private sectors of care. *Professional Psychology: Research and Practice, 26,* 229–234.

6. Cantor, D. W. (1997). Open letter to managed care. *APA Monitor, 28,* 2.

7. Cantor (1997). *ibid.*

8. Tomes, H. (1997). Concerns continue on managed care. *APA Monitor, 28,* 41.

Chapter Nine

1. Loganbill, C., & Hardy, E. (1983). Developing training programs for clinical supervisors. *Clinical Supervisor, 1,* 15–21.

2. Russell, R. K., Crimmings, A. M., & Lent, R. W. (1984). Counselor training and supervision: Theory and research. In S. D. Brown & R. W. Lent (Eds.), *Handbook of counseling psychology* (pp. 625–681). New York: Wiley.

3. Holloway, E. L. (1992). Supervision: A way of teaching and learning. In S. D. Brown & R. W. Lent (Eds.), *Handbook of counseling psychology* (2nd ed., pp. 177–214). New York: Wiley.

4. Russell, R. K., & Petrie, T. (1994). Issues in training effective supervisors. *Applied and Preventive Psychology, 3,* 27–42.

5. Cummings, N. A. (1995). Impact of managed care on employment and training: A primer for survival. *Professional Psychology: Research and Practice, 26,* 10–15.

6. American Psychological Association. (1996). *Book 1: Guidelines of principles for accreditation of programs in professional psychology.* Washington, DC: APA.

7. Stoltenberg, C. D., McNeill, B. W., & Crethar, H. C. (1994). Changes in supervision as counselors and therapists gain experience: A review. *Profes-sional Psychology: Research and Practice, 25,* 416–449. Krause, A. A., & Allen, G. J. (1988). Perceptions of counselor supervision: An examination of Stoltenberg's model from the perspectives of supervisor and supervisee. *Journal of Counseling Psychology, 35,* 77–80.

8. Boylan, J. C., Malley, P. B., & Scott, J. (1995). *Practicum and internship: Text-book for counseling and psychotherapy* (2nd ed.). Washington, DC: Acceler-ated Development.

9. Russell & Petrie (1994). *ibid.*

10. Russell & Petrie (1994). *ibid.* Borders, L. D., Bernard, J. M., Dye, H. A., Fong, M. L., Henderson, P., & Nance, D. W. (1991). Curriculum guide for training counseling supervisors: Rationale, development, and implementa-tion. *Counselor Education and Supervision, 31,* 58–80.

11. Russell & Petrie (1994). *ibid.*

12. Robiner, W. N., & Schofield, W. (1990). References on supervision in clini-cal and counseling psychology. *Professional Psychology: Research and Prac-tice, 21,* 297–312.

13. Goodyear, R. (Producer). (1982). *Psychotherapy supervision by major theo-rists* [Videotape series]. Manhattan: Instructional Media Center, Kansas State University.

14. Bernard, J., & Goodyear, R. K. (1992). *Fundamentals of clinical supervision.* Boston: Allyn and Bacon.

15. Yutrenska, B. A. (1995). Making a case for ethnic and cultural diversity in increasing treatment efficacy. *Journal of Consulting and Clinical Psychology, 63,* 194–206.

16. Yutrenska (1995). *ibid.* LaFromboise, T. D., & Foster, S. L. (1992). Cross-cultural training: Scientist-practitioner model and methods. *Counseling Psychologist, 20,* 472–489. Ridley, C. R., Mendoza, D. W., & Kanitz, B. E. (1994). Multicultural training: Reexamination, operationalization, and integration. *Counseling Psychologist, 22,* 227–289.

17. LaFromboise & Foster (1992). *ibid.*

18. Lefley, H. P. (1985a). Impact of cross-cultural training on black and white mental health professionals. *International Journal of Intercultural Relations, 9,* 305–318. Lefley, H. P. (1985b). Mental-health training across cultures. In P. B. Pedersen (Ed.), *Handbook of cross-cultural counseling and therapy* (pp. 259–273). Westport, CT: Greenwood Press. Lefley, H. P., & Bestman, E. W. (1991). Public-academic linkages for culturally sensitive community mental health. *Community Mental Health Journal, 27,* 473–488.

19. Mio, J. S. (1989). Experimental involvement as an adjunct to teaching cul-

tural sensitivity. *Journal of Multicultural Counseling and Development, 17,* 38–46.

20. Merta, R. J., Stringham, E. M., & Ponterotto, J. G. (1988). Simulating culture shock in counselor trainees: An experiential exercise for cross-cultural training. *Journal of Counseling and Development, 66,* 242–245.
21. Russell & Petrie (1994). *ibid.*

Chapter Ten

1. Lamb, D. H., Cochran, D. J., & Jackson, V. R. (1991). Training and organizational issues associated with identifying and responding to intern impairment. *Professional Psychology: Research and Practice, 22,* 291–296.
2. Welfel, E. R. (1992). Psychologist as ethics educator: Successes, failures and unanswered questions. *Professional Psychology: Research and Practice, 23,* 182–189.
3. American Psychological Association. (1992). Ethical principles of psychologists and code of conduct. *American Psychologist, 47*(12), 1597–1611.
4. American Psychological Association. (1987). *General guidelines for providers of psychological services.* Washington, DC: Author.
5. Rest, J. R. (1984). Research on moral development: Implications for training counseling psychologists. *Counseling Psychologist, 12,* 19–29.
6. Kohlberg, L. (1969). Stage and sequence: The cognitive- developmental approach to socialization. In D. Goslin (Ed.), *Handbook of socialization theory and research* (pp. 347–480). Chicago: Rand McNally.
7. Kitchener, K. S. (1992). Psychologist as teacher and mentor: Affirming ethical values throughout the curriculum. *Professional Psychology: Research and Practice, 23,* 190–195.
8. Hall, J. E. (1998). Protection in supervision. *Register Report, 14*(4), 3–4.
9. Lamb, Cochran, & Jackson (1991). *ibid.*
10. Saccuzzo, D. (1996). *Liability for failure to supervise adequately mental health assistants, unlicensed practitioners and students.* Unpublished paper, San Diego State University.
11. Leong, F. T. L. (1996). Toward an integrative model for cross-cultural counseling and psychotherapy. *Applied and Preventive Psychology, 5,* 189–209.
12. Association for Counselor Education and Supervision. (1989). *Standards for counseling supervisors.* Alexandria, VA: Author.
13. Saccuzzo (1996). *ibid.*
14. *Masterson v. Board of Examiners of Psychologists,* WL 790949 (Del. Super 1995).

15. *Tarasoff v. Regents of the University of California*, Tarasoff II, Vacating Cal. 3rd 117, 529 P. zd553, 118, Cal. Rptr. 129 (1974) (Tarasoff I).

16. Saccuzzo (1996). *ibid.*

17. Kitchener (1992). *ibid.*

18. Association of State and Provincial Psychology Boards. (1979). *Guidelines for the employment and supervision of uncredentialed persons providing psychological services.* Montgomery, AL: Author.

19. American Psychological Association (1992). *ibid.*

20. American Psychological Association (1992). *ibid.*

21. Lamb, Cochran, & Jackson (1991). *ibid.*

22. Lamb, Cochran, & Jackson (1991). *ibid.*

23. Vasquez, M. J. T., & McKinley, D. L. (1982). Supervision: A conceptual model: Reactions and an extension. *Counseling Psychologist, 10,* 59–63.

Epilogue

1. Stein, D. M., & Lambert, M. J. (1995). Graduate training in psychotherapy: Are therapy outcomes enhanced? *Journal of Consulting and Clinical Psychology, 63,* 182–196.

2. Watkins, E. (1996). Psychotherapy supervisor and supervisee: Developmental models and research nine years later. *Clinical Psychology Review, 15,* 647–677.

—w— References

Abadie, P. D. (1985). *A study of interpersonal communication processes in the supervision of counseling*. Unpublished doctoral dissertation, Kansas State University, Manhattan.

American Psychological Association. (1980). *Criteria for accreditation of doctoral training programs and internships in professional psychology*. Washington, DC: Author.

Atkinson, D. R., & Thompson, C. E. (1992). Racial, ethnic and cultural variables in counseling. In S. D. Brown & R. W. Lent (Eds.), *Handbook of counseling psychology* (2nd ed., pp. 349–382). New York: Wiley.

Aubrey, R. (1978). Supervision of counselors in elementary and secondary schools. In J. Boyd (Ed.), *Counselor supervision: Approaches: Preparation: Practices* (pp. 292–338). Muncie, IN: Accelerated Development.

Baker, S. A., & Daniels, T. G. (1989). Integrating research on the microcounseling program: A meta-analysis. *Journal of Counseling Psychology, 36*(2), 213–222.

Barak, A., & LaCrosse, M. (1975). Multidimensional perception of counselor behavior. *Journal of Counseling Psychology, 22,* 471–476.

Barrett-Lennard, G. T. (1962). Dimensions of therapist response as causal factors in therapeutic change. *Psychological Monographs Applied, 76*(43, Whole No. 562).

Bartell, P. A., & Rubin, L. J. (1990). Dangerous liaisons: Sexual intimacies in supervision. *Professional Psychology: Research and Practice, 21*(6), 442–450.

Battle, C. C., Imber, S. D., Hoehn-Saric, R., Stone, A. R., Nash, E. R., & Frank, J. D. (1966). Target complaints criteria of improvement. *American Journal of Psychotherapy, 20,* 184–192.

Behling, J. C., Curtis, C., & Foster, S. A. (1982). Impact of sex-role combinations on student performance in field instruction. *Journal of Education for Social Work, 18*(2), 9397.

Bem, S. L. (1981). *Bem Sex Role Inventory: Professional manual*. Palo Alto, CA: Consulting Psychologists Press.

Benshoff, J. M., & Thomas, W. P. (1992). A new look at the counselor rating scale. *Counselor Education and Supervision, 32*(1), 12–22.

Berkman, A. S., & Berkman C. F. (1984). The supervision of cotherapist teams in family therapy. *Psychotherapy, 21*(2), 197–205.

Bernard, J. M. (1979). Supervisory training: A discrimination model. *Counselor Education and Supervision, 19,* 60–68.

Bernard, J. M., & Goodyear, R. K. (1992). *Fundamentals of clinical supervision.* Needham Heights, MA: Allyn & Bacon.

Blocher, D., Christensen, E. W., Hale-Fiske, R., Neren, S. H., Spencer, T., & Fowlkes, S. (1985). Development and preliminary validation of an instrument to measure cognitive growth. *Counselor Education and Supervision, 25*(1), 21–30.

Blumberg, A. (1980). *Supervision of teachers* (2nd ed.). Berkeley, CA: McCutchan.

Borders, L. D. (1989a). A pragmatic agenda for developmental supervision research. *Counselor Education and Supervision, 29,* 16–24.

Borders, L. D. (1989b). Developmental cognitions of first practicum supervisees. *Journal of Counseling Psychology, 36*(2), 163–169.

Borders, L. D. (1990). Developmental changes during supervisees' first practicum. *Clinical Supervisor, 8*(2), 157–167.

Borders, L. D. (1991a). A systematic approach to peer group supervision. *Journal of Counseling and Development, 69,* 248–252.

Borders, L. D. (1991b). Supervisors' in-session behaviors and cognitions. *Counselor Education and Supervision, 31*(1), 32–47.

Borders, L. D., & Fong, M. L. (1989). Ego development and counseling ability during training. *Counselor Education and Supervision, 29,* 71–83.

Borders, L. D., Fong-Beyette, M. L., & Cron, E. A. (1988). In-session cognitions of a counseling student: A case study. *Counselor Education and Supervision, 28,* 59–70.

Borders, L. D., Fong, M. L., & Neimeyer, G. J. (1986). Counseling students' level of ego development and perceptions of clients. *Counselor Education and Supervision, 26,* 36–49.

Borders, L. D., & Usher, C. H. (1992). Post-degree supervision: Existing and preferred practices. *Journal of Counseling and Development, 70,* 594–599.

Bridge, P., & Bascue, L. O. (1990). Documentation of psychotherapy supervision. *Psychotherapy in Private Practice, 8*(1), 79–86.

Brodsky, A. (1980). Sex role issues in the supervision of therapy. In A. K. Hess (Ed.), *Psychotherapy supervision: Theory research and practice* (pp. 509–524). New York: Wiley.

Buhrke, R. A. (1989). Lesbian-related issues in counseling supervision. *Women and Therapy, 8,* 195–206.

Buhrke, R. A., & Douce, L. A. (1991). Training issues for counseling psychologists in working with lesbian women and gay men. *Counseling Psychologist, 19,* 216–234.

Burns, C. I., & Holloway, E. L. (1990). Therapy in supervision: An unresolved issue. *Clinical Supervisor, 7*(4), 47–60.

Carey, J. C., Williams, K. S., & Wells, M. (1988). Relationships between dimensions of supervisors' influence and counselor trainees' performance. *Counselor Education and Supervision, 28,* 130–139.

Carney, C. G., & Kahn, K. B. (1984). Building competencies for effective cross-cultural counseling: A developmental view. *Counseling Psychologist, 12*(1), 111–119.

Carrol, M. (1988). Counseling supervision: The British context. *Counseling Psychology Quarterly, 1*(4), 387–396.

Chelune, G. J. (1976). The self-disclosure situations survey: A new approach to measuring self-disclosure. *JSAS Catalog of Selected Documents in Psychology, 6,* 111–112 (Manuscript No. 1367).

Chickering, A. W. (1969). *Education and Identity.* San Francisco: Jossey-Bass.

Cook, D. A., & Helms, J. E. (1988). Visible racial/ethnic group supervisees' satisfaction with cross-cultural supervision as predicted by relationship characteristics. *Journal of Counseling Psychology, 35*(3), 268–274.

Crane, D. R., Griffin, W., & Hill, R. D. (1986). Influence of therapist skills in client perceptions of marriage and family therapy outcome: Implications for supervision. *Journal of Marital and Family Therapy, 12*(1), 91–96.

Cross, D. G., & Brown, D. (1983). Counselor supervision as a function of trainee experience. *Counselor Education and Supervision, 4,* 333–341.

Cummings, A. L., Hallberg, E. T., Martin, J., Slemon, A., & Hiebert, B. (1990). Implications of counselor conceptualizations for counselor education. *Counselor Education and Supervision, 30*(2), 120–134.

Danek, T. A., Barnes, A., & Freeman, F. E., Jr. The intensive supervision experiment: An historical review. *Evaluation Review, 14*(6), 607–611.

Davis, A. (1984). *Counselor expectations of supervision and counselor burnout.* Unpublished doctoral dissertation, University of Georgia, Athens.

Davis, A. H., Savicki, V., Cooley, E. J., & Firth, J. L. (1989). Burnout and counselor practitioner expectations of supervision. *Counselor Education and Supervision, 28,* 234–241.

Delaney, D. J., & Eisenberg, S. (1977). *The counseling process* (2nd ed.). Chicago: Rand McNally.

DeLucia, J. L., Bowman, V. E., & Bowman, R. L. (1989). The use of parallel process in supervision and group counseling to facilitate counselor and client growth. *Journal for Specialists in Group Work, 14*(4), 232–238.

Derogatis, L. (1977). *SCL-90 administration, scoring, and procedures manual—I.* Unpublished manuscript, Johns Hopkins University School of Medicine, Clinical Psychometrics Research Unit, Baltimore.

Dodds, J. B. (1986). Supervision of psychology trainees in field placements. *Professional Psychology: Research and Practice, 17*(4), 296–300.

Dole, A. A., et al. (1982). Six dimensions of retrospections by therapists and counselors—A manual for research. *JSAS: Catalog of Selected Documents in Psychology, 12,* p. 23 (Manuscript No. 2454).

Efstation, J. F., Patton, M. J., & Kardash, C. M. (1990). Measuring the working alliance in counselor supervision. *Journal of Counseling Psychology, 37*(3), 322–329.

Ellis, M. V. (1988a). Counselor trainees' perceptions of supervisor roles: Two studies testing the dimensionality of supervision. *Journal of Counseling Psychology, 35*(3), 315–324.

Ellis, M. V. (1988b). The cognitive development approach to case presentation in clinical supervision. *Counselor Education and Supervision, 27*(3), 259–264.

Ellis, M. V. (1991a). Research in clinical supervision: Revitalizing a scientific agenda. *Counselor Education and Supervision, 30*(3), 238–251.

Ellis, M. V. (1991b). Critical incidents in clinical supervision and in supervisor supervision: Assessing supervisory issues. *Journal of Counseling Psychology, 38*(3), 342–349.

Ellis, M. V., & Dell, D. M. (1986). Dimensionality of supervisor roles: Supervisors' perceptions of supervision. *Journal of Counseling Psychology, 33*(3), 282–291.

Ellis, M. V., Dell, D. M., & Good, G. E. (1988). Counselor trainees' perceptions of supervisor roles: Two studies testing the dimensionality of supervision. *Journal of Counseling Psychology, 35*(3), 315–324.

Erickson, E. H. (1968). *Identity, youth, and crisis.* New York: Norton.

Ericson, P. M., & Rogers, L. E. (1973). New procedures for analyzing relational communication. *Family Process, 12,* 245–267.

Everett, C. A. (1980). An analysis of AAMFT supervisors: Their identities, roles, and resources. *Journal of Marriage and Family Therapy, 6,* 215–226.

Everett, C. A., & Wayland-Seaton-Johnson, A. (1983). An analysis of pastoral counseling supervisors: Their identities, roles and resources. *Journal of Pastoral Care, 37*(1), 21–25.

Eysenck, H. J., & Eysenck, S. B. J. (1969). *Personality structure and measurement.* San Diego, CA: Knapp.

Fassinger, R. E. (1991). The hidden minority: Issues and challenges in working with lesbian women and gay men. *Counseling Psychologist, 19,* 157–161.

Fenell, D. L., Hovestadt, A. J., & Harvey, S. J. (1986). A comparison of delayed feedback and live supervision models of marriage and family therapist clinical training. *Journal of Marital and Family Training, 12*(2), 181–186.

Fisher, B. L. (1989). Differences between supervision of beginning and advanced therapists: Hogan's Hypothesis empirically revisited. *Clinical Supervisor, 7*(1), 57–74.

Fleming, J. (1953). The role of supervision in psychiatric training. *Bulletin of the Menninger Clinic, 17,* 157–159.

Fong, M. L., Borders, L. D., & Neimeyer, G. J. (1986). Sex role orientation and self-disclosure flexibility in counselor training. *Counselor Education and Supervision, 25*(3), 210–221.

Fransella, F., & Bannister, D. (1977). *A manual for Repertory Grid Technique.* Orlando, FL: Academic Press.

Friedlander, M. L. (1982). Expectations and perceptions of counseling: Changes over time in relation to verbal behavior. *Journal of College Student Personnel, 23,* 402–408.

Friedlander, M. L. (1984). Hill Counselor Verbal Response Category System–Revised. *Tests in microfiche.* Princeton, NJ: Educational Testing Service. (Test Collection, No. 012397, Set I).

Friedlander, M. L., Siegel, S. M., & Brenock, K. (1989). Parallel process in counseling and supervision: A case study. *Journal of Counseling Psychology, 36*(2), 149–157.

Friedlander, M. L., & Snyder, J. (1983). Trainees' expectations for the supervisory process: Testing a developmental model. *Counselor Education and Supervision, 22,* 342–348.

Friedlander, M. L., Thibodeau, J. R., & Ward, L. G. (1985). Discriminating the "good" from the "bad" therapy hour. *Psychotherapy, 22,* 631–642.

Friedlander, M. L., & Ward, L. G. (1984). Development and validation of the supervisory styles inventory. *Journal of Counseling Psychology, 31,* 541–557.

Gallant, J. P., & Thyer, B. A. (1989). The "bug-in-the-ear" in clinical supervision: A review. *Clinical Supervisor, 7*(2,3), 43–57.

Garfield, S. L., & Kurtz, R. (1976). Clinical psychologists in the 1970s. *American Psychologist, 31,* 1–9.

Gazda, G. M., Asbury, F. R., Balzea, F. J., Childers, W. C., & Walters, R. P. (1977). *Human relations development* (2nd ed.). Needham Heights, MA: Allyn & Bacon.

Gelso, C. J., & Fassinger, R. E. (1990). Counseling psychology: Theory and research on interventions. *Annual Review of Psychology, 41,* 355–386.

Gerkin, C. (1969). An objective method for evaluating training programs in counseling psychology. *Journal of Counseling Psychology, 16,* 227–237.

Gilbert, L. A. (1992). Gender and counseling psychology: Current knowledge and directions for research and social action. In S. D. Brown & R. W. Lent (Eds.), *Handbook of counseling psychology* (2nd ed., pp. 383–418). New York: Wiley.

Gilligan, C. (1982). *In a different voice.* Cambridge, MA: Harvard University Press.

Goodyear, R. K. (1982). *Psychotherapy supervision by major theorists* (Videotape series). Manhattan, KS: Kansas State University, Instructional Media Center.

Goodyear, R. K., Abadie, P. D., & Efros, F. (1984). Supervisory theory into practice: Differential perception of supervision by Ekstein, Ellis, Polster, and Rogers. *Journal of Counseling Psychology, 31,* 228–237.

Grotjahn, M. (1955). Problems and techniques of supervision. *Psychiatry, 18,* 9–15.

Guest, P. D., & Beutler, L. E. (1988). Impact of psychotherapy supervision on therapist orientation and values. *Journal of Consulting and Clinical Psychology, 56*(5), 653–658.

Harvey, O. J., Hunt, D. E., & Schroder, H. M. (1961). *Conceptual systems and personality organization.* New York: Wiley.

Heath, A. W., & Storm, C. L. (1985). From the institute to the ivory tower: The live supervision stage approach for teaching supervision in academic settings. *American Journal of Family Therapy, 13*(3), 27–36.

Heppner, P. P., & Handley, P. G. (1981). A study of the interpersonal influence process in supervision. *Journal of Counseling Psychology, 28*(5), 437–444.

Heppner, P. P., & Handley, P. (1982). The relationship between supervisory behaviors and perceived supervisor expertness, attractiveness, or trustworthiness. *Journal of Counseling Psychology, 28,* 47–51.

Heppner, P. P., & Roehlke, H. J. (1984). Differences among supervisees at different levels of training: Implications for a developmental model of supervision. *Journal of Counseling Psychology, 31,* 76–90.

Hess, A. K. (1986). Growth in supervision: Stages of supervisee and supervisor development. *Clinical Supervisor, 4,* 51–67.

Hess, A. K., & Hess, K. A. (1983). Psychotherapy supervision: A survey of internship practices. *Professional Psychology: Research and Practice, 14,* 504–513.

Hiebert, B. (1987). Exploring changes in cognitive structure of counselling practicum students. *Alberta Psychology, 16,* 3–7.

Hill, C. E. (1978). Development of a counselor verbal response category system. *Journal of Counseling Psychology, 25,* 461–468.

Hill, C. E. (1985). *Manual for Hill Counselor Verbal Response Category System.* College Park, MD: Author.

Hill, C. E. (1986). An overview of the Hill Counselor and Client Verbal Response Models Category Systems. In L. S. Greenberg & W. M. Pinsof (Eds.), *The psychotherapeutic process: A research handbook* (pp. 131–159). New York: Guilford.

Hill, C. E., Carter, J. A., & O'Farrell, M. K. (1983). A case study of the process and outcome of time-limited counseling. *Journal of Counseling Psychology, 30,* 3–18.

Hill, C. E., Grenwald, C., Reed, K. A., Charles, D., O'Farrel, M. K., & Canter, J. A. (1981). *Manual for the Counselor and Client Verbal Response Category Systems.* Columbus, OH: Marathon Consulting and Press.

Hill, C. E., Helms, J. E., Spiegel, S. B., & Tichenor, V. (1988). Development of a system for categorizing client reactions to therapist intervention. *Journal of Counseling Psychology, 35,* 27–36.

Hill, C. E., Helms, J. E., Tichenor, U., Spiegel, S. B., O'Grady, K. E., & Perry, E. S. (1988). Effects of therapist response modes in brief psychotherapy. *Journal of Counseling Psychology, 32,* 222–233.

Hill, C. E., & O'Grady, K. E. (1985). List of therapist intentions illustrated in a case study and with therapists of varying theoretical orientations. *Journal of Counseling Psychology, 32,* 3–22.

Hillerbrand, E. (1989). Cognitive differences between experts and novices: Implications for group supervision. *Journal of Counseling and Development, 67,* 293–296.

Hillerbrand, E., & Claiborn, C. D. (1990). Examining reasoning skill differences between expert and novice counselors. *Journal of Counseling and Development, 68,* 684–691.

Hogan, R. A. (1964). Issues and approaches in supervision. *Psychotherapy: Theory, Research, and Practice, 1,* 139–141.

Holloway, E. L. (1984). Outcome evaluation in supervision research. *Counseling Psychologist, 12*(4), 167–174.

Holloway, E. L. (1987). Developmental models of supervision: Is it development? *Professional Psychology: Research and Practice, 18*(3), 209–216.

Holloway, E. L. (1988). Models of counselor development or training models for supervision? Rejoinder to Stoltenberg and Delworth. *Professional Psychology: Research and Practice, 19*(2), 138–140.

Holloway, E. L. (1992). Supervision: A way of teaching and learning. In S. D. Brown & R. W. Lent (Eds.), *Handbook of counseling psychology* (2nd ed., pp. 177–214). New York: Wiley.

Holloway, E. L., Freund, R. D., Gardner, S. L., Nelson, M. L., & Walker, B. R. (1989). Relation of power and involvement to theoretical orientation in supervision: An analysis of discourse. *Journal of Counseling Psychology, 36*(1), 88–102.

Holloway, E. L., & Wampold, B. E. (1983). Patterns of verbal behavior and judgements of satisfaction in the supervision interview. *Journal of Counseling Psychology, 30,* 227–234.

Holloway, E. L., & Wampold, B. E. (1986). Relation between conceptual level and counseling-related tasks: A meta-analysis. *Journal of Counseling Psychology, 33*(3), 310–319.

Hogan, R. A. (1964). Issues and approaches in supervision. *Psychotherapy: Theory, Research, and Practice, 1,* 139–141.

Horvath, A. O., & Greenberg, L. (1989). Development and validation of the Working Alliance Inventory. *Journal of Counseling Psychology, 41,* 438–448.

Hostford, R. E., & Barmann, B. (1983). A social learning approach to counselor supervision. *Counseling Psychologist, 11*(1), 51–58.

Hunt, D. E. (1971). *Matching models in education: The coordination of teaching methods with student characteristics.* Toronto: Ontario Institute for Studies in Education.

Hunt, D. E., Butler, L. F., Noy, J. E., & Rosser, M. E. (1978). *Assessing the conceptual level by the paragraph completion method.* Toronto: Ontario Institute for Studies in Education.

Hutt, C. H., Scott, J., & King, M. (1983). A phenomenological study of supervisees' positive and negative experiences in supervision. *Psychotherapy: Theory, Research and Practice, 20*(1), 118–123.

Iberg, J. R. (1991). Applying statistical control theory to bring together clinical supervision and psychotherapy research. *Journal of Consulting and Clinical Psychology, 59*(4), 575–586.

Kaslow, N. J., McCarthy, S. M., Rogers, J. H., & Summerville, M. B. (1992). Psychology postdoctoral training: A developmental perspective. *Professional Psychology: Research and Practice, 23*(5), 369–375.

Kennard, B. D., Stewart, S. M., & Gluck, M. R. (1987). The supervision relationship: Variables contributing to positive versus negative experiences. *Professional Psychology: Research and Practice, 18*(2), 172–175.

Kiesler, D. J. (1985). *Research manual for the Impact Message Inventory*. Palo Alto, CA: Consulting Psychologists Press.

Kiesler, D. J. (1966). Some myths of psychotherapy research and the search for a paradigm. *Psychological Bulletin, 65,* 110–135.

Kivlighan, D. M., Jr. (1989). Changes in counselor intentions and response modes and in client reactions and session evaluation after training. *Journal of Counseling Psychology, 36*(4), 471–476.

Kivlighan, D. M., Jr., Angelone, E. O., & Swafford, K. G. (1991). Live supervision in individual psychotherapy: Effects on therapist's intention use and client's evaluation of session effect and working alliance. *Professional Psychology: Research and Practice, 22*(6), 489–495.

Krause, A. A., & Allen, G. J. (1988). Perceptions of counselor supervision: An examination of Stoltenberg's Model from the perspectives of supervisor and supervisee. *Journal of Counseling Psychology, 35*(1), 77–80.

Kruger, L. J., Cherniss, C., Maher, C. A., & Leichtman, H. M. (1988). A behavior observation system for group supervision. *Counselor Education and Supervision, 27,* 331–343.

Kurpius, D. J., Benjamin, D., & Morran, D. K. (1985). Effects of teaching a cognitive strategy on counselor trainee internal dialogue and clinical hypothesis formulation. *Journal of Counseling Psychology, 32*(2), 263–271.

Kurpius, D. J., & Morran, D. K. (1988). Cognitive-behavioral techniques and interventions for application in counselor supervision. *Counselor Education and Supervision, 27,* 368–376.

LaForge, R., & Suczek, R. (1955). The interpersonal dimension of personality: III. An interpersonal checklist. *Journal of Personality, 24,* 94–112.

Lambert, M. J. (1980). Research and the supervisory process. In A. K. Hess (Ed.), *Psychotherapy supervision: Theory, research, and practice* (pp. 423–450). New York: Wiley.

Larson, L. M., Suzuki, L. A., Gillespie, K. N., Potenza, M. T., & Betchel, M. A. (1992). Development and validation of the Counseling Self-Estimate Inventory. *Journal of Counseling Psychology, 39*(1), 105–120.

Leary, T. (1957). *Interpersonal diagnosis of personality*. Somerset, NJ: Ronald Press.

Littrel, J. M., Lee-Boden, N., & Lorenz, J. (1979). A developmental framework for counseling supervision. *Counselor Education and Supervision, 19,* 129–136.

Loesch, L. C., & McDavis, R. J. (1978). A scale for assessing counseling orientation preferences. *Counselor Education and Supervision, 17,* 262–271.

Loevinger, J., & Wessler, R. (1970). *Measuring ego development* (Vol. 1). San Francisco: Jossey-Bass.

Loganbill, C., & Hardy, E. (1983). In defense of eclecticism. *Counseling Psychologist, 11*(1), 79.

Loganbill, C., Hardy, E., & Delworth, U. (1982). Supervision: A conceptual model. *Counseling Psychologist, 10*(1), 3–42.

Maguire, G. P., Goldberg, D. P., Hobson, R. F., Margison, F., Moss, S., & O'Dowd, T. (1984). Evaluating the teaching method of psychotherapy. *British Journal of Psychiatry, 144,* 575–580.

Mahler, M. S. (1979). Separation-individuation. *The selected papers of Margaret S. Mahler, M.D.* (Vol. 2). New York: Wiley.

Martin, J. S. (1985). Measuring clients' cognitive competence in research on counseling. *Journal of Counseling and Development, 64,* 126–130.

Martin, J. S., Goodyear, R. K., & Newton, F. B. (1987). Clinical supervision: An intensive case study. *Professional Psychology: Research and Practice, 18*(3), 225–235.

Martin, J., Martin, W., Meyer, M., & Slemon, A. (1986). Empirical investigation of the cognitive meditational paradigm for research on counseling. *Journal of Counseling Psychology, 33*(2), 115–123.

Martin, J., Slemon, A. G., Hiebert, B., Hallberg, E. T., & Cummings, A. L. (1989). Conceptualizations of novice and experienced counselors. *Journal of Counseling Psychology, 36,* 393–396.

Maslach, C., & Jackson, S. (1981). The measurement of experienced burnout. *Journal of Occupational Behavior, 2,* 99–113.

McAuliffe, G. J. (1992). A case presentation approach to group supervision for community college counselors. *Counselor Education and Supervision, 31,* 163–172.

McColley, S. H., & Baker, E. L. (1982). Training activities and styles of beginning supervisors: A survey. *Professional Psychology: Research and Practice, 13,* 283–292.

McNeill, B. W., & Stoltenberg, C. D. (1992). Agendas for developmental supervision research: A response to Borders. *Counselor Education and Supervision, 31,* 179–183.

McNeill, B. W., Stoltenberg, C. D., & Pierce, R. A. (1985). Supervisees' perceptions of their development: A test of the counselor complexity model. *Journal of Counseling Psychology, 32*(4), 630–633.

McNeill, B. W., Stoltenberg, C. D., & Romans, J. S. (1992). The integrated developmental model of supervision: Scale development and validation procedures. *Professional Psychology: Research and Practice, 23*(6), 504–508.

McRoy, R. G., Freeman, E. M., Logan, S. L., & Balckmon, B. (1986). Cross-cultural field supervision: Implications for social work education. *Journal of Social Work Education, 22,* 50–56.

Miars, R. D., Tracey, T. J., Ray, P. B., Cornfeld, J. L., O'Farrell, M., & Gelso, C. J. (1983). Variation in supervision process across trainee experience levels. *Journal of Counseling Psychology, 30,* 403–412.

Miller, P. H. (1989). *Theories of developmental psychology* (2nd ed.). New York: Freeman.

Myers-Briggs, I. (1962). *The Myers-Briggs Type Indicator.* Palo Alto, CA: Consulting Psychologists Press.

Myrick, R. D., & Kelly, F. J. (1971). A scale for evaluating practicum students in counseling and supervision. *Counselor Education and Supervision, 10,* 330–336.

Neimeyer, G. J., & Neimeyer, R. A. (1981). Personal construct perspectives on cognitive assessment. In T. Merluzzi, C. Glass, & M. Genest (Eds.), *Cognitive assessment* (pp. 188–232). New York: Guilford.

Nelson, M. L., & Holloway, E. L. (1990). Relation of gender to power and involvement in supervision. *Journal of Counseling Psychology, 37*(4), 473–481.

Newman, F. L., Kopta, S. M., McGovern, M. P., Howard, K. I., & McNeilly, C. L. (1988). Evaluating trainees relative to their supervisors during the psychology internship. *Journal of Consulting and Clinical Psychology, 56*(5), 659–665.

Newman, J. L., & Fuqua, D. R. (1988). A comparative study of positive and negative modeling in counselor training. *Counselor Education and Supervision, 28,* 121–129.

Nichols, W. C., Nichols, D. P., & Hardy, K. V. (1990). Supervision in family therapy: A decade restudy. *Journal of Marital and Family Therapy, 16*(3), 275–285.

Norcross, J. C., Prochaska, J. O., & Gallagher, K. M. (1989). Clinical psychologists in the 1980s: Theory, research, and practice. *Clinical Psychologist, 42*(3), 45–53.

Penman, R. (1980). *Communication process and relationships.* Orlando, FL: Academic Press.

Piaget, J. (1970). *Structuralism.* New York: Basic Books.

Piaget, J. (1971). *Biology and knowledge: An essay on the relations between organic regulations and cognitive processes.* Chicago: University of Chicago Press

Ponterotto, J. G., & Zander, T. A. (1984). A multimodal approach to counselor supervision. *Counselor Education and Supervision, 24*(1), 40–50.

Putney, M. W., Worthington, E. L. Jr., & McCullough, M. E. (1992). Effects of supervisor and supervisee theoretical orientation and supervisor-supervisee matching on interns' perceptions of supervision. *Journal of Counseling Psychology, 39*(2), 258–265.

Rabinowitz, F. E., Heppner, P. P., & Roehlke, H. J. (1986). Descriptive study of process outcome variables of supervision over time. *Journal of Counseling Psychology, 33*(3), 292–300.

Raven, B. H. (1992). A power/interaction model of interpersonal influence: French and Raven thirty years later. *Journal of Social Behavior and Personality, 7*(2), 217–244.

Reid, E., McDaniel, S., Donaldson, C., & Tollers, M. (1987). Taking it personally: Issues of personal authority and competence for the female in family therapy training. *Journal of Marital and Family Therapy, 13*(2), 157–165.

Reising, G. N., & Daniels, M. H. (1983). A study of Hogan's model of counselor development and supervision. *Journal of Counseling Psychology, 30,* 235–244.

Rickards, L. D. (1984). Verbal interaction and perception in counselor supervision. *Journal of Counseling Psychology, 31*(2), 262–265.

Robiner, W. N., & Schofield, W. (1990). References on supervision in clinical and counseling psychology. *Professional Psychology: Research and Practice, 21*(4), 297–312.

Robinson, S. E., & Kinner, R. T. (1988). Self-instructional versus traditional training for teaching basic counseling skills. *Counselor Education and Supervision, 28,* 140–145.

Robyak, J. E. (1981). Effects of gender on the counselor's preference for methods of influence. *Journal of Counseling Psychology, 28*(1), 7–12.

Robyak, J. E., Goodyear, R. K., & Prange, M. (1987). Effects of supervisors' sex, focus and experience on preferences for interpersonal power bases. *Counselor Education and Supervision, 26*(4), 299–309.

Robyak, J. E., Goodyear, R. K., Prange, M. E., & Donham, G. (1986). Effects of gender, supervision, and presenting problems on practicum students' preference for interpersonal power bases. *Journal of Counseling Psychology, 33*(2), 159–163.

Rodenhauser, P. (1992). Psychiatry residency programs: Trends in psychotherapy supervision. *American Journal of Psychotherapy, 46,* 240–249.

Rogers, L. E. (1979). *Relational communication control manual.* Unpublished manuscript, Cleveland State University, Department of Speech Communication.

Rokeach, M. (1973). *The nature of human values.* New York: Free Press.

Rokeach, M. (1979). *Understanding human values.* New York: Free Press.

Ronnestad, M. H., & Skovholt, T. M. (1993). Supervision of beginning and advanced graduate students of counseling and psychotherapy. *Journal of Counseling and Development, 71,* 396–405.

Rotter, J. B. (1966). Generalized expectancies for internal versus external control of reinforcement. *Psychological Monographs: General and Applied, 80*(1, Whole No. 609).

Russel, R. K., Crimmings, A. M., & Lent, R. W. (1984). Counselor training and supervision: Theory and research. In S. D. Brown & R. W. Lent (Eds.), *Handbook of counseling psychology* (pp. 625–681). New York: Wiley.

Sansbury, D. L. (1982). Developmental supervision from a skills perspective. *Counseling Psychologist, 10*(1), 53–57.

Schiavone, C. D., & Jessell, J. C. (1988). Influence of attributed expertness and gender in counselor supervision. *Counselor Education and Supervision, 28,* 29–42.

Schroll, J. T., & Walton, R. N. (1991). The interaction of supervision needs with technique and context in the practice of live supervision. *Clinical Supervisor, 9*(1), 1–14.

Shaw, B. F., & Dobson, K. S. (1988). Competency judgements in the training and evaluation of psychotherapists. *Journal of Counseling Psychology, 56*(5), 666–672.

Skinstad, A. H. (1993). Practicum supervision in Norway and the United States. *Journal of Counseling and Development, 71,* 406–408.

Smith, K., Pickering, M., Crago, M., & Naremore, R. (1990). Patterns and challenges in supervision: Research in human communication disorders. *Clinical Supervisor, 8*(2), 185–193.

Sperling, M. B., Handen, B. L., Miller, D., Schumm, P., Pirrotta, S., Simons, L. A., Lysiak, G., & Terry, L. (1986). The collaborative team as a training and therapeutic tool. *Counselor Education and Supervision, 25*(3), 183–190.

Sternitzke, M. E., Dixon, D. N., & Ponterotto, J. G. (1988). An attributional approach to counselor supervision. *Counselor Education and Supervision, 28,* 5–13.

Stiles, W. B., & Snow, J. S. (1984). Counseling session impact as viewed by novice counselors and their clients. *Journal of Counseling Psychology, 31,* 3–12.

Stoltenberg, C. D. (1981). Approaching supervision from a developmental perspective: The counselor complexity model. *Journal of Counseling Psychology, 28*(1), 59–65.

Stoltenberg, C. D., & Delworth, U. (1987). *Supervising counselors and therapists.* San Francisco: Jossey-Bass.

Stoltenberg, C. D., & Delworth, U. (1988). Developmental models of supervision: It is development—Response to Holloway. *Professional Psychology: Research and Practice, 19*(2), 134–137.

Stoltenberg, C. D., McNeill, B. W., & Crethar, H. C. (1994). Changes in supervision as counselors and therapists gain experience: A review. *Professional Psychology: Research and Practice, 25,* 416–449.

Stoltenberg, C. D., Pierce, R. A., & McNeill, B. W. (1987). Effects of experience on counselor trainee's needs. *Clinical Supervisor, 5*(1), 23–32.

Stone, D., & Amundson, N. (1989). Counsellor supervision: An exploratory study of the metaphoric case drawing method of case presentation in a clinical setting. *Canadian Journal of Counselling, 23*(4), 360–371.

Strong, S. R. (1968). Counseling: An interpersonal influence process. *Journal of Counseling Psychology, 15*(3), 215–224.

Strong, S. R., Hills, H. I. (1986). *Interpersonal Communication Rating Scale.* Unpublished manuscript, Virginia Commonwealth University, Department of Psychology, Richmond.

Strong, S. R., & Matross, R. P. (1973). Change process in counseling and psychotherapy. *Journal of Counseling Psychology, 20,* 25–32.

Strozier, A. L., Kivlighan, D. M. Jr., & Thoreson, R. W. (1993). Supervisor intentions, supervisee reactions, and helpfulness: A case study of the process of supervision. *Professional Psychology: Research and Practice, 24*(1), 13–19.

Strupp, H. H. (1981). *Vanderbilt Psychotherapy Process Scales (VPPS): Rater manual* (Rev. ed.). Unpublished manuscript, Vanderbilt University, Nashville.

Sunland, D. M. (1977a, June). *Theoretical orientation: A multi-professional, American sample.* Paper presented at the meeting of the Society for Psychotherapy Research, Madison, WI.

Sunland, D. M. (1977b). Theoretical orientations of psychotherapists. In

A. S. Gurman & A. M. Razin (Eds.), *Effective psychotherapy: A handbook of research* (pp. 189–222). New York: Pergamon Press.

Swope, A. J. (1987). Measuring clinical competence in psychology graduate students: A case example. *Teaching of Psychology, 14*(1), 32–34.

Thyer, B. A., Sowers-Hoag, K., & Love, J. P. (1988). The influence of field instructor-student gender combinations on student perceptions of field instruction quality. *Clinical Supervisor, 6,* 169–179.

Tracey, T. J., Ellickson, J. L., & Sherry, P. (1989). Reactance in relation to different supervisory environments and counselor development. *Journal of Counseling Psychology, 36*(3), 336–344.

Tracey, T. J., & Sherry, P. (1993). Complementary interaction over time in successful and less successful supervision. *Professional Psychology: Research and Practice, 24*(3), 304–311.

Vasquez, M. J., & McKinley, D. (1982). A conceptual model—reactions and extension. *The Counseling Psychologist, 10*(1), 59–63.

Wetchler, J. L. (1988). Primary and secondary influential theories of family therapy supervisors: A research note. *Family Therapy, 15*(1), 69–74.

Wilbur, M. P., Roberts-Wilbur, J., Morris, J. R., Betz, R. L., & Hart, G. M. (1991). Structured group supervision: Theory into practice. *Journal for Specialists in Group Work, 16*(2), 91–100.

Wiley, M. O., & Ray, P. B. (1986). Counseling supervision by developmental level. *Journal of Counseling Psychology, 33*(4), 439–445.

Winter, M., & Holloway, E. L. (1991). Relation of trainee experience, conceptual level, and supervisor approach to selection of audiotaped counseling passages. *Clinical Supervisor, 9*(2), 87–103.

Worthington, E. L., Jr. (1984). Empirical investigation of supervision of counselors as they gain experience. *Journal of Counseling Psychology, 31,* 63–75.

Worthington, E. L., Jr. (1987). Changes in supervision as counselors and supervisors gain experience. *Professional Psychology: Research and Practice, 18*(3), 189–208.

Worthington, E. L., & Roehlke, H. J. (1979). Effective supervision as perceived by beginning counselors-in-training. *Journal of Counseling Psychology, 26,* 64–73.

Yogev, S., & Pion, G. M. (1984). Do supervisors modify psychotherapy supervision according to supervisees' level of experience? *Psychotherapy, 21*(2), 206–208.

Zucker, P. J., & Worthington, E. L., Jr. (1986). Supervision of interns and postdoctoral applicants for licensure in university counseling centers. *Journal of Counseling Psychology, 33,* 87–89.

⟶ Index

⟿ The Authors

CAL D. STOLTENBERG is professor of educational psychology and director of the Counseling Psychology Program at The University of Oklahoma and a licensed psychologist. He has contributed to more than fifty publications, including three other books. He is a fellow of the American Psychological Association, the American Psychological Society, and the American Association of Applied and Preventive Psychology. He serves as a clinical supervisor for all levels of graduate students, as well as postdoctoral clinicians.

BRIAN MCNEILL graduated from the Counseling Psychology Program at Texas Tech University in 1984. He has supervised psychotherapists in various applied and academic settings. Dr. McNeill is currently an associate professor and director of graduate training for the Counseling Psychology Program at Washington State University.

URSULA DELWORTH is a professor in the Division of Psychological and Quantitative Foundations at The University of Iowa. She is a fellow of the American Psychological Association and the American Psychological Society, a former president of Division 17 (Counseling) of the APA, and former chair of the Committee on Women in Psychology of the APA. Her scholarly interests focus on clinical supervision and issues of gender and ethnicity in counseling.